With Bold Knife and Fork

I then set a while at Coutts's, and then at
Macfarlane's, and then went to Davies's.
Johnson was gone to Oxford. I was
introduced to Mr. Dodsley, a good, jolly,
decent, conversable man, and Mr. Goldsmith,
a curious, odd, pedantic fellow with
some genius. It was quite a literary
dinner. I had seen no warm victuals for
four days, and therefore played a very
bold knife and fork. It is inconceivable
how hearty I eat and how comfortable I
felt myself after it. We talked entirely
in the way of Geniuses.

James Boswell
London Journal
ENTRY FOR 25 DECEMBER 1762

With Bold Knife and Fork

M. F. K. Fisher

COUNTERPOINT
Washington, D.C.
New York, N.Y.

Library of Congress Cataloging-in-Publication Data

Fisher, M. F. K. (Mary Frances Kennedy), 1908-1992
With bold knife and fork / M.F.K. Fisher.
    p.   cm.
Originally published: 1969.
ISBN 1-58243-187-6
1. Cookery, International. 2. Gastronomy. I. Title.
TX725.A1 F55 2002
641.5-dc21   2001008494

Jacket and text design by Wesley B. Tanner / Passim Editions

COUNTERPOINT
387 Park Avenue South
New York, NY 10016–8810

Counterpoint is a member of the Perseus Books Group
10 9 8 7 6 5 4 3 2 1
FIRST PRINTING

For my grandmother, born Mary Frances
Oliver, July 14, 1838, Dungannon,
County Tyrone, Northern Ireland;
died Mrs. Bernard David Holbrook,
April 15, 1920, Whittier, California, U.S.A.

Introduction

This book is about how I like to
cook, most of the time, for people
in my world, and it gives some of the
reasons. These have made life
enjoyable, so they may be of interest
to other human beings.

M. F. K. Fisher

Contents

❧ The Anatomy of a Recipe

IT IS MODISH IN THIS DECADE to refer to the anatomy of a thing or a problem, although Robert Burton really jumped the gun in 1621 with his philosophical exposition of melancholy. Lately there has been published and filmed a successful legal thriller called *The Anatomy of a Murder*, by Robert Traver. In March of 1966 a newsweekly printed an *Anatomy of Inflation*. And so on.

In turn, I plan to discuss the anatomy of a recipe. I could as easily call it a history, a study, an outline, but I like the sound of this.

According to dictionaries, *anatomy* concerns the standard makeup of a thing, or an examination of its parts, or the act of dividing it for observation. I think what I write will qualify in any of these definitions, and certainly it will be done with both passion and precision, for I feel strongly on the subject and consider myself experienced, if not skilled.

The reasons for the gradual changes in a basic recipe such as one for wheat bread, for instance, are inextricably tangled with man's history and assumed progress. A thing like soup, which Jacob sold to Esau for his birthright in the first Biblical reference to the restaurant trade, is too vague to trace unless one settles definitely upon the *kind* of soup, in this case a pottage of lentils, but really the method of making a good lentil soup, even as a loaf of good bread, has changed very little in the several thousand years since it was first mentioned. It is only the way of writing the recipe itself that has evolved, to be trimmed to our changing tempo of reading, preparing, producing.

Perhaps more amusing to contemplate than bread or soup is cheesecake, somewhat less than a staple, more like a treat, a delicacy. In one form or another, but almost always based on sweetened curds, it has been written about and even hymned for centuries. It moved with all the benign as well as corrupt attributes of culture from the East and the Near East into Greece and Rome, and in the almost intolerably lengthy banquet described by Athenaeus in the second century A.D. and called *The Deipnosophists*, many pages are devoted to it, and of course numerous classical references to it by the gabby guests, all of whom could apparently quote every writer of the ancient world, including themselves. One Alexis, for instance, sang from his own *Philiscus*:

> *Now is the time to clear the table, and*
> *To bring each guest some water for his hands,*
> *And garlands, perfumes, and libations,*
> *Frankincense, and a chafing-dish. Now give*
> *Some sweetmeats, and let all some cheesecake have.*

Athenaeus wistfully limited himself to listing only the names of the famous men who had written on the art of making cheesecake, but said that he would communicate to his guests at the banquet his personal appraisement, "not treating you as Socrates was treated in the matter of the cheesecake which was sent to him by Alcibiades; for Xanthippe took it and trampled upon it, upon which Socrates laughed (at his shrewish wife), and said, 'At all events, you will not have any of it yourself.' But I, so fond of cheesecakes, should have been very sorry to see that divine one so injuriously treated."

He wrote, among many other things, of how bridegrooms were presented with cheesecakes by their brides, in Argos, and how brides themselves, in another district, were given the cakes delicately shaped like breasts, by their maiden attendants. He listed the ingredients of many cakes, but few as concisely as this one from Crete:

> Take some nuts and some almonds, and also a poppy. Roast this last with great care, and then take the seed and pound it in a clean mortar; then, adding (some) fruits, beat them up with boiled honey, putting in plenty of pepper, and make the whole into a soft mass (but it will be of a black color because of the poppy); flatten it and make it into a square shape; then, having pounded some white sesame, soften that too with boiled honey, and draw it out into two cakes, placing one beneath and the other above (the poppy mixture) . . . and make it into a neat shape.

Athenaeus added that this was a recipe "of that clever writer on confectionery, Chrysippus"—who, as far as can be judged so long since, forgot to add any cheese at all to his cake. Sopater the farce writer, in his drama entitled *Pylae*, both of them equally unremembered except for loyal Athenaeus the name tosser, wrote:

> *Who was it who invented the first black cakes*
> *Of the uncounted poppy-seed? who mix'd*
> *The yellow compounds of delicious sweetmeats?*

It was Chrysippus, silly Sopater!

There are always a few people who will bother to keep ancient things alive, and through the Dark Ages and even now a curious nose can sniff out recipes which might possibly please Jasper Dillingham, Sr., as well as Sopater. It has been slow going. There was the medieval time-lapse to hinder things, when books went underground with much of the rest of civilized life. With light and the Renaissance, old manuscripts like Apicius' were pulled from the cells and cellars where they had been hidden, and the ancient rules were read out again to the illiterate cooks who must follow them: a little of this, some of that, baked long enough, and then served forth. It was a priest, or a steward, and gradually, as it proved profitable to marry a wife who could read and write, the lady of the house who directed the kitchen, and obviously it was assumed that the cooks knew basic principles to be followed in preparing any dish, whether baked or boiled.

By about 1650, ladies were keeping receipt books to hand on to their oldest daughters (Americans did this until past the turn of the last century, and I have both my grandmothers', stained, brittle, and shockingly archaic in their vagueness and confusion). Many collections got into print, as people of the new middle class learned to read and to ape the aristocracy. They were called tempting things like *A Closet for Ladies and Gentlemen* (Sir Hugh Plat, London, 1608) and *The Queen's Closet Opened* (London, 1687). Of all the "closets," the one I like best is Sir Kenelm Digby's, "published by his son's consent" in 1669. It has one recipe for Herring Pye, for instance:

> Put great store of sliced onions, with Currants and Raisins of the
> sun both above and under the Herrings, and store of butter, and so
> bake.

The fact that no crusts are mentioned proves that Sir Kenelm trusted his cook, to whom he read the instructions, to know that anything called a pie, and certainly any pie in *England*, had/has crusts above and below, perforce, of *course*.

The old receipt books, mostly kept by ladies instead of their husbands, are rare and crumbling by now, and very hard to read. One I have liked for a long time was finished in about 1694 by Lady Ann Blencowe, and was kept by her descendants and published in London by Chapman in 1925. It is plain that many of her recipes are much more precise, more detailed, than before. This was of course because her book was meant to be studied and understood by succeeding generations of housekeepers, although Ann Blencowe could not have conceived that her descendants would actually cook in their own kitchens, translating her receipts to cope with electric ranges, presifted flour, and the Servant Problem.

Here is a good "rule" she gave for Brandy Cake (Mrs. Morice's. This is a nostalgic trick of all the old receipt books . . . my own lists things like Aunt Evvie's Tipsy Parson, Mr. Pike's Indian Relish Not Bad . . .):

Take four pounds of flouer well dryed & sifted, seven pounds of curants washed & rubed clean, 6 pounds of butter, two pounds of almonds blanched & beat fine with orange flower water & sack. Then take 4 pounds of eggs, put away half the whites, 3 pounds of good lump sugar pound'd & sifted, mace and nutmegs to your taste, half a pint of Brandy & half a pint of sack & what sweetmeats you like.

How to mixt the cake: —

Work ye Butter to a cream with your hands, then put in your sugar and almonds; mixt these all well together & put in your eggs. Beat them till they look thick and white, then put in your sack & Brandy & shake in your flouer by degrees & when your oven is ready, put in your Curants & sweetmeats, just before you put it in your hoop. It will take four hours in a quick oven to bake it.

This recipe is a great improvement over one resembling it which can be found in almost any older book, from Apicius to Digby, but it still has several unfortunate things about it. They would be merely bothersome or

tedious to an experienced cook, which I am sure both Lady Ann and her kitchen helpers were, but it is irksome to have to reckon with her lack of time-logic, which is often present even in current procedures. The "flouer" is mentioned first in Mrs. Morice's recipe, and yet it is not shaken into the mixture until third from the last addition, just before the currants and the candied fruits. In mixing the cake, the mace and nutmegs which have been prescribed are not mentioned again. Any idiot knows that they could be sifted along with the flour, and that of course they would be grated or powdered . . . but as a spoiled idiot-child of the twentieth century I want to be *told*.

By now it is plain that there are some things I *demand* to be told, in a recipe. Basically they are two: the ingredients and the method. Ann Blencowe has done this better than heretofore at least, but she has not done the essential for me. She has not named the first in the order of their use as well as their correct measurements, and she has not seemed to use them in their natural order in the method for concocting the hoped-for results.

In 1816 an English eccentric if ever there was one (and there were, and fortunately there still are!), named Dr. William Kitchiner, published an extraordinarily amusing and informative book, and an important one in my own search for correction in a recipe's anatomy. It was called *The Cook's Oracle* (*Apicius Redivivus*), and it said farewell to "the rule of thumb" in cookery and gave exact measurements for every ingredient of a dish, as well as the order of their use. It is true that they were not listed first, as I prefer them to be, but at least a clear look at the recipe told the cook everything that would be called for, and he or more probably she could trust the good doctor (nonpracticing but always fired with profes-sional curiosity) to recount the method in its correct sequence. Myself,

I quibble at doing some of his tricks as they come along: I would like to have more of the additions prepared in advance, rather than let the whole business cool off while I brown one chopped onion in butter to add to a tureen of soup, for instance, and then mix curry powder with flour and three cups of the soup and add it to the same tureen. It is perhaps the fault of the modern tempo? I think the curry broth would profit by standing, for one thing . . . or even simmering a bit. But I bow to Dr. Kitchiner with respect and thanks, and with real regret that I cannot write a book about him and his quirks: the way he would lock his guests either in or out, depending upon their promptness, and the way he . . . But it is not for now.

Mrs. Isabella Beeton owed a lot to him too, just as we all do to her. Her *Book of Household Management*, which first came out in 1861 and is still in print in a "modernized" version that is not half as much fun, gave recipes adapted to middle-class English households with the minimum staff, a bare one in those days, of about three servants, but with the "lady" running the whole thing, from the bursting nursery high above-stairs to the bustling kitchen-scullery-buttery-pantry far below. Mrs. Beeton not only continued with the weird old doctor's ideas about precise measurements, but she also noted the correct cooking times (given a scullery maid who knew how to stoke the ranges properly), the number of servings (given family and guests who knew what was proper to take upon one's plate), the time needed for preparation (given a stern and experienced cook), and the approximate cost. This last is of course the main reason for preferring an old to a new edition of the encyclopedic work . . . fascinating financially!

It really took until 1896 for much order to jump the Atlantic into American kitchen records. This was the year Miss Fannie Merritt Farmer published at her own expense *The Boston Cooking-School Cook Book*. She insisted with clinical sternness that level and standarized measurements be used: eight ounces to a cup, for instance, and five grams or one half tablespoon to a teaspoon, not "some of this" and "a pinch of that."

She was the kiss of death, one would assume, to such sloppy recipe writing as kept on being published for brides like my maternal grandmother, whose copy of Marion Harland's best-selling manual, *Common Sense in the Household*, first published in 1871, is inscribed by an older brother: "Improve each shining hour." But even in the Harland *Dinner Year-Book*, brought out less than a decade later in New York and loyally purchased by my beldam in Iowa, there is little sign that Dr. Kitchiner and Mrs. Beeton had ever slaved over their measurements in London. Here is some of a Harland recipe for Chicken Scallop, to be served on the fourth Monday in July with "A Baked Soup, Green Peas, New Potatoes, Lettuce, Huckleberries, Cream, and Cake," a light hot-day snack compared with most of her suggested menus:

> Cut cold boiled chicken into pieces. . . . Have ready a cup of yesterday's soup in a saucepan—or some drawn butter—and, when hot, stir in the meat, just boil, and pour upon a beaten egg . . .

Then one put the mixture, "rather highly seasoned," into a bake dish, strewed it with crumbs, put "drops of butter over the surface," and baked it quickly half an hour, covered, before uncovering and browning it. Of course this was a recipe for leftover food, which always depends for its salvation upon the inner and spiritual temperature of the cook, no matter what the weather without . . .

And about thirty-five years after Miss Farmer had uttered in an authoritative and Bostonian tone the final dicta of *correct* American measurements, and about seventy-one after Mrs. Beeton had murmured them somewhat less scientifically but with almost equal effect to millions of British housewives, and at least one hundred and fourteen after Dr. Kitchiner had frowned forever upon "the rule of thumb" as applied to civilized dining, well-meaning ladies like my own mother were still copying recipes in much this fashion from their favorite sources:

> For a Nut Cake, cream butter and sugar. Beat egg whites and yolks separately. Fold. Add liquids. Sift flour and baking powder together and add gradually. Add nutmeg. Slice nuts, dust them and raisins with flour, and add. Grease loaf pans. Bake . . . etc., etc.

This recipe, once it has been put into some sequence of procedure and given correct quantities, is a good one, but I do not believe that it came, as my mother firmly did, from Mrs. William Vaughn Moody's *Cook-Book*. At least I cannot find it there. Mrs. Moody wrote in a genteel style, which I think pleased Mother because its somewhat rambling asides were refreshing in the no-nonsense pattern of American kitchen trusties. It had a little of the nonchalance of a Georgian duchess dictating to her head pastry cook a recipe already too familiar to both of them, but although her listings of needed ingredients tended to be erratic, most of her recipes are worth study and translation.

Fortunately I was a ruthless spotter of anatomical faults by the time Mrs. Moody's book was given to me in about 1944, and I knew a good basic pattern when I saw one. But worse than mayhem would face any inexperienced cook who tried to make a batter containing beaten eggs and liquids and baking powder and then put it aside to slice a large quantity of nuts, dust them and raisins in flour which had not been mentioned in the ingredients and must be sought out, and *then* grease loaf pans . . . and then, as far as can be known, heat the oven and bake, at an unspecified temperature and apparently "till done"!

A recipe is supposed to be a formula, a means prescribed for producing a desired result, whether that be an atomic weapon, a well-trained Pekingese, or an omelet. There can be no frills about it, no ambiguities... and above all no "little secrets." A cook who indulges in such covert and destructive vanity as to leave out one ingredient of a recipe which someone has admired and asked to copy is not honest, and therefore is not a good cook. He is betraying his profession and his art. He may well be a thief or a drunkard, or even a fool, away from his kitchens, but he is not a good *cook* if he cheats himself to this puny and sadistic trickery of his admirers, and no deep-fat kettle is too hot to brown him in.

Given such a simple definition of a recipe as the one Webster and I have settled on, and as culinary near-gods like Kitchiner and Beeton and Farmer have set forth, it seems exceeding strange that examples of abuse should continue to come so easily to hand. Even experienced cooks often err, but amateurs are of course the prime criminals. Of these last, I think their slim and beautifully printed volumes which float out of London, through wars and pestilence, are the most quotable. Usually they are on fine paper, with skillful and pleasing woodcuts and a tiny preface by somebody famous. Most of the recipes start out with the comfortably historical "Take": Take a pound of shrimps . . . take some lettuce. . . . The style is always informal: one is discussing, between peers, what was a *succès fou* at last night's little stand-up supper for Imogene (Lady) Craddo, or may be so tonight after Wallie's new opening. A few of the rules give more or less exact ingredients, but in most of them it would be a chancy path indeed from the first "Take" to the table, even for an old tired anatomizer like me. This is mainly because there is no time sequence, no logi-

cal progression . . . unless one perhaps had absorbed the right amount of
gin-and-lime. For instance, in a dish called *Veal Au Porto* in one such
"cabinet," after a vague outline for cooking the dish one is told to "arrange
the pieces [of meat] on your dish, let it get cold, and serve with mixed
vegetable salad. Pour the sauce over them." Over what? The mixed vegetables? When? After the veal has been served with the salad? How cold?
Which? Eh? What say?

Here is another prime example (but almost any page of a fashionable
cookery book will yield a juicy harvest of such plums) of this bland ambiguity:

> (For *Croûte au Jambon*) Take a few slices of lean cooked ham,
> cut them into small pieces and warm them in butter. Bind with a
> stiff and creamy horseradish sauce and serve on hot buttered toast.
> Then sprinkle the top with grated cheese which should be browned
> under the grill.

The time element is almost hysterically askew for anyone mercilessly
stone-cold sober. The "*croûtes*" are served, and then sprinkled with grated
cheese. But is it really the cheese which should be browned under the
grill before it is sprinkled upon the canapés of pieces of ham? And if so,
how would it then be sprinkled upon them, cheese behaving as it does,
and they waiting to be sprinkled but apparently already served . . . ?

Such culinary humor, almost always accidental, makes for innocent
merriment when read aloud, and most of it has a better spice and ring to
it from England than at home. Here, we tend to be less lightsome. There
are fewer elegant and giddy little books, partly because American mass
publishers are leery of them but mostly because the mainstream of our
seemingly endless flood of cookbooks comes from established "culinary
authorities," with large research staffs and definite "ideas" in mind. Gas-

tronomical guides in the United States are for the most part written in a flat undistinguished sameness, which can become a dangerous occupational hazard to people who must for professional reasons read them with conscientious attention. They are, in other words, rarely funny, and almost never witty.

Often they are coy or whimsical. More often they are larded with asides on the general worldliness of the compiler's background: Rome, Istanbul for the off-season, a villa on Crete . . . Most often they depend for their hoped-for appeal upon casual and even intimate folklore: how many oyster crabs Great-Uncle John speared the night he and Diamond Jim competed at a Saratoga dinner table; how Paw used to catch catfish for Maw to serve as *truites au bleu* when she ran the boardinghouse; how Missie Lou-Mary canned her dewberries . . . Rarely funny, anyway, for a *real* laugh. The formulas for the recipes themselves are often more suited to my demands, of course, thanks to eagle-eyed graduates on the publishing staffs who have been trained to modern patterns, but the usual make-up of "idea" books lacks the extra distinction which can occur inadvertently, as in some of the London books, or discreetly, as in Mrs. Moody's or even such a standard manual as *The Boston* or Mrs. Rombauer's *Joy of Cooking*.

A good recipe, for modern convenience, should consist of three parts: name, ingredients, method. The first will perforce give some sort of description: for instance, one does not simply say "Cake" or "Bread," but "Golden Sponge Cake," "Greek Honey Bread." The ingredients should be listed in one column or two, rather than in a running sentence, according to the order of their use, and with the exact amount of each ingredient given before its name. The method should in most cases tell the temperature of the oven first, if one is needed, and in a real kitchen guide should indicate in the simplest possible prose what equipment will be used: a saucepan rather than a double boiler, a shallow skillet, a large deep bowl. In the same way, a true manual, written to instruct every kind of reader from a Brownie Scout to a June bride to an experienced but occasionally unsure kitchen mechanic like myself, should indicate in some way the number of portions a recipe will make. In a book like this one in hand, though, I cannot feel it necessary, and certainly it would be guesswork, for if everybody at table is very hungry there should be "enough," and how can that be defined? And even a dolt must know, instinctively, that a six-egg omelet will not feed ten people . . .

One time, in the "phisical receipts" which were an essential part of any household manual in the medieval and Renaissance periods, I found an interesting recipe, or perhaps it could be called a prescription, which I rewrote to use as an example of what I try to prove in this personal anatomy of such a thing:

Name)	To Drive a Woman Crazy
Ingredients)	1 or more nutmegs, ground 1 left shoe, of 1 woman
Method)	Sprinkle small amount of nutmeg on left shoe every night at midnight, until desired results are obtained with woman.

There is an essential question about this arbitrary formularizing. Does a correct recipe also give the results, the desired end of the procedure? In the case of the woman and the shoe and the nutmeg, perhaps any kind of description is best left unattempted. Some good modern writers, even of

the sternly impersonal "standards," occasionally permit themselves a relaxed comment like, "This keeps well and is fine for picnics," or "Our First Lady once ate this and asked for more." In the uninhibited school of modern gastronomical chitchat, mostly from the gentlemen of course, the reminiscences and asides about a dish are bountiful, and often very entertaining, if one has the time.

There is increasing improvement in the style of cookery writing which falls between these two stools of strict manuals and charming kitchen talk. A few good books are being written and even published with the respect due any honest work, both of and about an art which may be one of our last firm grasps on reality, that of eating and drinking with intelligence and grace in evil days. The best of these, I think, are by practicing teachers. There is a current vogue for cooking schools, and infallibly the right pupils will seek out the best professors, the dedicated men and women with innate taste, rather than the snobbish showoffs who will give directions for making crêpes suzettes in ten minutes which "nobody will know from the real thing." The books by good teachers are scanty, but they are worth waiting for: they will be composed with unfaltering honesty and patience, and the quality of the cook will shine through, exactly as it still does in the textbooks of masters like Alexis Soyer, Escoffier, Mrs. Beeton . . .

I find all this new cool enthusiasm and detachment very refreshing, and cannot but believe that it is a promise for a much brighter future in what could and should be a part of our literature, which must be written by people who know and respect the language they are using and who have true humility, in their direct approach to something which is essential to life itself, the art of cooking.

Teasers and Titbits

IN PLUTARCH'S *LIVES* HE OBSERVED, "It is no great wonder if in long process of time, while fortune takes her course hither and thither, numerous coincidences should spontaneously occur." In other words, history repeats itself. Sometimes this can be leery, in even a tiny way. Occasionally it can be embarrassing, or funny. It can be good, too.

There is an unwritten law, as I assume it to be, that things go in threes, and in one week of my life three coincidences did "spontaneously occur," with such a subtle message that I felt instinctively I would prefer not to heed it. They sound innocent enough.

First, I was reading a collection of short stories written by authors of uneven quality in different decades of the past century, and near the front of the book was the term *félo de se*. It is seldom used in English, but this time it was perfectly in its place, and I enjoyed it, and thought about another one which rhymes with it and is only a little commoner: *auto da fé*. I wondered lazily why I had seen neither of these expressions for a long time. Would I ever write one of them? And then about three stories later in the book there was *auto da fé*. Full circle, I thought with the docility of anyone facing coincidence itself.

A couple of days later I was trying to remember the conclusion of a mistreated proverb beginning, "There is only one thing worse than a nagging woman, and that . . ." and I heard my father saying firmly, ". . . and that is one who *whangs* at you." I had not heard the word *whang*, even in my head, for at least twenty years. Dictionaries say that as a

noun it means a blow, a whack, but the way Father said it, the tone of
voice was what made it a verb: a loud, quarrelsome, stubborn punish-
ment of sound, with hopelessness and ugly despair in it. I pondered the
word, and the strangeness of its coming into my head . . . from a lost
dream of the night before, perhaps? In Mencken's *American Language* I
learned that in some prisons a whang is a dope addict, and that a
whangdoodle is a mystical creature devoted to lamentations, but still I
heard my father dismissing forever anyone, especially a woman, who
might whang. And there it rested until the evening, when a friend came
in for a glass of wine on the way home from work and said casually of
an unfortunate neighbor we share, "I heard Bella Dobson out whanging
away at her poor poodle." I felt a small peculiar shock, quasi-audible,
like the click of a safe being closed in a TV thriller. Half a glass later we
talked about the other words, about the oddness, the mystery, of coincidences in life, no matter how puny. That was all.

The next day, this harmless and pleasurable chitchat almost forgotten,
I started for the second or third time to write about what are correctly
called titbits, the "dainty morsels," the "small delicious nibbles" which
puritanical dictionaries prefer to spell tidbits to protect the salacious. I
myself think of titbits as little harmless appetite whetters served with
drinks before meals: salted nuts, small flavored wafers. Increasingly I regret the custom of presenting elaborate canapés, mistakenly called hors
d'oeuvres in our country, which more and more take the place of a first
course at table and often serve adequately as a full meal, washed along on
floods of strong drink instead of the once customary dry sherry or, for cel-
ebration, champagne. I feel almost violent about this, for personal and
obviously prejudiced reasons, and when I start to talk or write about it, I
am apt to grow malicious, or scoffing, or plain peevish.

This happened as I tried to compose a hopefully light and provocative article about titbits as such: I crossed out paragraphs, tore pages into scraps, made abortive new starts, with a special and mounting dislike for one word especially, the new American *dip*. Finally I found myself outlining an unpublishable credo of protest, based on the cold facts that I had never made a dip in my life, had never in my life tasted a dip (for I refuse to consider an honest guacamole as such, even though it is correctly eaten on the tip of a piece of crisp tortilla which, admittedly, must be scooped through the bowl of mashed avocado . . .), and was sure that never would I either make or taste a dip. I felt very firm and relieved about it, and turned my back smugly upon several new cookbooks with long chapters devoted to dips of varying extravagance. Men don't really like dips, I reminded myself. Dips are messy. The idea of all kinds of wafers and chips and vegetables and plastic skewers dabbling in a common bowl, and often breaking off in it, was repugnant. Down, down to hell itself, I said, with dips. Life tasted sweeter . . .

Then the telephone rang, and my Third Time had rolled around: a kind neighbor, who found herself expected to serve thirty instead of ten people, to raise money for an eminently worthy purpose . . . and would I possibly make some kind of . . .

I interrupted her rudely and fast, for I had a wild feeling that if she said the word, I would go off into a helpless scream of laughter and shake her even deeper than she already had been. ". . . some kind of canapé, some little nibbles?" I asked almost sternly, self-protectively.

"Oh, no, nothing like that," she said. "Nothing that takes any time, really. You can buy several kinds already made, in the supermarkets, and I thought perhaps you could just mix a few together and add a little something, and . . . really, just any kind of easy *dip!*"

I kept in control, and promised to bring a "little something," and hung up before she tried to help me any further.

It sounds silly to admit that I was upset by this last coincidence. I pulled my diatribe about teasers and titbits out of the typewriter and threw it away, and sat down with an out-of-date newsweekly and a glass of dry vermouth to air my spirits. The trick worked its usually twenty-minute magic, and I felt only an occasional wave of hysteria as I read carefully some of the new cookbooks I had dismissed with prejudice and impatience not long before. I scanned recipes for Bean-Bacon Chip-Dip and Saucy Crab-Clam Dip and Blue Cheese Chili Fluff and Pink Devil Dip-n-Dunk. I also read conscientiously the formulas for many other somewhat less outlandish mixtures to be paddled in by drinkers armed with everything from raw green beans to reinforced potato chips. I agreed that not only guacamole but a true Swiss fondue and even a currently fashionable *bagna cauda* demand this communal enjoyment which seems to have become such a lifesaver, apparently, to American party givers. I closed the books and went to two large markets and stared for some time at the pretty plastic containers of dips in the cold-bins. I bought one, made of sour cream with a great deal of monosodium glutamate and not many minced clams in it, and ate some of it for lunch. I then faced the fact that I still refused, as a matter of integrity, to concoct even a reasonable facsimile of such a thing.

I would and did make something rather soft, easy to spread . . . but to *spread*. I compromised with a Tried-and-True from my mother's old files, and poured it while still warm into two wide-mouthed bean pots, and served them at my harried neighbor's Bash with several kinds of new crackers, tasty but not faked with imitation bacon and Cheddar and suchlike flavors. In each chilled jar I stuck two or three old-fashioned butter knives, comfortably broad in the beam. Everything went well.

Here I give the original recipe, and then my "cocktail" version: &

This formula, especially in its first version, makes a good mild cheese for children's sandwiches, as the sharper one does a pleasant fabrication with fruit after a meal, in case straight honest-to-God material is unprocurable. It can also be a commendable after-dinner cheese if made of one part each of ripe Camembert and Roquefort to two parts of sharp American, melted gently into two parts of heavy cream and seasoned with a dash of cayenne, omitting the mustard and salt.

Recently I read a magazine advertisement asking what is the right cheese to serve with a martini (my beleaguered friend served a medium dry sherry with the Canadian Compromise . . .) and then suggesting several different kinds, such as nippy cheddar type in jars, or wedges of everything from Swiss to Edam garnished with crisp bacon curls, sliced olives, and so on. Me, I dislike with my mental palate the idea of *any* cheese with a martini, which in the eyes of the majority may be proof positive that I am not qualified to discuss titbits at all.

I repeat that I think most appetizers as we now present them would be better off served as a first course, and to people sitting down. But

& Edith's Canadian Potted Cheese
(Nobody knows why this is called Canadian . . .)

1 pound soft mild cheese (Tillamook, American, etc.)
1 small can unsweetened condensed milk
1 teaspoon Coleman's dry mustard
1 teaspoon salt
Any other seasonings to taste: dill, herbs, cayenne . . .

Heat milk gently in top of double boiler. Cut or grate cheese into milk, and stir until smooth and melted. Add seasonings. Pour into jars, and keep cool and covered.

& Canadian Pot-Cheese Compromise

3 pounds nippy American cheese
3 small cans unsweetened condensed milk
2 tablespoons Coleman's mustard
2 tablespoons salt
Generous shake of cayenne pepper
1 pint commercial sour cream

Make as in preceding recipe, stirring in the sour cream at the last. Keep chilled. Better after standing, but should be used within two weeks.

❧ *Shrimp Pâté*

4 pounds fresh shrimps, cooked and shelled, or 6 cans
     (4½ ounces) dry-pack shrimps
1 white onion, minced very fine
1 cup melted sweet butter (or more)
⅓ cup lemon juice
Salt, pepper, dry mustard
2 ounces good brandy

Mash the shrimps very fine in a big bowl, preferably with a potato masher or a pestle, and add the onion gradually to make a crumbly paste. Keep mashing, and slowly add the butter and then the lemon juice. Add seasoning according to taste, and the liquor. Pack the thick paste firmly into a greased mold or terrine, and chill for at least 12 hours. If in loaf form, turn out and slice thin with a sharp hot knife. For a cocktail accompaniment, scoop out of the terrine and serve on melba toast or little crackers.

❧ *Potted Shrimps Hyde Park*

2 cups very small cooked cleaned shrimps
½ cup fresh lemon juice
Coarsely ground black pepper
1 cup (or more) melted salted butter

Toss shrimps in lemon juice, most of which they should absorb. Drain in one hour, and pack lightly in small jars, with a generous grind of black pepper on top. Cover to top of jars with melted butter (which can have a dash of cayenne in it, or ½ teaspoon paprika for color). Chill until hard.

fashion is against me, and I bow to it and make several kinds which I think are delicious, and most of which are sturdy enough in flavor to stand up to the impact of hard liquor as well as to supplement the flavor of sherry or dry white wine (which are always on tap in my house for people who prefer them). I like to make things from shrimps, for instance, and here are a couple of good recipes: ❧

(The slow pounding together of this basically delicate mixture sounds tedious, but here it is essential. A blender will make a comparatively uninteresting and too unctuous paste . . . as is the case, I think, with some other things like guacamole, which need a certain texture impossible with automation.)

A much simpler kind of appetizer, but very good if one can find tiny "bay" shrimps, is this: ❧

This is very good with cocktails, or with French bread and a dry white wine for the first course of a meal. And another recipe which is higher in flavor, and very good indeed, seems to be a natural evolvement from what years ago I confidently called Shrimps Arnaud, married as I was to a formula that could easily have come from a little farther north *or* south than the New Orleans restaurant. In a bowl on chopped ice it makes a fine robust appetizer to be speared by hungry drinkers: &

Most shellfish, whole or chopped, raw or cooked, lend themselves to the titbits we now call hors d'oeuvres. A currently stylish thing is to serve seviche, tender bits of raw fish which have literally been cooked by bathing in lime juice or lemon juice: a basically primitive and good dish, to be caught on little skewers at a stand-up party or served as the first course of a meal . . . or, according to some authorities, as a prime booster after a strenuous night.

In Tahiti this simple "fish salad" or seviche is called I'a Ota, or at least it was when Charles Nordhoff wrote the recipe for it in the early 1930s for a seagoing friend. He needed about four pounds of unquestionably fresh fine fish, cut into fillets about one inch by one half inch, and covered with equally fresh lime or lemon juice for about

& Canal Street Shrimps

2 pounds raw shrimps or prawns, shelled
    and de-veined
1 cup olive oil
2 to 3 cloves garlic, minced
2 white onions, minced
6 scallions minced, green and white,
    OR
2 white onions, sliced very thin
½ cup wine vinegar
1 teaspoon salt
½ teaspoon black pepper
1 teaspoon dry mustard
¼ teaspoon cayenne

Prepare shrimps. Then heat ¼ cup of the oil in heavy skillet, add minced garlic and first onions, and stir constantly over moderate fire for 10 minutes. Add raw shrimps and sauté 5 to 7 minutes, always stirring. Remove from stove and cool. In large bowl make marinade of remaining oil, minced scallions or sliced onions, and vinegar and seasonings. Add shrimp mixture and toss thoroughly. Let chill from 6 to 24 hours, stirring occasionally, and serve very cold, with cocktails or as an hors d'oeuvre.

two hours, but never less than one. Then the fish is well drained and served either with thinly sliced raw onions and a simple vinaigrette or

A *Seviche of Scallops*

> 2 cups shapely morsels of fresh or frozen
>   scallops
> Fresh lime or lemon juice to cover
> 3 tablespoons minced parsley
> ½ cup minced green pepper
> ½ cup minced sweet pepper
>   OR
> 1 small jar minced pimiento
> ½+ cup olive oil
> Salt, freshly ground pepper
>
> *Cover scallops with juice and marinate about 2 hours. Drain. Add rest of ingredients, mix well, and chill for at least 1 hour. Serve in bowl on crushed ice with drinks or as first course. Very good in hot weather.*

with fresh coconut milk seasoned and mixed with onion slices. This simplicity is refreshing in the face of the modern temptation to add more and more fire to seviche, in the Latin American way: spices, mustards, powdered red peppers.

The secret of a good preparation of raw fish, besides serving it very chilled and new, is to let it act as a comforter rather than a whet, and I was pleased lately to find in a good new cookbook a trick I knew I had not invented but still had never heard about from anyone else: using fresh or frozen scallops instead of raw white fish or sometimes raw shrimps, for just such a gastronomical palliative. Of course little "bay" scallops are best, from Maine, and sometimes they can even be bought frozen. But the good big clumsy old ones, fresh or frozen, will do very nicely to please even a purist, if cut with moderate care and tedium into smaller prettier bits . . . *tit*bits, that is.

Of course I seem doomed to live without actual pain or deprivation, but with undying hope, from my last taste of caviar to the next one, so I cannot hold with any tampering with it, any more than I can approve of sweetened punches, or "cocktails" made from an honorable champagne. There are many pleasant things to be done with caviar, however, by people who respect the intrinsic fact that it must and can stand alone, un-

aided and unstretched by such deceivers as minced onion, chopped hard
eggs, strips of anchovy. Perhaps the most impressive such thing I have
eaten is a caviar pie made by a famous amateur chef. (I think it is an
awkward titbit to eat when one is standing up with drink in hand, as are
the stuffed hot snails in their shells he also produces happily. Both these
elegant dishes should be served at table, I would wish.) The pie is a gem
of simplicity: a baked pastry shell, filled with about a quart of commercial
sour cream stiffened with one tablespoon of dissolved gelatin and delicately seasoned with minced chives, and then a half pound, or more, of
good fresh caviar spread evenly over it. Come the Revolution. . . .

Most people who are roaming about, drinking, will eat almost anything that is discreetly thrust at them, unless they are the more actively
hungry ones who bend constantly over the tray or buffet table. Often they
seem to like raw things, what in France are stylishly served as *les crudités*,
and I have noticed that they really pounce on olives, which startle and
please them when treated as something besides a meaningless garnish.
Fortunately I live in a fertile wine valley where the Spaniards and then
the Italians and French and Germans brought their trees as well as their
vines with them, and my stores are rich because of my generous friends. I
can serve tiny pungent green olives, very salty, or big darkly mottled ones
cured until they fall easily from their stones, and all the colors and shapes
and flavors in between. And if I am out of my local supplies, I can buy
wrinkled mean black ones on Main Street . . . or I can open and drain a
can of something flat and tame called California Mammoth Jumbos, for
instance, and roll the gargantuan fruit around in some olive oil warmed
with a clove of garlic and a flick of tabasco. Even such emasculated giants
will come to life, which proves my native conviction that olives should
not be served chilled or on a bed of chopped ice, as they usually appear in

America in routine restaurant dining, flanked by a few radishes and a stalk or two of crisp and tasteless celery. Much in the same way, it is a pity to steal a good olive's flavor by taking out its stone, but the black and green pitted ones sold everywhere are very convenient at parties (and of course in some recipes). It is interesting, but a bore, to clean a room the day after several people have been drinking and nibbling, and discover those indestructibly pointy stones behind books, in potted plants, under sofa cushions. Olives, like many other things which have been reduced to near-oblivion by familiarity (potatoes served willy-nilly alongside meat!), or near-invisibility as garnishes to be pushed aside, deserve more respect than they get. They are as worthy of a rescue crusade as some other things any of us could mention . . .

ℰ *Olive Paste, Provençale*

4 to 6 peeled garlic cloves
Pepper, salt, cayenne as wished
1 to 2 cups olive oil
2 cups chopped black olives (canned)

Heat garlic and seasonings gently in olive oil until cloves take on some color. Remove them and let mixture cool slightly. Drain chopped olives, mix well in oil, and pack firmly into small pots or bowls. Press down to make oil rise for firm topping when frozen for a few hours or almost indefinitely.

Here is a fine thing to do with them, which pleases people because of its little trick, and who does not like a trick now and then? It calls for thorough freezing, contrary to my general feeling that warmth brings out the best in any honest olive, and this heathenish freezing is in order to keep the oil which holds the whole together as thick as soft butter, to be spread easily upon bread or wafers. I go one step further and sometimes put the pot or bowl of paste into a larger one filled with water and then put that in the deep freezer, but chopped ice serves as well. ℰ

This appetizer is simple to the point of crudeness, and is probably several thousand years old around the Mediterranean Basin, with packed snow to keep it properly chilled for the great eaters like Nero or Lucullus.

Plainly it is not a thing to eat slowly in a warm room, especially if one is wandering about with a glass in the other hand! A good compromise can be made by treating it like a shrimp pâté and using seasoned melted butter instead of olive oil. In this case I often mince the garlic and leave it in the butter instead of removing the whole cloves, and I add a can of chopped anchovies.

This compromise between natural melting points and social habits could well be the ancestor of the *tapénade*, which was first concocted in a famous restaurant in Marseille less than a century ago but tastes as subtly ancient as Time itself can taste. A tapénade is fun to make, and it keeps well in little pots, to be eaten like its simpler version on bread with drinks or as part of an hors d'oeuvre. In Provence it is served traditionally with hard-boiled eggs, which are often cut in halves and laid face down on a shallow dish thickly coated with the unctuous heady mixture. Sometimes it is simply spooned onto the open halves. Any way, it is good, and here is its basic recipe: ❧

In the recipe evolved by Chef Maynier of the long-gone Maison Dorée in Marseille, the pounded mixture was put through a sieve before the olive oil and brandy were added, but true to form I prefer it with a somewhat rougher consistency. Like all the other concoctions made with olives, it is a fine companion alongside a drink or two at any party, and for

 Tapénade

1 cup pitted chopped black olives
    (canned will do)
½ cup fillets of anchovy, drained of oil
½ cup tinned tuna
1 scant teaspoon dry mustard
Pepper to taste
½ cup capers, drained
1 scant cup olive oil
¼ cup lemon juice
1 jigger good brandy

Pound in a mortar the first six ingredients, to make a thick and fairly smooth paste. Gradually add the olive oil, as for a mayonnaise. Add the lemon juice slowly, then the liquor, mix well, and store in a covered jar in the icebox.

a country luncheon or picnic, with or without its trusted hard eggs but with plenty of crusty bread and perhaps some sun-ripe tomatoes, it assumes its rightful position, as to the meadows if not the manor born.

In this same homely category are eggs, of course. What can be done to a hard-boiled egg is a mercifully limitless mystery. They too are fine in meadows. They are indispensable, in one guise or another, on fashionable buffets, as well as in humble and great kitchens. *La Cuisinière Provençale,* one of my favorite cookbooks, discussing hors d'oeuvres in general, says something that pertains especially to the egg, I think: "The field is immense, unlimited . . . but an ingenious and appreciative cook can give himself free rein, and vary to infinity this category of sophisticated fantasies . . ." And here is a recipe which I suspect would astound even old J.-B. Reboul, tolerant as he felt himself to be about the whimsies now called "appetizers." It is distant cousin to the hard-boiled eggs once found sitting in jars of beet-juice vinegar on bars in American saloons, and I have always wanted to make it, perhaps because I am a soy addict:

Pungent Tea Eggs, Mandarin

1 dozen fresh eggs of any uniform size: duck, hen, goose . . .
Water to cover
4 tablespoons black tea leaves
½ cup soy sauce
1 teaspoon salt
Tangerine peel, cinnamon, if wished

Bring eggs to rapid boil in cold water to cover, and then cook gently for 5 minutes. Save water, and cool eggs under tap. When thoroughly cold, roll gently on board or tap with fork to crackle but not loosen shell. Make strong broth with reserved water, tea leaves, soy, and any added spices. When thoroughly brewed, add crackled eggs and simmer, covered, for 1 hour. Let stand in liquid overnight. Best in 48 hours, but will keep many days in broth. Drain, and serve peeled, in halves, for appetizers, or unpeeled for picnics.

What keeps me from trying this probable amusement? It is a very simple pattern. It would be interesting, and perhaps a little startling, and certainly delicious. . . . Why do I not make it in secret, starting with two eggs, two pinches of tea?

One of the trusted standbys of eaters who like to tease and please their
palates with the subtle whips of richness and rare flavors is what we call a
pâté. In the classical sense, a pâté is always enclosed in and under the
crust it is baked in, while a terrine is made without any crust at all but is
sealed (for days or even months) by a layer of fine fat. Also, a real pâté can
often be served hot as well as cold. By now, in spite of raised eyebrows and
shudders from the gastronomical purists, a pâté can mean a terrine and
vice versa, almost everywhere outside of France perhaps. They are entertaining and interesting to assemble and then make, and are an unfailing
reward to the cook's ego when served forth. Probably the most impec-
cable basic recipe for a terrine (of duck), to my mind, can be found in the
American or French editions of *Larousse Gastronomique,* and any honest
kitchen manual will supply endless variations on the theme.

A "pâté," then, in our current sense, if it is properly molded and
chilled, can be served without plates at a stand-up party, in little smears
and dabs, on morsels of crisp baked starch of various kinds. It can as well
(or better, depending upon one's prejudices) be served at table, cut or
spooned simply from its terrine or sliced elegantly from a truffled loaf
upon a bed of aspic. It is almost as much fun to make as good bread, although usually harder on the purse, even if some kind friends of the cook
bring game to go into it in the hunting season. Pictures of its myriad
forms are dazzling in any stylish cookbook, and recipes are about the
same now as they were a few centuries ago when making a pâté was one
sure way to preserve hare or pheasant, or duck, venison, even goose, for
the long winters and their therapeutic holidays. Good materials, and a
generous but firm hand with both the oven and the liquor bottle, are pre-
requisites of even a simple pâté, and orthodox creators spurn "stretching"
its forcement with carrots, celery, any kind of starch.

Even a casual reading in a few good cookbooks will make it plain, of course, that a terrine or pâté is not something to be tossed together while the kettle boils for tea, but it will be equally obvious that such a cunning dish can be either extravagantly elegant or "home style." Often in France I have used a rather ruthless gauge of a restaurant's worth, no matter what its class or reputation, by ordering a portion of the "pâté maison," and as is often the case in other fields, I have found some of the best in the most unpretentious eating places. They are usually rougher in texture and heartier in flavor than in a fine restaurant, but not masked by stretched ingredients and elaborate garnishings.

I like very much to make terrines now and then. In small pots they are fine for presents, and it is reassuring to hold on to one family-size mold at the back of the icebox, ready for unexpected friends who are thirsty and hungry. For special things like weddings and christenings and such, a true pâté in a fine crust, rich perhaps with truffles, shimmering both inside and out with an artful aspic, is no more than fitting . . . if one has the ingredients and the wish! Or a terrine like the one of duck, in *Larousse* . . . But for one of the nicest celebrations I ever went to, small and quiet and vitally important, as all such things should be (it was the marriage of my younger daughter), we ate perhaps the simplest pâté ever evolved over several thousand years by a wandering people. It was exactly right: light and fresh. It was made with loving care by an Orthodox Jewish godmother and eaten by an ecumenical crew of Presbyterians, Episcopalians, Orthodox Greeks, Catholics, atheists, and backsliders, with equal pleasure. Here is the recipe for it, and may it be savored in good health! ❧

There is no doubt about it: ethnic forces have joined with modern tensions to make it compulsive that most Americans who drink before a meal drink standing up, with strong liquor in one hand and a series of little nibbly things in the other. The more potent the drink, the fiercer and firier the bits of food. A few decades ago, a martini was made care-

fully with about three parts of dry but mellow gin to one of moderately dry vermouth. Now it is concocted of high-proof vodka with perhaps a sixteenth of extra-dry vermouth flipped into it for custom's sake. In scale, the casual bowl of salted almonds or, in some bars after ladies began to share them, the fresh potato chips have come increasingly to resemble a buffet-style meal, in even half-fashionable cocktail lounges, and sometimes in our own homes.

Predominantly Anglo-Saxon or Germanic or Nordic or Slavic in origin, we are in many ways, including the alcoholic, hoist with our own atavistic and gastronomical petards. Our ancestors from the northern countries knew and liked the warmth that strong fermented brews and distillations could give them, and they learned quickly that both wits and swords dulled quickly if whiskey or schnapps or aquavit or vodka sloshed around an empty belly. They drank fast, standing near a simple or elaborate board of the kind of food that could be eaten fairly neatly with the free fingers . . . and they still do.

I have never seen a buffet table in Russia, either White or Red, except in movies, but I have read about them in everything from Tolstoi to *Newsweek,* and a few times in Paris I have been in Russian bar-restaurants

 *Doro's Chicken Liver Spread*

1 large white onion, finely diced
4 tablespoons chicken or goose fat
1 pound fresh chicken livers
Salt, pepper
4 hard-boiled eggs
Pinch of nutmeg
¼ cup brandy or rye whiskey
　　("Not too much!")

Sauté onion in fat until transparent. Add livers, salt, and pepper, and simmer until cooked through. Place in refrigerator overnight, and do same with cooked eggs. The next day chop the eggs finely, add to the livers and onion, and chop all again. Mix lightly, adjust the seasoning, and add a little nutmeg and the liquor. Blend well, but "Do not make it too firm or too loose," and chill before serving.

and wandered about as my hosts were doing, with many small glasses of cold smooth vodka and many generous mouthfuls of the pressed caviar and smoked fish and all the spiced and salty titbits from the bar. In Sweden I have been served awkward large canapés to eat with the fancy sweet cocktails made in my national honor, and in Denmark have tasted from at least eight kegs of different picklings of herring and eight different bottles of aquavit, before dinner . . . fortunately seated at the table!

I have never drunk schnapps before a meal in Germany, and the nearest I have come to a Teutonic version of our American adaptation of racial alcoholic stamina was between the two world wars on North German Lloyd ships, which for some oblique reason I rode a few times. The heavy drinkers of spirits and wines were, it seems odd now to me, mostly very important rich brewers of beer. They drank in a fashion which if it had been more attractive I would call gargantuan but which was only gross: before lunch, and before dinner and often between meals, three or four at a time of "Ohios," from double-sized champagne glasses heavily rimmed with sugar and filled with an intricate syrup of several liquors and liqueurs in which floated brandied cherries. As I remember, the men usually sat down for these beakers. It was stylish, the bartender told me, to drink "American style" instead of ordering the out-of-date quick belt of schnapps washed down with beer, like our own "boilermakers."

As for England, I have usually drunk there with fairly conservative or even abstemious natives, and since I like the old-fashioned type of carefully measured martini and I prefer my drinks uniced, it is simple for everyone trying to please a Yank! In the few good pubs I have come to know, mostly in Liverpool and Penzance, "snacks" could and should be avoided, laid out along the bar itself: open tins of cold Boston-style baked beans, for instance. They had to be paid for, a few pennies a helping, but in Liverpool a dish of little boiled winkles could be brought to my table in the Ladies', with a long pin for digging them out of their last refuge. Very good with gin-and-It, especially sitting down . . .

Here at home I am seldom in a bar (seeming to run my own unlicensed one!), but lately I have spent some agreeable time in two or three in San Francisco, and I am surprised by the amount of temptingly offered food which is consumed, and even gobbled, by people stopping on the ways from their offices for a couple of drinks before dinner. I am too young and of course of the wrong sex to remember the fabulous Free Lunches of the old-time saloons, but the display of hot and cold appetizers I have observed lately in the City is impressive to my naïve eye. I am far from naïve, though, about the danger of pure altruism in any restaurateur's heart and budget, and can see how his highly spiced titbits might well be of latently inferior quality and still appetizing to a hungry and soon numbed palate. Still, they are offered copiously, and accepted with bland and overt greediness, and I think the people lured into ordering three or four drinks instead of two are more relaxed than if they were gulping for a weary trek to the suburbs, or fidgeting with a bored business prospect, with nothing but stone-cold liquor as a standby.

Myself, I have no interest in the sizzling salty lures offered to me from chafing dishes and steaming wagonettes. Possibly my entire attitude toward them, narrow and prejudiced and sardonic as it may be, is summed up in my bothering to outline the following recipe, which is printed seriously in a modern cookbook and which I have actually seen presented, with my own astonished eyes, and smelled with my affronted but still wondering nose. It is called something like Shrimps Aflame with Dip, and is dramatic, to describe it most discreetly.

Shrimps Aflame calls for shrimps, of course, marinated in a vinai-

grette. The dip is made of sour cream with plenty of curry powder, and there must also be a large cabbage, either white or red, toothpicks of course, and a can of Sterno. Sterno is a kind of impregnated wax that burns in a little can, and Skid Row veterans sometimes strain it through the toe of an undamaged sock for its dribbles of often lethal alcohol. The cabbage is made with the help of iced water into a petaled rose. Its hard core is hollowed at the top so that the can of Sterno will fit into it, and then the shrimps skewered on what are elegantly called cocktail picks are stuck into this hopefully firm base. The flammable wax is lighted. *Oh,* cry the guests. *Ah,* they murmur as they bend over the fuming flame, broiling their shrimps in its gases and then dipping them. *Amusing,* they shriek and occasionally, *Ouch.*

In self-defense I now speak gently of what were the most delicate and appetizing of all the teasers and titbits I have ever been offered. It happened in the old Palm Court of the old Palace Hotel in San Francisco, now a Garden Court in a Sheraton Palace. Lucien Hérault still ruled the kitchens there, and when he stopped his royal procedures to make about two dozen of his own *croque-monsieurs* for my pleasure, he was coping skillfully with the black market of World War II and was pleased to please my host, his skillful attorney. In spite of my dogged resolve not to tangle with such a social and legal problem, I managed this late afternoon to eat the old chef's canny offering as if it had been patriotically paid for with ration stamps . . . as if much better people than I were not capitulating to their own hungers . . .

The Palm Court was dim and quiet in the lull before dinner. An occasional shadowy waiter pussyfooted in the edges of light and sound, checking on tables, flowers, unlighted candles. Our small table was an island in a hushed sea. We drank slowly from almost invisible glasses, so thin, a *blanc de blanc* champagne. It was balm to my thirsty spirit, too long in the jumping-off place for all the young recruits being shipped West to the East. M. Hérault scudded toward us with a plate in a huge napkin and then rushed off after postlegal compliments from my host, and we unveiled the prettiest pile of the tiniest sandwiches in the whole world, I am sure. They were delicately brown, very crisp, hot, and precisely the thickness and width of a silver dollar. Unbelievably, they were made of an inner and outer slice of white bread, with a layer of Parma ham and one of Gruyère cheese between. They were apparently tossed in a flash of sweet butter and rushed to be eaten. They seemed to evaporate in the mouth, like fried mimosa blossoms. They were an astonishing thing, in fact . . . minute and complete.

I was told, as I snatched amazedly at them and sipped the beautiful wine, that once they had been much in demand in the Palm Court by the top-level courtesans, who measured them sternly with a stack of dollars alongside, and that the cooks hated to make them, demanding as they did most infinite care. The day I tasted them, the same legendary Chinese bread man who sliced for the gay ladies of the last century still sat behind his knives in the basement kitchen of the hotel, making melba toast like no other, and it was he alone who could cut the bread thin enough, and plainly M. Hérault was the last of the great chefs to have time enough to see that the titbits were properly constructed and then pressed under weights to the right thickness and then fried correctly so as not to gain a millimeter in height. It was, in other words, a historical moment.

I am glad it happened, just as I am glad that not long ago I went to a student *self-service* in Aix-en-Provence and pulled out from the glass counter a lukewarm lump labeled Croque-Monsieur, an inch-thick slab of bread overlaid with a dangling slice of pale ham and topped with a gluey cap of leathery melted cheese. I took it and a glass of tepid white wine out into the pure sunlight of a little courtyard and sat down under the leaves of a sickly palm tree, and part of me was back at the old Palace in the hushed gloom, reaching for another minute gilded dollar, sipping a finer wine in a thinner goblet, and I was happy for such a coincidence to warm my soul. It was not eery or funny or embarrassing. It was good. It is a fine thing that history repeats itself occasionally.

✺ | Especially of the Evening

ANY HALF-DECENT APPROACH TO MATURITY in the use of words. is as mysterious as that of sex initiation into a Congolese tribe, but slower. Of course I can only judge at first hand by the former, but books tell me that it is apparently much easier to learn marital protocol in a jungle clearing southeast of Lambaréné than it is to accept reasons for some of the sounds we use in communications.

My first hint of puzzlement ahead came long before I could spell or read, when I felt bothered, irked, perhaps slightly wounded by the rhyme scheme of:

> *I love little Pussy! Her coat is so warm!*
> *And if I don't hurt her, she'll do me no harm.*

Since then, I have listened to several kinds of accents tackle this, and never have they coped with the basic problem.

About a decade later in my semantic—or, at least, phonetic—education, after I had survived the hazards of "Gladly the Cross-eyed Bear" and suchlike hymns I could sing without reading, I met a professionally mad Basque, really a nice, mild Spanish aristocrat raised in Paris, who shocked me almost silly by prattling persuasively at my first grown-up dinner party about the pity of wasting the word "iodine" on a foul medicament. "Correctly pronounced," he cried, "it would grace any lovely woman! If I should ever have a daughter, I would call her *Yo-deen!*"

I have never recovered from this part of the initiation, and I still trans-

fer common sounds into real or imaginary languages, even subconsciously. Once, in a repaired attic room in Aix-en-Provence, I awoke to the Matins from St. Jean-de-Malte, which rang a few dozen feet from me, and I was saying aloud, "Avocado . . . ah-vo-caa-doh." It was beautiful. I was making progress. (It lasts, so that now deep bells sound very softly when I see the fruit or taste it.) My teachers were leading me from the jungle. Sometimes what they showed me was clear, as with Yo-*deen*, but why the matins in the cool morning sounded avocado "ah-vo-caa-doh" to me I do not yet understand.

One of the last teachers was an Algerian with a bright eye and ear. "What," he asked me with a subtle air of impudent challenge, for he was politically wary and liked to ascribe this wariness to cultural gaps (mine, not his), "is a beautiful sentence to you—a perfect phrase?" Without any thought, I answered, "Soup of the evening, beautiful Soup." We were astounded, both of us, if for different reasons. We talked about it, and I have often pondered it since then. Basically, it can be left alone, like a fragment of Etruscan pottery, and the Algerian had no real need to point out to me, as he did very skillfully, how dull it would be in translation. (Italian and Spanish sounded better than French.)

Of course it was the Mock Turtle, singing for Alice when she was in Wonderland, who gave me the phrase. The peevish Gryphon had maliciously suggested the subject to the poor creature who represented soup itself in those Victorian days, and it was a kind of melancholy wail, a musical moan, he managed to produce. But it still sounds in my ears, "more and more faintly . . . carried on the breeze":

> *Beautiful Soup! Who cares for fish,*
> *Game, or any other dish?*

Who would not give all else for two p
Ennyworth only of beautiful soup?

....

Soo-oop of the e-e-evening,
Beautiful, beautiful Soup!

That is exactly how I feel about it. I like it best without further courses
like "fish, / Game, or any other dish." I know that tuppence would not
buy much today, but when I am tired and cold and hungry, poor or rich, I
would rather drink a bowl of hot broth than confront any meal ever devised. And I feel confident that I would be a useful provider in times of
hardship, for it is challenging, even when I need not scratch for tuppence, to steep the last drop of nourishing flavor from a bone, a cabbage
leaf. There is excitement and real satisfaction in making an artful good
soup from things usually tossed away: the washed tops of celery stalks,
stems of parsley, skeletons of fowl, bones of animals. This cannot be done
in a public eating place, because of modern laws of sanitation as well as
ancient ones of common courtesy, but at home I do not hesitate, if a fine
T-bone lies fairly naked on the platter, to make a stock from it, remove
any fat when it is chilled, and use it within a few days for a soup base or a
sauce. It is, as Mrs. Beeton would say in her Victorian cooking manual, "a
sustaining broth."

For simple living, when one is alone or with children or other people
who must sleep sweetly and then rise to face school or jobs, the supper of
our European forebears is a good one, and when one feels jaded from too
many pressures it seems even more beneficent: all one wants to eat of a
plain soup, some bread or toast, perhaps, then a compote of cooked fruits
or a little custard if indicated by habit or hunger, and then *bed*—unless
there is in the family somewhere an Austrian or a Frenchman who will

enjoy, and gently initiate the others to enjoy, a fuming cup of the mild infusion of various dried herbs and leaves and berries called a tisane. This is a delicate belly-wash indeed, good for quiet talk with friends before a slowing fire, or alone between the sheets.

 *A Life Saver*

> *1 part good stock*
> *1 part tomato juice or V-8*
> *1 part clam juice*
>
> Mix, heat to simmer point, and serve, seasoning and garnishing as wished. Good alone or with a sandwich for lunch.

There are several kinds of soup I consider excellent for such gentle suppers. When I am alone and perhaps a little low, it is good to heat a can of cream of tomato and some milk or water, pour them into a warmed bowl with a sprinkle of cinnamon in it, and go to bed with it. (A small, widemouthed pitcher is easy to drink from, especially if I am reading a good book.) Any mild, smooth soup will serve as well, and I usually keep a jar or two on hand. I make them from leftover vegetables and good basic stock, all put in a blender so that no spoon is necessary when I am half stretched out. I also give the bland, delicious mixtures to my friends, but usually as the sole dish for lunch—hot on a cold day, chilled, of course, in summer.

Another good soup for any weather is made either slowly or quickly, according to one's speed of life. Here is my quick way: ℰ

This can be varied for grown-ups, and indeed made quite sophisticated, by substituting for the tomato juice one part dry white wine added at the last; the soup should be brought just to the steaming point and served immediately. It is also good very hot, in mugs, or it can have things added to it and be eaten properly from a consommé cup or soup plate, at luncheon or dinner. Chopped watercress is a fine, pungent addition. Or why not a spoonful of fresh caviar, if it is there handily growing on the nearest bush?

Plainly there are many tricks, self-taught or stolen from other magicians of any standing in the soup circuit. One good amateur cook who makes the best split-pea soup I ever tasted—and split-pea soup can be a fine thing—adds a quart of strong beer or ale to every gallon of his production before its final half hour of simmering. Why? What does this mean? I cannot possibly say, but certainly the stuff is good, with a nice bite to it. He serves this restorative as the main course of a long, gabby supper, with plenty of pumpernickel and ripe cheeses, or after a lengthy session of music and more talk, when people begin to feel a predawn intimation that they are not immortal.

It is hard to remember the worst soup I ever ate, but easy to give a near-exact date for the best, the most memorable: April or May in 1921. I have eaten many more cunning broths and brews since then, both plain and fancy, but that was a soup that I still dream for when I think about it.

I had been in bed for perhaps five days with some kind of flu, and except for an occasional remote word of sympathy from my parents, who had to remain antiseptic because of all the younger siblings and who therefore could get no closer to me than it takes to use a thermometer, I was *alone*; even my sister had been moved relentlessly into the spare room. This was a test of my being the oldest and the nearest to grown up, and it was perfect for the first four days: I was a sick little animal, lying under the bushes farthest from the pack. Floods of watered fruit juices stood by my bed, for the version of the adage practiced in our house was "Starve a fever and also starve a cold, but more so." (Does this explain why we had few of either, and with no lingering aftereffects to plague us once we got some meat back on our bones?) The fifth day, I felt as pure as a mountain stream, and eager for company, and almost wildly hungry.

From out the kitchen windows and across the roof and into my pri-

vate pest ward came a breeze of delight—a beef broth was in the making! Could I stand to wait for it without howling aloud? I lay for several
hours, obedient to family law but increasingly peeved, for nobody had
bothered to take my temperature or say good morning. Did they not understand what I had gone through? Had they forgotten me perhaps?
About noon, my father came home from his job as editor, occasional
pressman, and volunteer paper boy on the daily *News* and right to my
room, and gave me a bone-cracking hug, but my resulting elation
slumped badly when I heard everyone murmuring down in the dining
room. He had not reminded them that I lay alone—weak, starved, almost sobbing, *alive*.

And then my mother came. She put down a little tray with a big bowl
on it and gave me the second hug of the week and my first kiss and went
away. There, alone with me, waiting for me, was the biggest bowl—a
kitchen bowl—of the most beautiful soup I had ever seen or smelled, of a
clear color like strong tea, with other glowing colors not too far below the
surface, and a pearly vapor rising straight up. At first, I ate it properly, with
a large spoon (the Irish pattern, which was usually saved for Occasions).
Then, aware that things were going exactly as my mother had meant
them to, I picked up the bowl in both hands and sucked at it the way a
half-drowned cow or sailor will suck at the air. It filled me with bliss. I
drank all the dark, heady broth—slowly, no doubt noisily, and very voluptuously. I lay back. Then I returned to the delicious engagement and ate
the freshly cooked morsels of half a dozen vegetables at the bottom of the
bowl, and the bits of meat that had been cut from the big bones I had
smelled rolling in their kettle. I tipped down the last drop, put the kitchen
bowl neatly on its tray, and sank back again for a long, sweet nap. I was

sure that more soup would be there for supper ("Soo-oop of the e-e-evening, / Beautiful, beautiful . . ."), and that my little sister would be sleeping in her bed beside mine. Fate could not harm me.

There is no secret in making such a magic potion, and it is not necessary to be convalescent to respond to it. I know from experience that something almost like it can be contrived quickly from cans and frozen packages and perhaps a pressure cooker. Given the time and the ingredients, though, it is at its best as I ate it that day, made of a strong bouillon of meat bones, and then fresh vegetables: carrots, green beans, slices of zucchini if possible, mild onions, peeled tomatoes perhaps, celery, cabbage leaves. If everything is basically good, there seems little need for salt, but some herbs and celery tops in the stock are one more addition to the savor. The kettle is kept at a slow boil for three or four hours, and then the bouillon is strained, and skimmed of fat when it cools. Good bits of meat are chopped and set aside. The vegetables go into the stock, which is once more boiling, according to their times for being done. The bits of meat are added. The brew is ready, to cheer and succor.

As for the worst soup I ever ate, a merciful and apparently impenetrable veil has been drawn over this event by my highly self-protective nature. I can state, however, that a kind of thin-thick whitish stuff served mostly in Swiss boardinghouses and third-class station restaurants in France should be courteously shunned unless one is almost falling-down hungry. I know its secret—a gritty meal called *semoule*, much like our cream of wheat, which is employed to thicken and stretch pale broths, usually made even paler by a little blue-gray milk. That covers the subject, I think.

The Swiss seem prone to serve thick soups. They always taste as if they had been affronted in some way by the compulsive national addition of starches. They are of various colors, but of a generally indistinguishable flavor. Often they look like a poor American gravy. Here, though, is one recipe that can be delicious:

Alpine Mushroom Soup

½ pound mushrooms
2 cups chicken stock
2 cups milk
5 tablespoons butter
5 tablespoons flour
Salt, pepper
½ cup light cream
¼ cup dry white wine
OR
3 tablespoons dry sherry

Chop clean mushrooms and simmer for 20 minutes in chicken stock and milk. Rub through coarse sieve (I prefer to skip this step). Melt butter and blend in flour. Add liquid mixture slowly and cook over low heat, stirring constantly until thick. Season. Just before serving, add cream and wine.

Most Swiss, and I believe most alpine people, also like to stir things—edible things, that is—into strong, hot broth: droplets of various batters, cubes of soft cheeses, broken lengths of vermicelli. All this must be eaten as fast and hot as one can safely swallow it, which is as it should be in high, snowy country. One fine trick I learned when I lived there, and often play when I am far away, is to beat an egg lightly with a little broth or wine and stir it into a cup of steaming consommé, to make a quick restorative from cold or weariness.

The first time I ever drank this comforting potion was the evening I reached, on shanks' mare, a small unfashionable inn, in the cold dark, wearing a pack and carrying skis, which were also unfashionable in those long-gone days. I must have looked as tired and lost as I felt, for when I asked the sleepy but pleasant innkeeper if she could scare up something simple to eat, she brought me almost at once a big bowl of strong consommé with a milky look to it and told me to drink it all while she scouted the kitchen for some scraps from the family supper. I did. It was enough for my needs, but by the time she came back with a little omelet stuffed with chicken livers, as I remember, and then a piece of apple tart, I felt ready to tackle them and the whole strange business of being a camp follower to a bunch of mountain buffs. (I was never any good on skis, except to stay vertical on the meadows and wait in the huts. "Mush on," my husband would sing out as he went swooping off with the pack. "Good girl! Mush on!" And there I would be, by a fine fire, when they all swooped in again—food ready, heart ready.)

The innkeeper told me what she had done, when I paid my bill the next morning and noticed "Plain Consommé" marked on it, for something like twelve cents. "But that was not plain," I said. "That was special, extra." She laughed a little sidewise and said I had looked as if I could do with a couple of fresh eggs—even with an omelet afterward. Not everybody is that nice.

I don't think we eat enough soup here in the States. It can, and often should, be a meal in itself, as an occasional good book devoted to the subject tries to prove. What is better, more reassuring, on a Sunday night than a tureen of steaming buttery oyster stew, plenty of little round crackers, and some cold white wine or lager beer? Or a chowder—New England style or New York or plain American? Or a reasonable approximation of a West Coast *cioppino*, a Louisiana gumbo, a bouillabaisse more or less *marseillaise?* None of these heady, sustaining concoctions is what my young daughters once described as "innocent," as is a plain broth with an egg in it. There are as many recipes for them as there are cooks, almost, and they are absorbing of time and wit, but worth what one has to spare of both.

There are reliables, standbys, tried-and-trues, in any repertory, public or private, and it is amusing to observe their popularity wax and wane. For some time now, for instance, weight watchers who must lunch often

in upper-class restaurants have shunned the lately fashionable vichyssoise, which is usually served very cold but can be good in winter, hot from a tureen. It is a potato-leek soup that has been either glorified or emasculated, according to one's taste, from its first hearty beginnings to its present genteel position in a small cup embedded in chopped ice, and since it is already on the skids because of its caloric menace, I feel enough loyalty to suggest that a good sturdy old-fashioned version of it be made occasionally by every self-respecting cook who wants to satisfy and soothe a hungry family.

The best version I ever ate was created by a Hollywood star who mistakenly gave up forever the kitchen, in which she could outshine herself, for her figure's sake. She and any peasant farmwife worth her salt would agree on several basic points about their *potages bonne femme*: the potatoes must be of good quality, and raw to begin with; the milk must be fresh; the onions or leeks (or scallions) must be simmered too gently to risk turning golden. In France, as in Switzerland, there seems to be a national temptation to put soups through strainers. I like a soup like this to have more definite texture, with the potatoes melting somewhat stubbornly into the creamy stock and delicate shreds of the onions still wandering through.

Another soup, much more stylish currently than any version of vichyssoise because it can be less fattening, is gazpacho. Again, there are almost as many recipes as there are cooks, and I seriously doubt that such a thing as a classic and firm formula exists, in spite of the Andalusian purists. It is a cold gruel made with fresh vegetables and herbs, bound by a kind of vinaigrette of olive oil and lemon juice or vinegar. It should rest and "marry" for a time before being eaten. In Spain—a more austere country than ours when left to its own devices—gazpacho has a water base and is served, most elegantly, with one or two cubes of ice in it. Here, a private poll lasting some thirty-five years has made it plain to me that my compatriots prefer it made with a fairly strong stock, even a little jellied, and never with the last-minute piece of ice to thin it. But in Spain or in California it is very good after a night in the icebox, and I am told it is balm of Gilead to a hangover. I have tried making it in a blender, urged on by my enthusiastic and otherwise reliable kitchen pals, but to me this forms a basically unattractive mess, without true colors or textures of all the bits of tomato, green and red pepper, onion, herbs that swim refreshingly in the more old-fashioned version. I like to make a rough thick paste of the herbs and seasonings and oil in a big mortar and gradually add the stock, and then stir the minced raw vegetables into it vigorously, to bruise them a little. And it is a personal and nonclassic preference to leave out the sprinkling of dry crumbs that most recipes ask for. It is correct that they will make any extra oil vanish, but the test of a true gazpacho for me is that although it can contain more than its fair share of good olive oil, none will ever make a droplet on its surface if the mixing has been slow and full.

Recipes for this honorable cold reviver are everywhere, especially in the modishly enormous and expensive books now being written by gentleman chefs and lady globe-trotters, but I cannot withstand the temptation to print one version never to appear again, I feel fairly sure. It is, plainly, a freak. It is not even a soup, technically, since it can be eaten with a fork. But it was a standard dish in a hush-hush military enclave of engineers and technicians and their ladies sweltering somewhere between Florida and the Bahamas one long summer of about 1950, and a friendly survivor gave me the recipe. I admit firmly that it has not been "kitchen tested"—in my own laboratories, anyway—but our friendship has, and my brave little donor is one of the best cooks in my experience, as well as loyal and true.

Guzpatchee

2 large hardtack
(keeps well in tropics)
4 fresh ripe tomatoes, chopped
1 cucumber, sliced or chopped
1 green pepper, chopped
Bottled mayonnaise
(can't make *it in tropics)*
Salt and pepper

Soak hardtack in water until soft. Squeeze dry and add vegetables. Mix in plenty of mayonnaise and season well. Chill at least 4 hours or overnight. Fine for the hottest of days.

This repulsive-sounding mess is a mercifully far cry from an Andalusian or even a Californian gazpacho, but it is basically recognizable, and borsch (or borsht) is another one of the soups we can all nod to in this shrinking world. Of course! Vichyssoise is white, gazpacho is red and green, and borsch is plain red. Vichyssoise has little flashes of chives on it. Gazpacho has crumbs, usually. Borsch has a dollop of sour cream—and if it is not red, it is not a borsch, or so most people believe.

Once, to honor a Russian Jewish guest, I made a "big" borsch rather than a little one, and as I remember it I spent about as much time and energy on it as an Irish boiled dinner would take, or a *potée Normande*. It was a masterpiece, and strictly kosher in every sense. But it was not the thin fluid of beet juice flavored with sour salt and swirling with thick cream that my friend and everyone else expected—a tart, refreshing fillip before the meal. It was the meal itself, and the beets were there—but artfully prepared to be added by each person, not the *raison d'être* of the show. Thanks to well-conditioned reflexes, ethnic and otherwise, the show was a delicious flop. We ate it all, but later the star confessed to me that he had never seen such a filling but edible meal and could not possibly think of it with the word "borsch," which had been in his childhood a term for water with a beet boiled in it, to warm and fill the stomach.

I often serve variations of his original version, because the color is pleasant and I can use it to mask amiably a dozen mixtures of meat and vegetable and even fish broths, especially helped by sour salt or lemon juice. Of course I cheat—canned beets are good, sliced or chopped, and so easy! I heat them in their own vivid juices, well seasoned with bay, a flick of cayenne sometimes, and the salt. The liquid will go into whatever broth I have on hand, and the well-drained beets into a vinaigrette while they are still hot, to make a delicious chilled salad. This is a bald-faced trick—as basic as juggling three oranges, I suppose.

Here is a more classic variation on the same Slavic theme, and it has often been approved by both Polish and Georgian friends. For it, the young beets should be either raw and scrubbed or parboiled just enough to let their skins slip off. &

Plainly this recipe is not flimflam. There is some up my sleeve, though, which I disclose less openly. Many people, for instance, are repelled by the idea of eating anything raw, such as an egg yolk. Others will reel with disgust at the word "buttermilk." Such problems are largely semantic

✌ A Little Borsch

14 crisp beets
2 cups vinegar
2 large sweet onions, chopped
2 to 3 leeks, thinly sliced
2 to 3 carrots, thinly sliced
1 cup chopped parsley, with some
  tarragon if possible
3 tablespoons butter
2 tablespoons flour
1 tablespoon salt
½ teaspoon pepper
2 to 3 bay leaves
2 to 3 quarts beef broth
1 pint sour cream

Put 2 beets aside. Grind rest coarsely and cover with vinegar for 2 hours. Braise onions and then leeks, carrots, and herbs in butter until rich brown. Add flour, taking care not to let it burn. Drain beets and shake dry in sieve, and add to vegetables. Add salt, pepper, bay leaves, and then the broth. Let simmer until beets and carrots are tender. Grate the 2 remaining beets, and add with a dash of vinegar. Pass the sour cream separately.

For a heartier dish, make small quenelles of sausage meat, rolled in flour and then poached in boiling water, and add at last.

and best left in silent limbo—the unmentionables. And meanwhile, just as I sometimes add a barely coddled egg, or even a couple of completely unbothered yolks, to a hearty salad that is to be the main dish at lunch, I continue without a sound to make and serve several soups like the two following ones. I forget the name for the Russian recipe on which they are based (an *okrashka?*), which I am told is currently stylish with jet-set chefs, but there is a sour-cream version in Polish cooking called *chlodnik*, or something like that, very cool and rich and suave. &

I usually mix this soup in a pitcher, which takes up less space in the icebox than a tureen, and chill it overnight, stirring it when I remember. It should be *yellow*, so more mustard can be added—a typical "hot dog" type, mild and garish with turmeric.

The second recipe is a personal invention and depends upon the fresh materials at hand. It is very good the next day, and, like the shrimp cucumber soup, it is recommended—along with gazpacho and, I suppose, borsch, too—as a bracer after a heavy night. I assume that all these concoctions could be made most simply with a blender, but I know, even without trying, that I prefer the contrasting textures and flavors of a rougher dish. &

Watercress is a lovely thing, especially so to me because often in my

& Shrimp Cucumber Soup

> 2 tablespoons mild prepared mustard
> 1 large cucumber, peeled, seeded,
>   and coarsely chopped
> 1 cup or 1 can peeled shrimp, with juice
> 1 quart buttermilk

Mix mustard, cucumber, and shrimp in bottom of tureen. Add buttermilk and stir well. Chill at least 6 hours.

& A Summer Soup

> 1 to 2 tablespoons prepared mild mustard
> 1 cup chopped tomato
> 1 cup chopped watercress
> ½ cup chopped scallions and tops
> ½ cup chopped fresh herbs, if possible
> 1 quart buttermilk

Mix all together roughly. Chill at least 3 hours. Then season to taste, which will depend upon strength of watercress and so on.

life it has been as scarce as rubies. When I was little, it was forbidden fruit, since my grandmother abhorred it for growing along the banks of streams where cows might stand—uncontrolled cows, that is. And then I lived often in very dry countries. I like this peppery little weed any way at all, and more than several times have embarrassed people by eating what was meant as a garnish on a plate. A quick fine soup can be made by chopping about a cupful and adding it at the last to heated and seasoned canned soups: cream of chicken or tomato, plain beef or chicken consommé. And here is a good, reliable recipe, open to budgetary or coincidental changes, of course, which has often pleased people I like. (It interests me—egocentrically, at least—that I seldom think of making a soup for people who bore me or to whom I feel indifferent. In the same way, I do not waste a good soup on people I love dearly who, poor souls, detest the stuff.) ஃ

Chowders are homely fare, no matter how distinguished their ingredients. I suppose baked beans, stews, desserts like Brown Betty, are in the same delicious category. Like all basically honest things, they can be perverted and desecrated by human stupidity-cupidity, but it is hard to think of making a bad one on purpose.

 ## Green Garden Soup

1 bunch watercress
½ head solid lettuce
4 scallions and tops
4 green celery tops
4 green cabbage leaves
10 to 12 sprigs parsley
1 sprig fresh thyme, if possible
3 to 4 tablespoons butter
1 quart (or more) strong chicken broth
1 egg yolk
½ cup cream
Salt, pepper

Chop all vegetables and herbs fine and simmer gently in butter for about 10 minutes, stirring to prevent burning. Add broth. Cover and simmer slowly about 30 minutes. Beat yolk and cream together, add desired seasoning to broth, and then stir in the egg mixture. Serve at once.

This soup can be put through a sieve or into a blender and then reheated before the egg and cream are added, to make a more elegant and equally delicate dish.

✑ A Clam Chowder

½ pound very lean bacon, cut in ½-inch
*   pieces*
2 mild onions, minced or
2 bunches scallions, green and white,
*   split and cut in ½-inch pieces*
4 large potatoes, peeled, cut in 1-inch
*   cubes, boiled 5 minutes*
2 cans (4 cups) cream-style corn
2 quarts hot water, stock, or water
*   from potatoes*
2 cans (2 cups) minced clams and juice
Salt, pepper
1 cup sliced red pimiento, optional
*   but recommended*
1 pint, cream or top milk, heated
Butter, in lump size of egg
Paprika

Cook bacon slowly in big pot, remove when crisp, and drain on paper towels. Keep warm. Cook onions gently in hot fat. When limp, add drained potatoes and mix well. Add corn and continue thorough mixing, and then add hot stock. Simmer 15 minutes or until potatoes start to melt. Add clams, and season. Add pimientos and the cream or rich milk. Pour into hot tureen when well blended and top with lump of butter freely doused with good paprika. (Scatter bacon crumbs as last garnish.)

Once, in Paris, at Prunier's, I ordered a clam chowder, New England style. (It was on the menu, although, of course, unrecognized as such in *Larousse Gastronomique*.) There were several other things I would have preferred to eat in that happy temple, but I felt a patriotic curiosity—what would a great French fish cook do with a Yankee dish? It was superb, the best and purest I have ever eaten, kept very simple and made with salt pork, clams freshly minced, crackers crumbled on top, all according to kitchen Hoyle. It put my own slapdash floutings of regional tradition into shameful shade, but I continued to play with them, depending upon the weather and my company, and here is one sturdy skeleton from the classic mayhem which can be clothed more or less at will: ✑

Obviously, this is a hearty mish-mash. The clams can go, or the corn can go, and surely the pimientos and the paprika can go, but the bacon, the onions, the hot milk, must *stay*, for reasons of gastronomical, regional, and even national honor and integrity.

This chowder is much like one we used to call a Harlequin, for some reason vague but probably Anglophiliac—lots of chopped fresh vegetables, braised gently in butter or good fat and then simmered in stock, with milk or cream added at the last. The first recipe is certainly naïve, but a Harlequin has more real innocence.

It is true that in our country many people do not think much about soups as a pleasant and healthful part of their daily fare. They are a boringly correct prelude to a meal in public, and few families serve them. I know of almost nobody who makes a winter or summer soup the whole meal, as can so easily be done, and I cannot find the reasons for this almost studied unawareness of a simple enjoyment. Very young and very old people find it much easier to drink a soup from a properly designed cup than to eat it with a spoon from bowl or plate, and often I serve brews, thick or thin, from mugs fitted to the drinkers' sizes and skills, and watch them smile. At boarding school we were given a thin, tedious consommé before the main course of dinner six nights a week, from large flat plates, and our manners were closely watched by the head of each table of eight shy, clumsy, splashing girls. I suppose I can feel some thanks at this safe distance for such training, but I am always glad when I can get people of any age to enjoy a good pottage without their worrying about spots, spills, shaking hands.

Most people, especially men, seem to feel safer with a thick soup than a thin one, as far as table habits go, and in winter I like to please them with lumpy chowders and their ilk. But there are many soups that can well be put in a blender and then *drunk*, no matter how thick. It is nice sometimes to serve a big hot pitcher of one of these, and another pitcher of a clear broth, when people are standing around talking after a concert or a late meeting of Puzzled Moms and Dads, Ltd. They take care of themselves and drink with one hand left free for the oyster crackers or the brown-bread-and-butter sandwiches.

For fun, here is another way to serve a more impressive buffet, either stand-up or with small tables where people can sit with their plates and/or mugs. A good white wine is fine with it, and a fruit compote afterward—cookies with that, and coffee, and of course crusty bread or crisp buttered toast with the soup. &

❧ A Chicken Soup Supper

Make a rich chicken broth, from any classic recipe. A pressure cooker is useful for this.

Cut the meat from the bones, chop it coarsely, and put it aside.

Skim and season the broth, saving the fat.

To serve: Put the heated broth in pitchers. On the buffet table with them, have hot rice or kasha (cooked preferably in chicken broth instead of water), the chopped and seasoned chicken tossed in some of the fat, and smaller bowls containing chopped parsley, chopped chives or scallions, perhaps capers, thick fresh cream (flavored lightly with curry if wished), chopped hard-boiled eggs, sautéed mushrooms, finely ground pecans or almonds. The broth can be drunk, plain, from mugs, or it can be poured over any mixture the guest may wish to make from the bowls of chicken and so on, and in any amount.

This is a fairly easy and entertaining meal to assemble. It tastes fresh and tempting, and seems to please people. It can be developed, up or down, but for myself I like it to remain simple, with things hot and well seasoned, or chilled, according to their natures.

And there are a thousand other good games to play around the soup kettle. Gather a few good basic recipes, and the field is open: a Greek *avgolemono*, which can be served very cold as deliciously as hot; a minestrone stiff enough to stand a spoon in, as friend Nino says it must be (wonderful chilled for breakfast on a hot day!); a soothing and baffling garlic soup from Provence, or one *au pistou*. They wait in good cookbooks, to try for size, as any good cook will and must do—a gastronomical tailoring, to fit the cloth to the suit, or something like that. And then there are the plain curiosities, like Guzpatchee, or like the caraway soup I'll note for possible titillation or nostalgia, and the elegant buckle or frill for armchair epicures, sidewalk chefs, like a consommé Talleyrand, possible to savor with the mind's ear and tongue, but not available in two-pennyworth portions. Soups of the evening—soups of the morning, of noon, but especially of the evening! Oh . . . beautiful Soups!

"A cure for colds or malaise," says the family recipe.

And at the other end of the stick, far from sniffles and homely remedies for them, is an equally simple but infinitely less attainable broth, which I feel sure would do much to ease my malaise, whatever that might be: 🙵

🙵 Caraway Soup

¼ cup butter
2 tablespoons flour
1 tablespoon caraway seeds
2 cups hot water
Salt
Rye bread croutons or toast

Brown the butter, stir in the flour and caraway, and brown again until the seeds pop. Stir in the water carefully. Bring to boil, and then simmer 10 minutes. Season, and serve with toast.

🙵 Consommé Talleyrand

4 large fresh (or canned) truffles, grated
½ cup very dry sherry (or more)
Cayenne pepper, a pinch
3 pints strong veal or beef consommé
2 tablespoons tapioca

Put grated truffles in tureen, cover with sherry, and add pepper. Cover closely and let stand one hour. Boil consommé with tapioca until it is transparent, and pour over the truffles. Serve at once.

How to Spring Like a Flea

I KNOW A MAN WHO GAVE UP what could be called an enviable life in central Nevada because he refused to eat any sea fish more than a day old and got tired of the fresh trout which often leaped in mountains all around him. He was rich, powerful, famous, sadly limited, and now he is dead. He reminds me of one of Brillat-Savarin's anecdotes about a devout gastronomer who had been given a political appointment in Périgueux, the capital of good living according to the Périgordins: truffles, turkeys stuffed with truffles, red partridges stuffed with goose livers stuffed with truffles, people stuffed . . . The new tax assessor sighed. "Nonsense and alas! How can I possibly be sure that anyone could survive, in a country where there is no fresh sea fish?"

As an elderly child of this century, I do and can accept many gastronomical vagaries which a true gastronome would not condone. I do not eat as much fresh fish as I would like to, because my friends who tickle the streams of the Sierra and the mouth of the Russian River grow fewer with the years and because most of the pitiable stuff called by name in the local markets is beneath my stove's contempt. It has been frozen, perhaps when caught and perhaps not, and then thawed again. It does not smell right. It does not feel right to my disdaining but always hopeful finger. Then it does not taste right, once cooked. A pox on it.

But I do use *frozen* fish, which I myself can pick up like bleak logs now and then in the markets. They tease my inventiveness. And of course

I use canned and pickled and smoked fish as the spirit moves me, with no feeling of betrayal to my inner standards.

Here in my town we can occasionally buy fresh salmon, and more rarely the excellent rex sole, with its blunt taste of iodine. In season, if we are lucky, there are shipments of cooked crab, best eaten cracked in the San Francisco fashion, with lemon juice and a mayonnaise firm in its taste of olive oil. (This calls imperatively for crusty bread, and to my mind none is better than the flat loaves of "sourdough" sold on Fisherman's Wharf, which fortunately can be bought in our whole area if people are insistent and persistent. Any light dry wine will do, but a Grey Riesling from Livermore Valley is traditional in our family.)

There used to be a good fishman in this little town, but he has gone from my scene. He would blow a horn here and there inside the city limits, the way the mobile merchants did when I lived on a farm in Provence. It was fun, forewarned and armed with my wallet and a tray or basket, to meet him at the curb. Neighbors would gather, and of course our cats. He had his own two-legged pets, nice old ladies who had been buying from him for fifty years and got the best of his family's catch before we ever even heard about it. Still, we fared well. I miss him. He used to plunge onto the dark roads up to Napa Valley right from his brothers' boat at the Wharf, and as early morning traffic grew thicker his outdated driving habits failed him, and he and all the freshly caught fish got spilled a few times too many . . .

I can still fake a lot, thank God. I can make a very decent oyster stew, for instance, with the Western Olympias shucked and packed into glass jars and kept chilled in reputable markets, and even canned ones will do, if one is fortunate with the brand. Often large coarse-seeming oysters, fresh or canned, prove very rewarding in flavor when chopped finely or put through a food grinder and then added to a basic cream soup. Purists strain most such blends, but at home I like them "rough." And here is a good recipe, unorthodox as All Get Out (a tantalizing comparison from unknown but not too remote ancestral sources), for a kind of stew that might raise eyebrows if not shoulders and hackles of Escoffier et Cie. It is one of those things easy to assemble and serve forth on buttered toast . . . and it is as good made with clams, chopped or whole, fresh or canned: &

✌ *Sunday Night Oysters*

3 tablespoons butter

1 small chopped onion or

6 whole scallions, thinly sliced

1 #2 can tomatoes with juice (2 to 3 cups)

Salt, pepper

½ cup chopped parsley and/or other
       herbs, to taste

1 pint canned oysters with juice
       (about 3 cups)

4 eggs

Hot buttered toast

Melt butter. Cook onion slowly until translucent. Add tomatoes and heat until bubbling. Season and add herbs. Simmer 8 to 10 minutes, add oysters, and mix well. Carefully break eggs into bubbling sauce. Cover, remove from stove, and let stand until eggs are set. Serve over and with hot toast.

Once I got caught up in a wild correspondence about how to tell when an oyster is bad. It involved all the old wives' tales, including the trick of seeing if a silver coin would turn black if left with the opened mollusks in a covered dish. One experienced old trencherman/chef advised me to drink copiously of the lowest type of rotgut red wine if ever I suspected that I had downed a potential murderer, and thus flush it out of my system on an almost equally lethal flood of tannic acid. And perhaps the most stoical counsel, especially since I had just swallowed the oyster I at once suspected to be bad, and had at least nine more on my plate (they were flown to Berne from Bordeaux that morning, the maître d'hôtel had assured us...), was a cool remark which still has almost the ring of an adage to it: "As in

certain other forms of physical assault, sit back and enjoy it. You will either be dead or feeling fine, in exactly six hours . . ." I finished my plate,
and I still feel fine, several decades later.
One must suffer to be beautiful, I have been
told, and since then I know that one must
occasionally risk trouble to be happy, and I
was very happy that day in the Swiss bar
where all the best spies ate lunch.

    Every everyday cook has her own ways of
saving that everyday, and here is one of
mine, made to please people now and then,
Fridays or any day. Obviously, since I seem
to have lived most of my life removed from
the seashores, what I name as raw oysters in
the recipe usually come from the half-
frozen jars I can often find, and the raw
peeled shrimps and the scallops have been
frozen. These are logistical hazards. ℰ

ℰ A Scramble

2 cups buttered crumbs, preferably made
*   from stale bread*
2 cups defrosted raw scallops in bite-size
*   pieces*
2 cups raw peeled shrimps, same size
2 cups raw oysters, small or cut in halves
Soft butter
Salt, pepper
1 cup cream

Put thin layer of crumbs in buttered baking dish, then
scallops, then crumbs, shrimps, crumbs, oysters,
crumbs, dotting each layer with butter and seasoning
it. Fill dish, moisten with cream, and bake in
preheated 400° oven for 30 minutes.

    This is a kind of "scallop" in the old-
fashioned sense, and simple, and open to infinite change.

    As I have already said, I like raw scallops (the ones from the sea) tossed
quickly with plenty of butter and paprika, to be tossed then with rice. I
like scallops uncooked, in a kind of seviche. (I like *scallops!*) I also like
shrimps and their myriad disguises, and I like oysters and theirs, and mussels whenever and however procurable. I do not know of their being
frozen, perhaps because the American demand is a thin one, but sometimes from Holland or Japan I can get very decent canned and smoked
ones, and meanwhile thank my stars that I was raised in Southern Califor-

nia before its coastal waters developed whatever ugly thing it is that makes mussels poisonous for so much of every year . . . if indeed it does. We were ignorant and well fed, and from about my fourth year until whatever may be my last, I'll have known that uncounted mussels steamed open on a bed of fresh seaweed, and eaten hot from the shell with plenty of melted butter and lemon juice, make a supper fit for dreaming.

✑ *Annie's Clam and Sausage Patties*

1 egg, lightly beaten
1 #7-ounce can minced clams, with juice
1 pound pork sausage
10 soda crackers, crushed
¼ to ½ cup minced parsley
½ cup finely chopped onion
Thin lemon slices
1 scant cup dry white wine or vermouth

Mix first six ingredients lightly but well. Chill about 1 hour. Make into small patties in shallow baking dish, with a spoon. Put lemon slice on each, and add wine. Bake 45 to 50 minutes in preheated 350° oven.

I think that all these briny titbits should be cooked quickly and lightly, and eaten soon, whether fresh or frozen. The same is true of bigger crustaceans; nobody can persuade me that an instant-frozen lobster claw is quite the same as from this morning's catch, but I feel able to help it into an honorable dish, and even enjoy it, as long as it has kept somewhere about it the secret freshness of the sea, which speed and my hopeful skill will manage to hang on to for a fleeting time.

About clams, now: there are noted ones along this coast, and I have friends who pursue them at the right times of the year, but I really do not like them as much as the more delicate ones from other parts of the world, except perhaps minced in cans. I often use these in one way or another, mostly in variations on the Chowder Theme. Their bottled juice is a staple on my shelves and has saved many a flat broth or sauce with its pungent natural salts. And here is a recipe which always seems improbable to me, but is dependable and interesting for an occasional change of flavor and texture: ✑

Who on earth ever thought of this? But then, what bold man first put love apples into a cream soup . . . or ate an oyster?

> *(The man had sure a palate covered o'er*
> *With brass and steel, that on the rocky shore*
> *First broke the oozy oyster's pearly coat,*
> *And risked the living morsel down his throat.*
> John Gay said this, perhaps in 1660?)

It is almost painful not to give more ways to play with the fertile and ubiquitous shrimps. They are plentiful in brooks all over the world and in salt waters and bays. They are the fleas of the seas, someone has said before me, and of course they are shameless scavengers. They are pretty little creatures in their way, and Oriental brush-painters dote on them as models, with their vanishing fragile parts. I can feel dotish too, in a more destructive way, when I confront a little pile of them, freshly caught and cooked to gray or rosy, and a pat of fresh butter, and some bread and copious pale cool wine. I like to eat them thus simply, as we used to along the canal in Burgundy, and in Paris and Marseille. They seem scarcer now. Manners have changed, and of course the streams are not as sweet. Here on the West Coast the tiny "bay" shrimps have disappeared completely from the once welcoming waters of San Francisco, thanks to heedless pollution, and the little ones caught and frozen off the northern bays do not have the same almost decadent succulence. (In Venice, the shrimps caught in unmentionable locations in the canals had somewhat the same allure, and I think I have never eaten better ones or more enjoyed them, served peeled in a bowl with enough herbs to mask the dangers and enough wine in the glass to counteract them . . .)

There are many books written about shrimp cookery, for anyone who wants to go further afield or astream, and meanwhile here is one delicious way to prepare the large gray prawns (also called "green") which are easily found in markets, frozen or thawed. (I buy them in five-pound blocks and ask my friend Remo to break them into two or three rocklike chunks. Then I thaw one to use right away and put the others in the reefer . . .)

 Baked Scampi

6 to 8 large prawns per portion
Olive oil
Salt, pepper
¼ cup chopped parsley per portion
1 clove garlic per portion
¼ cup bread crumbs per portion
Butter (optional) or olive oil

Split prawns in two down back, and take out vein if necessary. Place with cut side down, in their shells, in large cookie pan generously covered with olive oil. Let stand 5 to 10 minutes, then turn over, oily side up. Season to taste, and sprinkle generously with parsley. Mince or grate garlic into dry crumbs. Put prawns with parsley into hot (450°) oven for 4 to 5 minutes. Remove, and sprinkle garlicked crumbs over each prawn. Dot with butter or olive oil if wished, and place close to broiler until crumbs are brown and prawns begin to curl. Serve immediately, from the pan or piled on a platter.

Another good trick is to marinate uncooked peeled prawns, split if they are large, in sherry and lemon juice, and then drain and pack them into an unbaked pie shell with some sliced olives, cover them with strips of more pastry (or not), and bake them in a quick oven for a delicious tart . . .

Ah, well, there are other fish in the sea . . . with fins and scales, for instance! Hilaire Belloc once wrote that:

> *The Whale that wanders round the Pole*
> *Is not a table fish.*
> *You cannot bake or boil him whole*
> *Nor serve him in a dish.*

Of course this is true, in terms of pots and dishes, but not of skillets, for I know from experience that steaks are made from whale meat, and my knowledge is rather dismal: the meat is very oily, and unless cooked gently for a long time it results in nothing but a tough hunk of ugly-colored fibers, floating in a pan of peculiar grease. I have one Eskimo recipe for white whale, which says to cut the meat in pieces, put it into the pot, and boil it with salt and, fortunately, water. Then the blubber inside the whale's small intestine is added for richness and savor, and all is cooked again. Ah, yes?

My personal interest in fish, as in other functional beings, is dispassionate, as I suppose it is toward birds: they inhabit somewhat the same world, if not the same elements, as I try to do too, and if they wanted to eat me, as I occasionally do them, I am sure they would find a way. Since I do eat them, I prefer that they possess certain qualifications of edibility, to make them what Samuel Johnson would call *foody*. Any dead fish, for instance, whether of the fresh waters or the salt, should have a bright and firm if staring eye. It should not feel slimy to the touch, and its flesh when poked with the finger (human) should spring back like a healthy living human's or fish's flesh. In some fish one can lift the cheek and look for a bright red gill. If a live sea monster has been caught for religious or gastronomical reasons, a carp for instance, and put thoughtfully into the bathtub until slaughter time, it should swim about, no matter how despairingly, and not lie sunk in despond at the bottom. And above all a fish should smell fresh.

A FISH SHOULD SMELL FRESH.

It is perhaps impossible to say what "fresh" smells like, except that it smells right, not dubious. It smells like new-cut grass, newmown hay, an innocent brook, or a child emerging from his bath, or almost any happy clean thing for that matter. But when a fish smells wrong, it is not for buying or for burning. It should be tossed away ruthlessly, where not even a fatalistic cat would deign to touch it.

People have used the smell of spoiled fish as a simile for rottenness since words first started floating through the air. Perhaps the most pun-

gent dismissal of a political rival I ever heard or read is one made in 1806 by Senator John Randolph: "He is a man of splendid abilities, but utterly corrupt. He shines and stinks like rotten mackerel by moonlight." This might be called gentlemanly anathema, or even understatement!

There are plenty of quotations, some of them called adages or proverbs, about the spoiling of the delicate flesh of a fish, and usually they relate themselves to human behavior. Fish meat is called "white," lacking or thin in red blood, and it can and will die early . . . like lettuce or eggs, the flesh of lambs and fowls, even certain parts of our bodies such as the brain. The tide should not go out on a fish, say people along the world's coasts, before it is in the pan . . . just as modern surgeons say that a body's blood should not stay too long away from such complex tissues as may make up Man. All this is dictated by ancient wisdom, sometimes called self-preservation, and not by the abrupt contradictions of modern storage techniques. Now, though, we can keep quick-frozen fillets of fish, not to mention other bits and pieces, for almost indefinite times, and treat them with rays to make them last in time capsules for other civilizations to wonder at, if not consume.

One of the most apt and sardonic proverbs I have ever heard has been said in one form or another by every culture I know about, even the suave and courteous Chinese, and it is as direct as one wishes it to be, and an excellent rule to recall in times of duress: Fish and guests grow stale in three days.

It is wrong to imply that I have known this all my life, for I was raised in a kind of backwash of the nineteenth-century custom of spending several months at a time with relatives whose physical or spiritual climates were sympathetic. We ourselves stayed home. We never went anywhere. Maybe it was because we felt all right *there*. But we had regular visitors

who escaped to us from Iowa winters, London and Dublin and Hong
Kong fogs, Chicago riots and strikes, and other more personal embarrass-
ments, for whole winters, long summers. It was wonderful: stress and
storm at times, mostly for my parents, but wonderful.

This is almost a vanishing custom, now that houses are smaller and
transportation is quicker and people have air conditioners and credit
cards and such. I remember one winter when my Uncle Park lost not one
but three trunks in his biennial trek from the Midwest to our Whittier
ranch, and as far as I know they were never found, having been shunted
off perhaps in Sioux Falls or even Albuquerque, but he barely missed
them for the necessities of life he had brought along in several more.
When he returned to the pleasant spring weather of his little prairie town,
three or four months later, he simply bought a cheap valise or two to hold
his usual esoteric tribute of tree-ripe oranges . . . Then of course there
were many cousins who went to Western universities and spent all their
vacations with us. And there were old friends of my parents who were recovering from major surgery on their bodies or souls, and young friends
whose parents had died or gone away otherwise. It was all part of living in
a big, confused, cluttered warm house, inadequately staffed by hired
saints and sinners who today would literally prefer being shot at dawn to
the hours they kept then and the jobs they had to do. (We had one cook,
who stayed for a phenomenal three years or more, who to relax and rest
herself would make a great pile of crullers or six pans of date bars . . .
Mad! Gone!)

Obviously we did not think of our visitors as *guests*. In fact, my mother
was known for her disinterest in such transients, and was even counted in-
hospitable by local observers, the while her house teemed continually
with long stayers. She who hardly blinked at having ten steady customers

for three meals a day would go into a nervous activity which was foreign to our habits if "company" had been invited to dinner, and as we grew used to this phenomenon in such a generous woman we easily convinced her that she need not fret and fume: *we* would protect her, by not letting her invite people for less than a month! We were protecting ourselves, for it was amusing to live as we liked, which meant easily and well, if with certain strong elements of politeness and protocol. It was understood, for instance, that on the Friday nights (no school the next day) when Uncle Evans was there from Michigan, he would peel countless apples for us in the sunroom after supper, instead of our eating dessert at the table . . . so we did not ask what the dessert might be, even if the apples got rather boring. And when Mother's school friend Miss Whitby was there, recovering as usual from a love affair or something like that, we ate without a whimper the pureed and mashed bland foods her emotional colon needed.

As far as I know, it never occurred to us that this steady stream of visitors could be connected with stale fish . . . and yet that has been a firm opinion for centuries. My friend Georges said to me, many years after my apprenticeship in keeping a live and open house, "I must remind you that a guest is like a freshly caught trout, delicious and rewarding the first day. The second day either one will seem subtly flat, and in need of extra flavorings. The third day, my dear, he like the fish will *stink*." Georges was in the process of installing himself for at least six weeks with us, while he lectured in California. I said to him, "But then you don't qualify?" And of course he did not.

It is unfortunate that fish must wear this cloak of unpleasantness, but in a way it is our safeguard against possible poisoning, for there is no way to disguise the honest stench of rotting flesh, and that, I suppose, is why many women of the Midwest pretended to abhor all swimming things, when I was growing up. We almost never ate fish at home, as I

recall . . . at least while Grandmother was alive. Certainly there must
have been good ones in the rivers that swept through Iowa, but the
people who caught them were not of her class. She depended upon an
occasional exotic can of salmon to serve creamed on toast, and salted
and dried fish sent from the East, that never-never land on the other
side of the Mississippi. That is why, when I was little, we occasionally
ate finnan haddie and codfish, always boiled until almost tasteless and
then swimming in a "white sauce" and served with little pale potatoes.
Otherwise we lived happily without, between her occasional whims. But
surely there must have been people all about us, in Whittier, who
caught or bought and then cooked the creatures of the nearby Pacific
and our deep occasional lakes?

Grandmother, and my mother, and several of our cooks, disliked the
smell in the house of frying or grilling fish, even if they liked fish as such.
I still know people in this sad state of gastronomical dichotomy. Sometimes I prepare sole or mackerel or trout for them, which they lap up like
the proverbial cat who "would eate fish, and would not wet her feete."
There are several tricks about this knavery in a wide-open house, with the
finicky guests by the parlor fire and the fish blatantly in the next room,
but the main one, not a true trick at all, is that the fish must be *fresh*.
Then, and this is especially true of a whole fish or one in thick slices
which must perhaps be kept overnight from a fortunate catch, a quick
thin painting of soy sauce will hold in the natural odors and still not alter
the flavors of the prospective dish in any way. I would not use this coat of
soy on a dainty fish like sole, for instance, already filleted . . . but then I
would not buy it at all if I would have to hold it too long.

Frozen fillets can be very good, with a certain amount of skullduggery.
It is well, for instance, to read about herbs and seasonings now and then, to
refresh oneself about such maneuvers as using dill with sole. This always

astonishes me, but I do it, somewhat cautiously . . . except once when I invented an impressive dish of the fillets wrapped around pieces of dill pickle, the whole covered with a rich sauce, with mushrooms and olives and cheese and God knows what, I feel sorry about the whole thing, if I let myself brood about it. I did it to an unmitigated cad I wished to discourage from the life of a close friend, and he soon disappeared. She felt happier almost at once, and we can recall with equanimity that he loved every lick of the barbarous dish. But I am regretful to have stooped so low.

(Dill with so fine a flesh as sole is no more preposterous, or at least mysterious, than the Provençal way of grilling the *loup*, most precious of the Mediterranean catch, over dry twigs of fennel . . .)

No fish is much more delicious than freshly caught salmon, poached and served cool with a good mayonnaise and cucumbers, but good things can be made with the varying qualities of canned salmon from grocers' shelves, and here again dill and fennel, and many other herbs, stand guard for the questing palate and the curious nose. In Simon's *Concise Encyclopedia of Gastronomy*, Section II, *Fish*, the whole potential is nicely summed up: "Salmon may be boiled, poached, grilled, stewed, baked, fried, and prepared in ever so many ways. It is excellent both hot and cold: also smoked, potted, and pickled." And it is also excellent tinned! Almost any cook will vouch for this and keep one or two kinds on hand. Decent salads can be made, with care of course to remove hints of skin and those strange chalky bones that used to tantalize me when I was very small and occasionally was sneaked one by an accomplice in the kitchen. Nice "scallops" can be made with the drained fish and crumbs, butter, mushrooms, what you will. And so can commendable "loaves," and stuffings for hollowed baked potatoes, and mixtures to spread on canapés or between bread slices for sandwiches. I have even eaten one good *lomi* of canned salmon, made patiently by an Islander with her hands, in the correct way. She shrugged a little impatiently about it, but I found it delicious, and here is the way she compromised with her native recipe (which would use salted fish, well refreshed by soaking): &

The working with the hands (lomi-lomi) is by far the best way to make this good soup, but a potato masher or pestle will do for the squeamish. A blender is not at all right, because the texture becomes nearly unpleasant, and the color too uniform. As for the final addition of crushed ice, there are some Mainlanders who do not like this, any more than they do in a correct gazpacho, but they seem easily convinced if not consulted beforehand! A salmon lomi is eminently refreshing and most pleasant on a hot day or night . . . or regretful morning!

What André Simon's *Fish* says about salmon is true of fish in general: they are good, prepared in countless ways . . . as long as they are good to begin with, of course. He forgot to mention soups in his list of attributes of the fish under discussion, but almost every coastal culture has its own version of what in San Francisco is called *cioppino*, in Marseille a bouillabaisse, in Boston a chowder, in Stockholm an *älsoppa*. The herbs in it will depend upon its country and climate, and a Swede would no more add garlic than a Provençal would use dill . . .

Some fish soups limit themselves to one breed of beast at a time: clams in a chowder, for instance, and eels in an älsoppa or matelote. Myself, I like to play the field and see what happens, but there are certain tacit

 *A Mainland Lomi*

1 large can (2 to 3 cups) good salmon
2 to 3 cups ripe tomatoes, peeled and
 mashed
4 to 6 scallions with green tops, finely
 minced
1 mild medium onion, finely chopped
Salt to taste
1 cup crushed ice (also to taste)

Drain and flake the fish, and mix it thoroughly with the mashed tomatoes and then the finely minced scallions and onion, working slowly with the hands. Salt to taste. Let chill for several hours, mix lightly again, and serve at once with crushed ice stirred in.

rules: do not mix freshwater fish with those from the sea; do not mix coarse fat fish with delicate ones; do not combine fresh and canned fish. Here, though, is a list of combinations I have kept since it was given to me in about 1932 by a famous woman cook of Martinique. It contradicts every possible rule, in her case for the construction of what is called on the island a bouillabaisse, more or less correctly since it is indeed a fish soup brought quickly to the boil and then simmered: (1) white fish, fresh salmon, lobster; (2) flounder, perch, scallops, lobster; (3) freshened dried codfish, tuna, smoked salmon, canned crabmeat; (4) lobster, shrimps, oysters, clams; (5) halibut, trout, bass, pompano. This last is perhaps the oddest, to my mental palate, although (3) does not allure me. I always think of halibut as a strong meaningless fish, probably because I doubt that I have ever tasted a small freshly caught "chicken." Trout I think of as a freshwater fish, and although I have only caught lowly rock bass along the cliffs of Laguna, I do know that it too can be good from lakes and rivers. But with halibut? And then pompano, that dainty fragile creature? This makes a combination to ponder on, certainly, but I would choose (2) or (4), if I had the wherewithal. And meanwhile I would follow the original recipe from Madame La Perle, which calls simply for three pounds of any good fish at all, and lobster if possible, and plenty of lemon juice. It also needs olive oil, onions, leeks, tomatoes, garlic, and of course some water! What better? It would raise the hair on a Provençal's bald head, but at least it is cooked the same way as his own bouillabaisse, fast and then slow.

Sardines in cans have a special quality which one either pines for or despises. Of course canned salmon and tuna are completely different from the fresh fish, and I have eaten fresh sardines a few times and found them as different, but there is something mysterious that happens to a sardine in a can, quite beyond the expected fishy changes. I must admit to a flash of fondness now and then for the tiny ones, luxuriously packed and priced,

and occasionally sent to me in a tuck box by rich uncles. I like to eat them
when I am alone, either straight from the can with a toothpick or laid
neatly, olive oil and all (it would be a pity to mash such exquisite little
corpses!), on a large diagonal slice of toasted French bread. This is perhaps
coarse behavior on my part, but at least I do not like the coarser fish! They
are too plump, too strong in taste and smell, too often packed in low-grade
oils or coated with an ersatz tomato sauce. Horrors indeed! The truth is
that I could live easily without any of them, even the wee ones . . .

It would be harder for me to forgo anchovies for the rest of my life.
I use them often in cooking, as they come from the can in flat fillets, or
mashed in a mortar, or occasionally in paste from a tube. I never seem to
have any use for the rolled fillets, and when a can of them turns up in a
tuck box I pass it along to some deserving friend who is garnish-prone.
I have never much liked the red pickled anchovies often found in small
stores in ethnic pockets here at home, and almost everywhere in France.
They are strongly spiced and rather slippery. As for the big barrels of the
salted fillets or whole fish which also stand in European grocery stores,
I long ago decided that if it were a case of cold economy I would simply
eat anchovies less often and buy them already prepared for me. This may
be an indication of some latent Rich American Syndrome . . . or plain
laziness. But soaking those unattractive smelly things, and scrubbing
them, and then clumsily boning them . . . ho hum.

I think one of my most useful kitchen capers with anchovies is to lay
them in a half-baked pie shell, with a cheesy custard and perhaps some
sliced olives, and bake them to serve warm or cold. And I almost always
have an anchovy butter on hand. It is useful: a dollop on a grilled lamb
chop, a bigger dollop with shrimps to serve hot on rice . . . It is a friend.

I know a fisherman in Monterey, very old now but still out on the
deep waters unless his sons say no, who sighs about two things: the grad-

ual pollution of his ocean and the dozens of wonderful fish that nobody but fishermen will eat. In most markets, even in Monterey and San Francisco, it is rare to find more than four or five kinds of fresh fish, any day of the week. "And now even good Catholics buy fish on *Thursdays*," my friend says scornfully. "They should be ashamed to serve old fish on Fridays!"

It is strangely reassuring to a frustrated Anglo-Saxon gourmande like me to be told by an Italian that he and thousands of other Mexican-Japanese-French-Hawaiian-Cuban-etc.-etc. dwellers along the West Coast go quietly about their own cooking of every single one of the true fruits of the sea, even while I must "make do" with frozen fillets of sole . . . and an occasional spree in a restaurant in the City where Dover sole is actually from Dover and not more than thirty-six hours old, and in another one where a local pride, the rex sole, can actually be ordered in advance now and then and served with the fresh butter in which it was sautéed rather than in a thick close-fitting bathrobe of spongy, oily batter.

In general, however, I must draw my immediate comfort from cans and the freezer, and refresh myself as needed with what a Japanese poet wrote long ago. There is a blithe poignancy about this *hokku*. It lightens my palate:

> *Young leaves everywhere;*
> *The mountain cuckoo singing;*
> *My first bonito!*

Another poet, English this time, once wrote that after a good fish dinner a man would spring like a flea. Me, I would rather leap like a bonito . . .

Some Seeds of This Planet

THE LITTLE SEEDS CALLED RICE, pearl white when they are husked, are among a good cook's best friends. They can appear in elaborate or completely simple dishes, from one end of a meal to the other, and familiarity with their uses has never bred contempt in anyone who likes them to begin with. Such a poor wretch as a rice hater I have never met.

We used to eat rice often, in many delicious plain ways, when I was growing. It was tender but not overcooked, and with every grain separate, although an Oriental would have shuddered at the great amounts of boiling salted water that had danced about it, and a modern housewife would be shocked at the debilitating washings it went through before and after it was boiled. When done, it was poured quickly into a special collander with small holes, and cold water was run over it. Then the collander was swung over more boiling water, and a clean folded towel held the steam in until we were to be served. What was left from dinner went into a baked custard full of raisins, with nutmeg on top. Or into a meat loaf or a stuffing. Or into a rare treat on Saturday noons, pancakes stretched with the nutlike little grains and doused with maple syrup (always served hot at home). Excellent fare! Later I was to learn through experience that it possessed more texture than flavor, but still it was good.

Chinese and Japanese methods of cooking rice differ somewhat with regions and utensils and fuels, but comparatively little water is used, and once at a boil the kettle or pot or jar is tightly closed and is never opened again until the grains are "done." This doneness is inexplicable, of course,

71

and for myself, often coping with rice from undependable sources, I have made a few real mistakes by trusting to blind instinct. I think a lot of rice today has been treated in one way or another to look whiter or even browner as the purchaser wishes, and to cook faster than it naturally should, and of course in the Oriental method it is forbidden even to *peek*, much less take out a few seeds to test them. Occasional results: dismal.

One Chinese directive I have says to add two cups of rice slowly to two cups of boiling water, cover the pot tightly, turn heat to *medium* for ten minutes, to *low* for ten more, and then *off* for ten . . . and "Do not remove the lid at any time." Another instruction, from a vanished correspondent named only Akagi in Osaka, says to wash one cup of rice thoroughly (thereby removing most of its nutrients, as we always did at home), add it to two cups of fast-boiling water, and stir until it boils again. Then it must be covered tightly, put on an asbestos mat over the lowest possible flame, and "Do not peek!" Mr. Akagi says, "Truly it will be done in about forty minutes." Well . . . thirty-seven? Forty-three?

Lately I have kept a box of "minit" rice on hand! I do not approve of this emasculated and precooked stuff, but when treated with grudging respect, and occasional gratitude, it has saved face for me when something went wrong . . . and cooked with a good chicken or beef broth in place of water, and tricked out this way and that, at least one of the current brands is palatable and, even more important, edible.

There is a mischievous Caribbean song about a bride making peas and rice for her husband. She says, "I put de peas in de pot to cook, / An' at de paper I took a look. / My favorite horse was goin' to run, / An' de peas in de pot dey all got bu'n!" Naturally things went from bad to worse for her until the last stanza, but there *is* nothing much worse than the smell of peas burning, unless it is rice burning, and it is no wonder that her "malicious

neighbors" were laughing at her. A few times I have misjudged the nature
of the rice I was cooking, and the stench when it stuck to the pot and sent

out ugly brownish gas was unfriendly, to put
it in a mild unmusical way, although I heard
no actual laughter.

    Here is a good simple recipe, which
should allow a little time for the racing
form: ℬ

    The last sentence of this recipe is help-
ful, since I have never been in the Bahamas.
I prefer using whole dried peas to the ones
called "split," to keep more character in the
dish, but the one time I made it with chick-
peas (garbanzos) the verdict was that it
seemed *too* crude and heavy.

    Rice can be cooked in two basic ways,
right and wrong. *Right*, for me, results in a
mass of separate and unsoggy grains, tender
but still with a little elasticity in them. I
know this can be attained by cooking it in a
great deal of quickly boiling water and washing it before and after, thus robbing it of al-

 *Bahaman Peas and Rice*

2 cups dry pigeon peas
¼ pound salt pork, diced
1 large onion, chopped
1 cup canned tomatoes
1 small pod hot red pepper
¼ cup fresh thyme
2 cups rice
4 cups water

*Soak peas overnight, drain, and put on to cook until
almost tender in plenty of clean water. In a separate
pan fry the pork and onion together until golden. Add
the tomatoes, pepper, and thyme. Drain the boiled
peas, and put in the bottom of an ample pot. Add the
uncooked rice, and cover with 4 cups water. When it
boils, add the sauce and cover closely. Let cook
without stirring until rice is done and liquid is gone.
(Black-eyed peas or any similar dried pea may be used
if pigeon peas are not available.)*

most everything but its innate nature; that it can be done by using a West-
ernized version of the age-old Oriental method, to be found in any reputable kitchen manual; and that it can even be done, in a pinch, with a
packaged five-minute facsimile. *Wrong*, fortunately, seems to be without a
real recipe, but it is the way the Swiss like it. It is the way it is served in
Lucerne, Berne, Lugano, and perhaps Geneva, although I have not

stayed there long enough to be exposed to it. It can be a solid creamy rich mass if you eat it in a good restaurant or home, and a grayish lump of unidentifiable exnodules, very sticky, if you happen to come upon the rare but occasional place of culinary disrepute which is always found on a bad day.

I have looked for a formula in several Swiss cookbooks with no luck, unless one wants deliberately to tamper with something like the "Risotto in Bianco" I often ate in Lugano. Cruelly I could devise an alternative to this good recipe and produce almost exactly the drab glutinous blob I have been served at even famous tables in the country that has often been my home, but here is the noblest version of what is still not my own idea of the *right* way to cook rice, because the Swiss do not watch their watches! (The friend who gave this recipe to me really preferred it made with milk, but would bow to my preference for the consommé and wine when *gentlemen* were her guests.) ⅋

⅋ White Risotto (Risotto in Bianco)

2 tablespoons finely chopped onion
½ cup butter
1 cup rice
1 cup dry white wine and
1 cup good stock or consommé
    OR
3 cups rich milk
Salt, pepper
Grated dry white cheese (Gruyère,
    Romano, Parmesan . . .)

Cook onion in butter until soft, add rice, and stir until opaque. Heat wine and stock (or milk), season to taste, and stir into rice. Cover tightly over very low heat and cook for about 20 minutes or until rice is tender. Serve with cheese.

I cannot resist adding here that I have never had this recipe prepared correctly except when I made it myself. Even in the Ticino the Swiss seem unable to serve rice at that mysterious moment of *doneness* innate in the Chinese, but let it turn soft and sticky. They *like* it that way. And I like being there with them. So I eat it when it is set before me . . .

The few more recipes I have pulled from my Tried and Trues may differ, but only slightly, from the thousands of them in good kitchen "bibles" and special books written on and around the subject of rice cookery. Some start with raw grains, absorbing as they go whatever the cook plies them with. Some depend upon rice already cooked. Variations on the two themes are endless, obviously, and with any sense at all they are rewarding.

It is said that one-third of all this planet's people lean on rice as their staff of life. For the rest of us, who need not eat it for survival but may play with it to please our kitchen fancies, probably a third more will think of a *risotto* as the best and perhaps even the only way to start a good dish with the raw grain and be able to count on its easy and successful end. Like many other classical formulas, the one for a risotto varies this way and that with every cook who makes it outside of a great restaurant, and perhaps even there. For example, there are as many recipes for a "correct" risotto made in Milano and called *alla Milanese* as there are cookbooks to outline them, and one I found dares to omit any mention of the saffron that even a half-educated gourmand would consider its special mark.

Some recipes start *every* risotto with the raw dry rice, and others soak it fifteen minutes and then add it to the basic liquids or sauces. Some want the rice to be creamy but still firm, and others state that every grain should be separate. Some use pure olive oil, and others a variety of mixtures of butter, beef marrow, oil, chicken fat, salt pork, and so on. The end result can be the same: a delicious thing to eat, whether served at the beginning of a meal as in northern Italy, or as a meal in itself, both simply and luxuriously.

The first time I ever ate a true risotto was, properly enough, in Milano, in a sparkling restaurant in the Galleria Vittorio Emanuele. I felt almost blinded by the perfect weather and my own private happiness, being comparatively young and completely in love, and I assumed, perhaps rightly, that I was surrounded by princely silk-merchants, stars from La Scala, and hungry duchesses. It was the right time and the right place for the right dish, and although I suspected immediately that it was not very well made, it was no flaw in the general perfection. It was too hastily cooked, a little too much *al dente*, and there was too much saffron in it, all because I completely upset the kitchen at the noon hour by asking for something not on the lengthy menu. I behaved like a naïve tourist, which I was. And I am very glad I did . . . and was. The dish was at its simplest: rice made opaque in a light olive oil and then simmered with some white wine and chicken broth, with the moistened saffron added perhaps five minutes before the dreamily handsome waiter served it. Ambrosia . . . because everything was at its correct position in both Time and Space.

My Basic Risotto

¼ to ½ cup butter or olive oil

¼ to ½ cup finely minced or sliced onion

2 cups raw rice, preferably Carolina
    or Italian

1 scant cup dry white wine

4 to 5 cups hot chicken broth

2 tablespoons butter

½ cup grated Parmesan cheese

Heat butter or oil in heavy saucepan, and in it cook onion gently until golden. Add rice and stir constantly until opaque, about 5 minutes. Stir in the wine, and when absorbed add the hot stock, ½ cup at a time as it disappears, always stirring. In about 20 minutes or when done, stir in the butter and cheese and serve at once, with more cheese alongside.

Here is my own basic recipe for a risotto, which can be made plain or fancy, and named for any town between Milano and Los Angeles, according to the wind and the weather and what is in the cupboard: ❧

This is really a risotto *in bianco*, and is delicate enough to stand alone as an accompaniment to chicken, for instance. If a scant teaspoon of saffron, of course steeped in a little wine or broth, is added about five minutes before it is done, it will be the foundation for a risotto *alla Milanese*, to be eaten plain, with plenty of grated Parmesan or with mushrooms, chicken livers, little shrimps lightly cooked first and then added to it a few minutes before it is done. In Venice chopped ham and green peas are cooked in the butter before the rice is added (and at home I cook the fresh or frozen peas lightly, add plenty of butter, and toss them with the risotto just before I add the cheese).

This same basic recipe can be made with more onion, with herbs, and with beef broth or even tomato juice, for a lustier dish. A dry vermouth is good instead of white wine (but red wines should not be used because of the weird color the rice will take on). One or two cloves of garlic can be heated with the oil and onion and then re-moved before the rice is added. Dried mushrooms, softened first in warm water or wine, give an excellent hearty flavor to such a risotto. Fresh mushrooms, I think, are better sautéed separately in a sauce fitted to the flavors already in the rice. Naturally this sauce will be stronger for a risotto made with beef broth, bacon or ham, tomatoes, or herbs than for the more delicate "white" one.

There are many other dishes made with raw rice which simply put everything together and then cook it slowly, usually in the oven, until done. Here is a foolishly easy method, which obviously can be made more exciting with herbs, mushrooms, whatever, added before the final baking begins:

 *Baked Rice*

2 cups brown rice

3 cups beef stock

    OR

2 cups beef stock and 1 cup white wine

    OR

1 can condensed consommé and
      1 can water

2 to 4 tablespoons butter

Salt, pepper

Put rice in casserole, add liquid and let soak for 3 to 4 hours. Cover and bake in preheated 350° oven for 50 minutes to one hour. Toss with butter and seasoning, and serve.

A good jambalaya, which really can be called a *concoction*, since it depends for its furbelows upon the cook's mood as well as the cook's past history, can be made in the following way, which will horrify many purists by calling itself "Creole":

A Shrimp Jambalaya

3 medium or 2 large minced onions
½ cup good fat or oil
3 tablespoons flour
4 peeled chopped tomatoes
½ cup minced parsley, with thyme or basil as desired
1 minced or mashed clove garlic
½ teaspoon chili powder (optional)
1 cup rice
5 cups boiling water
1 pound fresh peeled shrimps (raw) or 1 large can of shrimps

Brown onions gently in fat, stir in flour, and brown again. Add tomatoes, parsley, garlic, and seasoning. Add rice and water. Cover, and let simmer for about 45 minutes. Add the raw or canned shrimps, heat rapidly, and serve when the raw shrimps are cooked through but not tough . . . perhaps 5 to 6 minutes.

One unorthodox but delicious trick to play on this recipe is to forget the shrimps! Instead, cook small sausages and put them hot over the dish before serving. They should be brown and plump . . .

A more elegant jambalaya, as served in the West Indies, can be a grand mixture of sautéed chicken, ham, shrimps, a sauce, all cooked with herbs and such vegetables as tomatoes and green peppers, and then blended with already cooked rice for the last five minutes. This can be impressive and delicious, but I like my so-called Creole version for more humdrum (and shorter) gastronomical flights.

Once a cook considers what to serve with rice which is already cooked, the field is limitless. Books about curries, for instance, are published continually, with the success of a well-ticking clock. Special restaurants all over the world serve nothing but curries. Spice merchants grow rich on making their regional and private blends of curry powder. In other words, reputations can and do depend upon the authenticity of the recipe first and then of the powder which goes into the sauce, the skill with which the sauce is made, and in many cases the atmosphere in which the whole is served.

The general flavor of curry powder is recognizable, and many people live happily with what comes out of any of a dozen bottles and tins of it to be found in general markets. I list myself in this humble class. I also claim that I sense at once when I am eating a sauce made with a special high-level powder, although I do not know what part of India its formula may have come from. It is much like realizing that one is in the immediate presence of a noble Burgundy without knowing (or even caring) on which side of which hill its grapes grew in the Côte d'Or.

Probably the "greatest" curry I ever ate was in London, in 1930. It was in a small private room in a famous Indian restaurant. It had been arranged days before we sat down on the low couches. I had been asked if I wanted "mild" or "hot" by our host, and having been raised in Southern California in the days before Mexican cooking adjusted itself to the timid palates of the invaders from Iowa, I felt qualified to say, "Oh, hot, of course." There were more servants than diners in the pukka-sahib treatment our host had dictated for us, and very soon, but with exquisite discretion, one of my attendants noticed that tears were silently running down my cheeks, for I was too young to admit that I had been both cocksure and ignorant. A bowl of finely cracked ice was put by my dishes, and every time I ate a mouthful of the curried whatever-it-was, I followed it with a mouthful of the temporary balm. The next day the insides of my lips were finely and thoroughly blistered, but nobody ever teased me, and I felt it was worth the anguish for that strange experience in the dim silky room, with the silent men moving above us on our divans.

It was the other end of the stick from the favorite dish we looked forward to when I was a girl between about eleven and eighteen, which we blandly assumed was a real curry. The recipe for it would stupify or at least shock any kitchen purist, and by now of course I myself admit to a certain embarrassment in printing its skeleton time after time. But it *is* good . . . if one likes the smell and taste of curry powder as such. (Not only the smell and taste but the word itself will make some people feel sick . . .) It is low class, coming to us from a big blowzy nice cook whose corporal-husband had died in Injah long before. It is what some people would damn as an economical dish, since it is a godsent vehicle for cubes of leftover steak or roast beef. And it is made with the powder that comes from an easily procurable tin box, correctly disdained by a curry connoisseur, and not a freshly contrived blend of paprika, chili, ginger, turmeric, garlic, onions, cinnamon, coriander, nutmeg, mace, pepper, allspice, pimiento, mustard, anise, fennel, saffron, cardamon, fenugreek, poppy seeds, asafetida . . . And here it is: ⅋

⅋ A Makeshift Curry

1 large onion, thinly sliced

½ cup fat or 4 slices chopped bacon

1 to 2 tablespoons good curry powder

¼ cup wine vinegar

¼ cup water

1 cup tomato sauce

Leftover meat in cubes

Leftover gravy

Fry onion golden in fat or with bacon. Mix curry with liquids and add to onion. Stir briskly over hot flame to develop flavor. Add tomato sauce and cook five minutes. Add meat in pieces, and any gravy, and stir until heated through. Simmer 10 to 15 minutes. Serve with fresh dry rice and one or more condiments, or a sweet preserve such as figs or peaches.

A poor imitation of a Madras Curry with Beef, certainly! But I am as loyal to it in December as I was in May.

It is wrong to think that curries are served only in India, and there are myriad recipes to prove this. I have one which is rightly called Hawaiian, although many other cultures could claim it, and which is very delicately made with coconut milk, fresh ginger root, and shrimps. There is one made with bamboo shoots, and another Chinese recipe for a chicken curry made with grated coconut and fresh red peppers. Their like appear every day in print, ready for the curry buffs like me.

And then there are all the combinations of meat and fish and poultry which can be served on cooked rice, with great success if one cooks the rice properly first and then concocts the rest with respect. Fats Waller sang a slyly libidinous song about seafood long ago, in which he stated, "Swimpses and rice / Are *very* nice!" And a great many of us agree with him, for the recipes for serving the two together are countless and often good.

They usually involve some kind of sauce, or even a form of gumbo made with green peppers, okra, and tomatoes, with the cooked shrimps added at the last, to serve with the rice. Once, though, I listened to some fishermen in a mean bar in Delaware, and I liked the simplicity of the recipes they were exchanging. The best, spoken gently,

 *Rice Fats Waller*

1 pound large shrimps or prawns
　　(or small scallops)
1 cup good butter
1 to 2 tablespoons good paprika
½ cup dry sherry
　　OR
¼ cup lemon juice
4 to 6 cups cooked fluffy rice

Peel and devein shrimps or prawns, and cut in two down backs. Heat butter, add shrimps and paprika, and shake over hot fire until shrimps curl and turn white. Take off fire and add wine or lemon juice. Shake again and pour over hot rice. Mix lightly and serve.

　This is a quick operation, and one should not stint on butter or paprika.

with the shot glass of bourbon warming in the hand for slow sips: "The goddamn rice is cooked and dry. I take my goddamn swimpses, all peeled and raw, and throw them with plenty butter over the rice and heat it until they curl right up, and then I throw in some goddamn sherry and it makes, man, well . . . *good.*"

I went on from that day, and here is my goddamn version, perhaps even better with fresh or frozen small scallops than with swimpses: ✆

Stuffed baked mushrooms are very good placed with all their delicious juices on a bed of hot cooked rice. So are all kinds of creamed
and even unsauced combinations of
chicken, vegetables, meats. One I consider
worth reminding people about is a mixture
called, mysteriously since no Japanese
friend has ever been able to explain its
name, Egg Muchi. It was a standard dish
for the Sunday night suppers a San Francisco hostess served for the several years I
was a standard Sunday night guest, and
while there was constant if subtle variation, the main rule was clear-cut: ✑

This is plainly a naïve dish, really nursery fare, a kitchen innocent. It is also useful. It will survive several hours in a chafing
dish, and it apparently reassures the somewhat jaded people who drift here and there
for a pre-Monday pickup in most towns. Of course it can be made richer
(although not much poorer!), and the ingredients can change with the
seasons, as long as the eggs and the honest sauce stay there to keep it forever a Muchi, *whatever* that is.

It is hard to limit myself with the equally "innocent" ways to use
cooked rice in baked casseroles, as we call them in America: dishes to act
as a main course or a filling accompaniment. Here is one which is made
often in my small town of predominantly Italian-style cooks, all good as
far as I know. (I have only known one bad one in my life, a shrewish

✑ Egg Muchi

2 to 3 cups good cream sauce (Béchamel)

1 cup small shrimps

1 cup crab meat

1 cup small oysters or mussels

½ cup chopped pimiento

½ cup dry sherry

Salt, cayenne

4 sliced hard-boiled eggs

Hot dry rice or buttered toast

*Heat sauce in double boiler. Drain canned or fresh
cooked seafood and stir in, with pimiento and sherry.
Season to taste. Add sliced eggs gently. Keep hot. Serve
on rice or toast.*

woman from the Piedmont who ran a hole-in-the-wall grocery store in Lugano and lived out her dyspeptic life on all the horrible shortcut packages of ersatz soups and suchlike that the local people would not buy from her.) ✑

And here is a good variation, a trusted friend for a long time, and delicious alone or with something delicate like sautéed or roasted chicken: ✑

The Chinese, not to mention the Portuguese and even the Californians, have good quick ways of making a basic kind of pancake with rice, and here is a familiar recipe that bears trying again, and even some more experimentation: ✑ [see p. 84]

This is one of those breathless operations which demand, as does all Oriental cooking, that the ingredients be prepared before anything starts the final gallop between the skillet and the table. I notice that years ago I wrote that this dish was good with cold chicken or ham "or both." It probably still is, but I think I prefer it alone, or with a little chopped meat inside instead of outside.

I have devised a scandalous marriage between Chinese and Provençale cooking

 Green Rice

1 or 2 cloves garlic
1 medium to large onion
½ cup butter or olive oil
2 cups cooked rice
2 cups grated cheese (Gruyère, mild
  American, Parmesan)
2 cups whole milk
2 eggs, beaten
2 cups chopped parsley, with extra fresh
herbs if possible
Salt, etc.

Chop garlic and onion and brown in butter or oil. Combine with all other ingredients and bake in oiled casserole at 350° until set, or about 45 minutes.

 Rice and Almonds

2 cups cooked brown rice
½ cup melted butter
1 cup cream
1 cup mild cheese in small pieces
1 cup blanched slivered almonds
½ cup buttered bread crumbs

Combine first five ingredients in buttered casserole, and cover with crumbs. Bake 30 minutes at 350° and then brown quickly under broiler.

❧ Chinese Pancakes

3 or 4 eggs

1 cup cooked rice

1 cup cooked bean sprouts (canned)

1 cup coarsely chopped parsley, green
pepper, mushrooms, pimiento, celery, whatever,
    all mixed

2 tablespoons soy sauce

3 to 4 tablespoons good fat, butter, or oil

Stir first five ingredients briskly together. Heat fat in heavy skillet until hot. Pour mixture into fat, and keep folding in the edges as they appear, to make a compact cake very fast. When it is firm and brown on the bottom, cut into four sections and turn each one over. Brown a little, and serve immediately.

❧ Eggs Sino-Aixois

4 tablespoons olive oil (or butter)

4 eggs

½ cup (1 small can) chopped black olives

1 minced garlic clove

Salt, pepper to taste

2 to 4 cups hot cooked rice

Warm oil or melt butter over low heat in large iron skillet. Beat eggs lightly, mix with olives and garlic, season, and pour into hot skillet, tipping to spread mixture evenly. Turn off heat when barely solid, and let cool in skillet. When cold, turn onto breadboard and slice very thinly into strips about ⅛ by 2 inches. Toss with hot dry rice and serve.

which I think is delicious with rice, and at the risk of some classical shrugs and shudders here it is: ❧

This can be delicious alone, with grated Parmesan cheese, with cold chicken, and perhaps with many other things which I have never yet tried because I seem to stop at the first step, with a green salad after. A nice thing about it, especially in the summer, is that it can be prepared early and then heated discreetly to combine with the rice. In fact, it will keep for a day or so, neatly cut, in the icebox. It might be very good mixed with seasoned rice and chilled, for a salad? There are several ways I like to make rice salads. A favorite one goes like this, although I am not sure about its origin: ❧

This is a fresh and pleasant accompaniment to cold meats in the summer, and makes a good hors d'oeuvre (in the European sense rather than as we think of one at home, a stand-up canapé).

In Provence such chilled rice

dishes are served often, perhaps because of the increasing rice fields in the Camargue, perhaps because of the many Algerians who moved to that part of France after the Second World War. The wonderful pungent tomatoes of the region are usually a main part of them, generously sprinkled with salt and pepper and minced fresh herbs: basil, tarragon, thyme, a little garlic. Underneath them is a bed of freshly cooked rice which has been tossed with the same oil and vinegar while still warm. Usually there are the small local olives somewhere, whole or cut into slivers, or a few strips of anchovy. I have never tasted two of these salads alike, but they have always been cold and fresh and pleasant.

Here is another version, often used in Mexico and especially good when a couple of firm ripe avocadoes can be sliced over the top at the last minute:

If avocadoes are not in season, we have often eaten this salad with

 ## Green Rice Salad

2 cups cooked rice
½ cup oil-vinegar dressing (vinaigrette) to taste
½ cup currants or raisins
½ cup dry vermouth
½ cup pine nuts or slivered almonds
Fresh chopped herbs as desired

Mix the rice when still warm with the vinaigrette. Let chill. Poach the currants or raisins in the vermouth until puffed. Chill, add nuts, and then mix all together, and chill again.

Cold Mexican Rice

2 cups cooked rice
1 cup thinly sliced green pepper
1 cup thinly sliced red sweet pepper
    OR
1 cup or 5-ounce can sliced pimientos
2 large or 4 small tomatoes, peeled, drained, cut in strips
4 to 6 green onions (scallions) split and
in 1-inch slices
½ to 1 cup chopped fresh herbs: marjoram,
basil, parsley, etc.
1 cup vinaigrette dressing (to taste)
1 clove well-mashed garlic

Mix first six ingredients lightly. Blend vinaigrette and garlic, pour over mixture, and toss again, Chill for at least six hours, turning up now and then from bottom of bowl, with fork.

a couple of hard-boiled eggs chopped and sprinkled over it before serving. It is very good the next day, a fine boost on a hot morning, and in the same general class as a gazpacho for post-party therapy.

⚘ Milk Rice

1 cup rice
6 cups hot milk
Salt if wished
2 to 3 tablespoons butter
Brown sugar

Cook rice and milk in double boiler, covered, for an hour or until tender. Stir often. When done, stir in salt if wished, and butter, and serve sprinkled with brown sugar.

Probably the simplest rice dish I have ever eaten (except for a bowl of it unadorned a few times to try to understand how I would feel if that were *all* for me for a few hours or even days) was served by a beautiful tall woman from India, who later died from a bee sting. Her name was Love, in English. We ate some little titbits, as I remember, and then she brought to the table a large round platter of rice with grated fresh coconut sprinkled thickly on it. She tossed it together. The rice was hot, and the coconut was cold, and both were very white and pure. There was sweetness, but subtly, with no interruption of condiment or sauce. It was an experience I have never tried to repeat, but I am unsure why not.

There are other simple ways to make what may have been a dessert to my Indian friend. Most of the ones we like are sweetened with honey and sugar and jams, and heightened with spices, for we are conditioned to expect a minor complication of flavors at the end of a meal, and even a childlike supper like the cold rice with milk and sugar we loved when I was little. We would put nutmeg on it, the way Father liked it best, or copy Mother and drop a dollop of fresh jam on top. When we stayed next door with Aunt Gwen while Mother was having babies, which happily for us at least seemed fairly often, we picked blackberries, too ripe to wash, and mixed them into a dusty purple mash . . . delicious.

Most people remember rice custard puddings from much the same eras in their own lives as do I. Such creations need good fresh eggs and a light hand with the baking and *plenty of raisins*. Recipes for them are in any stout kitchen manual, and in classical cookbooks there are formidable formulas for making elaborate structures named after long-dead beautiful women, concoctions built like the beauties into towers of disciplined artificiality, corseted with spun sugar and candied violets.

Somewhere in the fanciest of these pantry dreams is the stepchild of what is called Milk Rice, as plain a pudding as any nanny ever dished out in her nursery. I do not know why we so seldom ate it at home . . . except that Grandmother liked to drink rice water now and then for her Nervous Stomach, and this recipe would leave no such dividend: ℰ

This, I well know, is the kind of pudding pre-young people like to make and then play with: more butter, grated orange rind, vanilla, spices, honey, raisins . . . Within reason, such invention is both commendable and edible.

A combination of the milk and the custard methods which I have been loyal to for a long time, and itself a combination of about six old recipes plus my own comparatively mature invention, makes a pretty and artfully simple dessert (Sweetness and Rice!), served very cold. My family knows it as: ℰ

ℰ Rice and Spice

2 eggs

2 cups milk

¾ cup raisins or currants

1½ cups cooked rice

½ cup brown sugar

½ teaspoon cinnamon (or more to taste)

½ teaspoon each nutmeg, ginger,
*   salt (to taste)*

1 to 2 tablespoons powdered sugar

Separate the eggs, and mix 2 tablespoons of the milk with the yolks. Put rest of milk in double boiler, add the raisins or currants, and cook about 15 minutes or until tender. Add rice, cook 5 minutes more, then stir in yolks, brown sugar, and spices. Cook for 2 to 3 more minutes, stirring well, and pour into buttered serving dish. Beat whites, add powdered sugar to make stiff meringue, and spread over pudding. Brown delicately in oven, and serve after chilling well.

And sweet dreams! Sleep like happy spoiled children . . .

There are many grains other than rice, on earth, which have nourished us for countless centuries. Two of them I keep always on hand: whole roasted buckwheat groats, called *kasha* usually, and processed wheat, usually called *bulgur* in the ancient world and surely to be bought in many ethnic pockets in our big cities. As for kasha, the kind I use is prepared and distributed in New York State.

Either of these brown tough seeds can be used in place of rice, especially if one already prefers brown rice to white, as I do. They are fine substitutes for the comparatively rare and costly "wild rice" it is now fashionable to serve with game . . . not rice at all, of course. This strange elongated grain is the fruit of a grass that grows in the shallow waters of North American lakes, very difficult to harvest and finicky to market. There are recipes for cooking it in good cookbooks or on its packages, and I would gladly use them oftener . . . if I did not find it more sensible to adapt some of their suggestions to the relatively inexpensive groats and kasha.

Perhaps the most provocative of such directions that I have ever/never read is in André Simon's *Concise Encyclopedia of Gastronomy*, which says simply, "Wild Rice," without even a period after it, and not a word to tell how or what or why! As far as I know, this is the *most* concise reference in all the volumes of the fascinating work, although directions for chopped rue sandwiches, Scotch nettle pudding, roast hedgehog, and lampern pie are outlined in detail . . .

Both buckwheat and wheat, whole or cracked, roasted or otherwise "processed," can be used at will in place of rice, *except* in the most delicate and dainty dishes: Riz à l'Impératrice, for instance, or sweet soufflés. They should be cooked according to the basic directions given on their boxes, with due respect but with a look at other recipes. Both Fisher

Flouring and Wolff will send, for the asking, interesting and occasionally amusing little folders of variations on their themes, and I too, at the risk of having to sue myself for plagiarism (which sounds dangerously like the intramural procreation of an oyster or a snail), still use and refer to a recipe I first printed a couple of times in the 1940s. A near-relative to it is also in almost any book about Russian or Near East cooking, as well as on the paper boxes the stuff comes in!

When I was little, I counted it a meal well conceived to sit before a bowl of cold white grains of rice, half-floating in the creamy milk and the brown sugar I could add from my own little pitcher and dish. Long later, my own children sat with the same obvious contentment before such small feasts: rice less blanched and robbed than mine had been or, better yet, buckwheat groats of kasha cooked to tenderness. We were fortunate.

Kasha can be browned gently in oil or fat or butter, like a classic risotto, and then combined with a liquid and other things (herbs, mushrooms, tomatoes, on and on), or mixed *after* cooking with such ingredients as fish, onions, herbs, nuts, to be baked in casseroles and loaves and rings. It can be combined, when cooked, with first a vinaigrette sauce and then fresh vegetables, to make a good chilled salad. It is delicious with curries and stews and other dishes having their own ample sauces and juices. It will make highly commendable if somewhat coarse desserts, mixed with eggs, honey, spices, nuts.

All this is true of wheat groats but more so, at least in my private listing. I *like* them better, the way the Swiss like sticky rice better than the kind with each little seed separate. And here I feel compelled to say that it is a wise idea, in these days when food merchants seem dedicated to the frustrating proposition that it is shameful, embarrassing, crude, idiotic for people to spend any time preparing what they must eat, to READ THE

DIRECTIONS. Words like "precooked" and "instant" must be looked for with care, and it does not hurt to read the required lists of the package's ingredients as well. Many of them will be fairly meaningless, of course: things like the mono- and di-glycerides we can leave to graduate home economists, with a faint nod of recognition to thiamine, niacin, riboflavin, all of them familiar in the lip-lingo of modern packaged foods. Reassuringly, economy seems to make it all right to skip a name like sodium chloride for s-a-l-t . . .

❧ Basic Kasha for Breakfast and Other Dishes

1 cup buckwheat groats
2 cups rapidly boiling salted water
2 tablespoons butter, if wished

Add groats slowly to water, add butter, and stir until at full boil. Cover, stir occasionally, and remove from heat in 12 to 15 minutes. Uncover, loosen with fork to dry a little, and use.

But even people who make good foods and then hire experts to present them to the public are not infallible, and there one must use an inborn sense of deduction, perhaps. A case in point, for me at least, is the direction for making the basic recipe on the kasha package. I do not wish to *contradict*, sir and madam, *but* . . .

I have cooked groats and kasha for many years, to be eaten plain or used in other dishes, and I use the same proportions . . . two cups of water, one of the grain, a little salt, and butter if I feel like it and it is "indicated." The groats I start in cold water, because the package says to, and I haven't time to argue. The kasha I add gently to the rapidly boiling water, because that is the way I started out to do it, decades ago, and also because the package says to. And now I notice that the kasha directions say something like "½ cup *groats*, 2½ cups boiling water"!

Something rings a little warning bell in me. (It is the same bell that will go off like the noon whistle at the match factory if I notice, no matter how carelessly or casually, that a supper recipe to serve eight people calls for three cups of chili powder . . .) Have the directions been changed

since I first read them so long ago? Has the kasha been re-"processed"?
Five to one, instead of two to one? Have *I* simply slipped a notch or two,
gastronomically?

The only way to answer this little bell,
this conditioned reflex, is to follow directions. The result of my loyal spirit, my dedi-
cation, is a thin grainy gruel fit perhaps to
lull a gastric casualty at bedtime, but nothing I would ever offer my own household in
a healthy state.

I try again, with the same measurements but long cooking. It is even more disastrous, somewhat thicker but with most of
the little grains tired and swollen into a
hodgepodge.

I go back to the way I have been doing it
for years, and until I find out why the bell
rang at those strange proportions given on
the kasha package, I shall make the plain
kind this way: ℰ

ℰ Kasha

2 cups whole grain buckwheat
1 large or two small eggs
½ teaspoon salt, if wished
2 to 4 cups hot water
2 teaspoons butter or good fat (chicken,
    for instance)

*Put buckwheat in cold, ungreased heavy skillet. Break
in the egg and stir until each grain is coated. Heat
gently, stirring often, so that the grains become
separate and glossy. Season. When skillet is hot, add
water to cover grains, and stir in fat. Cover with tight
heavy lid. Reduce heat to minimum (or cook covered
in 325° oven) for about 40 minutes. Check now and
then and add more hot water if too dry, but shake the
skillet instead of stirring.*

This proves, for me anyway, that even printed directions must be
looked at with a sharp eye. It also makes a nutty dark delicious cereal, to
be eaten hot or cold . . . seasoned with salt and pepper and butter, or in a
bowl with milk and honey or sugar . . . in salads, casseroles, on and on.

Here, however, is the way to make *kasha* from kasha. It can stand alone
as an accompaniment to all but the most delicate of meats and fishes; it
can be combined with things to be a dish by itself; it can be stuffed into
various cavities besides the human maw (birds, things like that). ℰ

This recipe can of course be made richer and more elegant by using good meat stock or vegetable juices instead of water, an extra dollop of butter whenever more liquid is added, a little dry sherry. It is plainly much like making a good risotto, except for the slow careful browning at first, so that each grain is like a toasted nutkin.

When the kasha is finally cooked but not soft, I give it a good gentle stir and leave it uncovered to breathe for an hour or so before I pile it into a well-buttered casserole to heat through in a mild (350°) oven. If it is going to be a dish in itself, I add whatever herbs, onions, and so on that I may want, with the liquid at the beginning. If I am going to serve it with fowl, it is probably redundant of me to remark that I make it with chicken stock. Sometimes I use half clam juice and half water, and when it is ready to be reheated I stir into it chopped or very small clams heated in plenty of butter with a drop or two of tabasco. Or a couple of cups of chicken meat. Or a cup of slivered almonds or whole pinenuts. Or a half cup of toasted sesame seeds and/or a half cup of currants simmered for a few minutes in white wine or dry vermouth to cover. Or I pile it on a hot plate and surround it with sautéed mushrooms and onion rings, with a bowl of good sour cream alongside. Or I stuff things with it: birds, cabbage leaves, vegetables like eggplants and zucchini. Or . . .

All of which is some kind of proof, I hope, that at least three of the grains of this earth can be our allies, for frugal days as well as fat ones. And there are many more . . . both the days and the grains.

ℰ | Once a Tramp, Always . . .

THERE IS A MISTAKEN IDEA, ancient but still with us, that an overdose of anything from fornication to hot chocolate will teach restraint by the very results of its abuse. A righteous and worried father, feeling broad-minded and full of manly understanding, will urge a rich cigar upon his fledgling and almost force him to be sick, to show him how to smoke properly. Another, learning that his sons have been nipping dago red, will chain them psychologically to the dinner table and drink them under it, to teach them how to handle their liquor like gentlemen. Such methods are drastic and of dubious worth, I think. People continue to smoke and to drink, and to be excessive or moderate according to their own needs. Their good manners are a matter more of innate taste than of outward training.

Craving—the actual and continued need for something—is another matter. Sometimes it lasts for one's lifetime. There is no satisfying it, except temporarily, and that can spell death or ruin. At least three people I know very well, children of alcoholic parents, were literally born drunk, and after sad experience they face the hideous fact that one more nip will destroy them. But they dream of it. Another of my friends dreams of chocolate, and is haunted by sensory fantasies of the taste and smell of chocolate, and occasionally talks of chocolate the way some people talk of their mistresses, but one Hershey bar would damn him and his liver too. (Members of A.A. pray to God daily to keep them from taking that First Drink. A first candy bar can be as dangerous.) These people choose to live, no matter how cautiously, because they know that they can never be satisfied. For them real satiety, the inner spiritual kind, is impossible. They are, although in a noble way, cheating: an *honest* satyr will risk death from exhaustion, still happily aware that there will always be more women in the world than he can possibly accommodate.

Somewhere between the extremes of putative training in self-control and unflagging discipline against wild cravings lie the sensual and voluptuous gastronomical favorites-of-a-lifetime, the nostalgic yearnings for flavors once met in early days—the smell or taste of a gooseberry pie on a summer noon at Peachblow Farm, the whiff of anise from a Marseille bar. Old or moderately young, of any sex, most of us can forgo the analyst's couch at will and call up some such flavors. It is better thus. Kept verbal, there is small danger of indigestion, and in truth, a gooseberry pie can be a horror (those pale beady acid fruits, the sugar never masking their mean acidity, the crust sogging . . . my father rhapsodized occasionally about the ones at Peachblow and we tried to recapture their magic for him, but it was impossible). And a glass of *pastis* at the wrong time and with the wrong people can turn into a first-class emetic, no matter how it used to make the mind and body rejoice in Provence. Most people like to talk, once steered onto the right track, about their lifetime favorites in food. It does not matter if they have only dreamed of them for the past countless decades: favorites remain, and mankind is basically a faithful bunch of fellows. If you loved Gaby Deslys or Fanny Brice, from no matter how far afar, you still can and do. And why not? There is, in this happily insatiable fantasizing, no saturation point, no moment at which the body must cry: *Help!*

Of course, the average person has not actually possessed a famous beauty, and it is there that gastronomy serves as a kind of surrogate, to ease our longings. One does not need to be a king or mogul to indulge

most, if at all, of his senses with the heady enjoyment of a dish—speaking
in culinary terms, that is. I myself, to come right down to it, have never
been in love from afar, except perhaps for a handful of fleeting moments
when a flickering shot of Wallace Reid driving over a cliff would make
me feel queer. I know of women who have really mooned, and for years,
over some such glamorous shadow, and it is highly possible that my own
immunity is due to my sensual satisfaction, even vicarious, in such things

as potato chips and beluga caviar. This realization is cruelly matter-of-fact
to anyone of romantic sensitivity, and I feel vaguely apologetic about it. At
the same time, I am relieved. I am free from any regrets that Clark Mar-
lon Barrymore has never smiled at me. I know that even though I eat potato chips perhaps once every three years, I can, whenever I wish to, tap
an almost unlimited fountain of them not five hundred feet from my own
door. It is not quite the same thing with caviar, of course, and I have dug
into a one-pound tin of it, fresh and pearly gray, not more than eight or
nine times in my life. But I know that for a while longer the Acipensers of
the Black and Caspian seas will be able to carry out their fertility rites and
that I may even partake again of their delectable fruits. Meanwhile, stern
about potato chips on the one hand and optimistic about beluga on the
other, I can savor with my mind's palate their strange familiarity.

It is said that a few connoisseurs, such as old George Saintsbury, can
recall *physically* the bouquet of certain great vintages a half century after
tasting them. I am a mouse among elephants now, but I can say just as
surely that this minute, in a northern California valley, I can taste-smell-
hear-see and then feel between my teeth the potato chips I ate slowly one
November afternoon in 1936, in the bar of the Lausanne Palace. They
were uneven in both thickness and color, probably made by a new apprentice in the hotel kitchen, and almost surely they smelled faintly of ei-

ther chicken or fish, for that was always the case there. They were a little too salty, to encourage me to drink. They were ineffable. I am still nourished by them. That is probably why I can be so firm about not eating my way through barrels, tunnels, mountains more of them here in the land where they hang like square cellophane fruit on wire trees in all the grocery stores, to tempt me sharply every time I pass them.

As for the caviar, I can wait. I know I cannot possibly, ever, eat enough of it to satisfy my hunger, my unreasonable lust, so I think back with what is almost placidity upon the times I could attack a tub of it and take five minutes or so for every small voluptuous mouthful. Again, why not? Being carnal, such dreams are perforce sinful in some vocabularies. Other ways of thinking might call them merely foolish, or Freudian "substitutes." That is all right; I know that I can cultivate restraint, or accept it patiently when it is thrust upon me—just as I know that I can walk right down Main Street this minute and buy almost as many macadamia nuts as I would like to eat, and certainly enough to make me feel very sick for a time, but that I shan't do so.

I have some of the same twinges of basic craving for those salty gnarled little nuts from Hawaii as the ones I keep ruthlessly at bay for the vulgar fried potatoes and the costly fish eggs. Just writing of my small steady passion for them makes my mouth water in a reassuringly controlled way, and I am glad there are dozens of jars of them in the local goodies shoppe, for me not to buy. I cannot remember when I first ate a macadamia, but I was hooked from that moment. I think it was about thirty years ago. The Prince of Wales was said to have invested in a ranch in Hawaii which raised them in small quantities, so that the name stuck in my mind because *he* did, but I doubt that royal business cunning had much to do with my immediate delectation. The last time I ate one was about four months ago, in New York. I surprised my *belle-soeur* and almost embarrassed myself by letting a small moan escape me when she put a bowl of them beside my chair; they were beautiful—so lumpy, macadamian, salty, golden! And I ate one, to save face. One. I can still sense its peculiar crispness and its complete macadamianimity. How fortunate I am!

Many of the things we batten on in our fantasies are part of our childhoods, although none of mine has been, so far in this list. I was perhaps twenty-three when I first ate almost enough caviar—not to mention any caviar at all that I can now remember. It was one of the best, brightest days of my whole life with my parents, and lunching in the quiet back room at the Café de la Paix was only a part of the luminous whole. My mother ate fresh foie gras, sternly forbidden to her liver, but she loved the cathedral at Strasbourg enough to risk almost any kind of retribution, and this truffled slab was so plainly the best of her lifetime that we all agreed it could do her nothing but good, which it did. My father and I ate caviar, probably Sevruga, with green-black smallish beads and a superb challenge of flavor for the iced grassy vodka we used to cleanse our happy palates. We ate three portions apiece, tacitly knowing it could never happen again that anything would be quite so mysteriously perfect in both time and space. The headwaiter sensed all this, which is, of course, why he was world-known, and the portions got larger, and at our third blissful command he simply put the tin in its ice bowl upon our table. It was a regal gesture, like being tapped on the shoulder with a sword. We bowed, served ourselves exactly as he would have done, grain for grain, and had no need for any more. It was reward enough to sit in the almost empty room, chaste rococo in the slanting June sunlight, with the generous tub of pure delight between us, Mother purring there, the vodka seeping slyly through our veins, and real wood strawberries to come, to make us feel like children again and not near-gods. That was a fine introduction to what I hope is a reasonably long life of such occasional bliss.

As for potato chips, I do not remember them earlier than my twenty-first year, when I once ate stupidly and well of them in a small, stylish restaurant in Germany, where we had to wait downstairs in the tavern while our meal was being readied to eat upstairs. Beside me on a table was a bowl of exquisitely fresh and delicate chips, and when we finally sat down I could not face the heavily excellent dinner we had ordered. I was ashamed of my gluttony, for it is never commendable, even when based on ignorance. Perhaps *that* is why I am so stern today about not eating many of the devilish temptations?

There is one other thing I know I shall never get enough of—champagne. I cannot say when I drank my first prickly, delicious glass of it. I was raised in Prohibition, which meant that my father was very careful about his bootleggers, but the general adult drinking stayed around pinch-bottle Scotch as safest in those days, and I think I probably started my lifelong affair with Dom Pérignon's discovery in 1929, when I first went to France. It does not matter. I would gladly ask for the same end as a poor peasant's there, who is given a glass of champagne on his deathbed to cheer him on his way.

I used to think, in my Russian-novel days, that I would cherish a lover who managed through thick and thin, snow and sleet, to have a bunch of Parma violets on my breakfast tray each morning—also rain or shine, Christmas or August, and onward into complete Neverland. Later, I shifted my dream plan—a split of cold champagne, one half hour *before* the tray! Violets, sparkling wine, and trays themselves were as nonexistent as the lover(s), of course, but once again, why not? By now, I sip a mug of vegetable broth and count myself fortunate, while my mind's nose and eyes feast on the pungency of the purple blossoms, and the champagne stings my sleepy tongue . . . and on feast days I drink a little glass of California "dry Sauterne" from the icebox . . . and it is much easier to get out of bed to go to work if there is not that silly tray there.

Mayonnaise, real mayonnaise, good mayonnaise, is something I can dream of any time, almost, and not because I ate it when I was little but because I did not. My maternal grandmother, whose Victorian neuroses dictated our family table tastes until I was about twelve, found salads generally suspect but would tolerate the occasional serving of some watery lettuce in a dish beside each plate (those crescents one still sees now and then in English and Swiss boardinghouses and the mansions of American Anglophiles). On it would be a dab or lump or blob, depending on the current cook, of what was quietly referred to as Boiled Dressing. It seemed dreadful stuff—enough to harm one's soul.

I do not have my grandmother's own recipe, although I am sure she seared it into many an illiterate mind in her kitchens, but I have found an approximation, which I feel strangely forced to give. It is from Miss Parloa's *New Cook Book*, copyrighted in Boston in 1880 by Estes and Lauriat:

> Three eggs, one tablespoon each of sugar, oil and salt, a scant tablespoonful of mustard, a cupful of milk and one of vinegar. Stir oil, mustard, salt and sugar in a bowl until perfectly smooth. Add the eggs, and beat well; then add the vinegar, and finally the milk. Place the bowl in a basin of boiling water, and stir the dressing until it thickens like soft custard. . . . The dressing will keep two weeks if bottled tightly and put in a cool place.

On second thought, I think Grandmother's receipt, as I am sure it was called, may have used one egg instead of three, skimped on the sugar and oil, left out the mustard, and perhaps eliminated the milk as well. It was a kind of sour whitish gravy and . . . Yes! Patience is its own reward; I have looked in dozens of cookbooks without finding her abysmal secret, and now I have it: she did not use eggs at all, but *flour*. That is it. Flour thickened the vinegar—no need to waste eggs and sugar . . . Battle Creek frowned on oil, and she spent yearly periods at that health resort . . . mustard was a heathen spice . . . salt was cheap,

 Grandmother's Boiled Dressing

1 cup cider vinegar
Enough flour to make thin paste
Salt to taste

Mix well, boil slowly fifteen minutes or until done, and serve with wet shredded lettuce.

and good cider vinegar came by the gallon . . . And (here I can hear words as clearly as I can see the limp wet lettuce under its load of Boiled Dressing): "Salad is roughage and a French idea."

As proof of the strange hold childhood remembrance has on us, I think I am justified to print once, and only once, my considered analysis of the reason I must live for the rest of my life with an almost painful craving for mayonnaise made with fresh eggs and lemon juice and good olive oil: &

Unlike any other recipe I have ever given, this one has never been tested and never shall be, nor is it recommended for anything but passing thought.

Some of the foods that are of passionate interest in childhood, as potently desirable as drink to a toper, with time lose everything but a cool intellectuality. For about three years, when I was around six, we sometimes ate hot milk toast for Sunday night supper, but made with rich cocoa, and I would start waiting for the next time as soon as I had swallowed the last crumbly buttery brown spoonful of it. I am thankful I need have no real fear of ever being faced with another bowl of the stuff, but equally happy that I can still understand how its warmth and savor satisfied my senses then. I feel much the same grateful relief when I conjure, no matter how seldom, the four or five years when I was in boarding schools and existed—sensually, at least—from one private slow orgy to the next, of saltines and Hershey bars, bite for bite.

There is one concoction, or whatever it should be called, that I was never allowed to eat, and that I dreamed of almost viciously for perhaps seventeen years, until I was about twenty-two and married. I made it then and ate every bit of it and enjoyed it enormously and have never tasted it since, except in the happy reaches of my gastronomical mind. And not long ago, when I found a distinctly literary reference to it, I beamed and glowed. I love the reality of Mark Twain almost as much as I love the dream image of this dish, and when he included it, just as I myself would have, in a list of American foods he planned to eat—"a modest, private affair," all to himself—I could hardly believe the miraculous coincidence: my ambrosia, my god's!

In *A Tramp Abroad*, Twain grouses about the food he found in Europe in 1878 (even a god can sound a little limited at times) and makes a list of the foods he has missed the most and most poignantly awaits on his return. It starts out "Radishes," which is indeed either blind or chauvinistic, since I myself always seem to eat five times as many of them when I am a tramp abroad as when I am home. He then names eighty separate dishes and ends, "All sorts of American pastry. Fresh American Fruits. . . . Ice water." Love is *not* blind, and I do feel sorry about a certain lack of divinity in this utterance, but my faith and loyalty are forever strengthened by items 57 and 58: "Mashed Potatoes. Catsup."

These two things were printed on the same line, and I feel—in fact, I *know*—that he meant "Mashed Potatoes *and* Catsup," or perhaps

"Mashed Potatoes *with* Catsup." This certainty springs from the fact that there is, in my own mind and plainly in his, an affinity there. The two belong together. I have known this since I was about five, or perhaps even younger. I have proved it—only once, but very thoroughly. I am willing to try to again, preferably in "a modest, private affair, all to myself," but in public if I should ever be challenged.

We often ate mashed potatoes at home. Grandmother liked what my mother secretly scoffed at as "slip-and-go-easies": custards, junkets, strained stewed tomatoes, things like that, with mashed potatoes, of course, at the head of the list as a necessity alongside any decent cut of meat. But—and here is the secret, perhaps, of my lifelong craving—we were never allowed to taste catsup. Never. It was spicy and bad for us, and "common" in bottles. (This is an odd fact, chronologically, for all the housekeepers of my beldam's vintage prided themselves on their special receipts for "ketchups," made of everything from oysters to walnuts and including the plentiful love apple.)

I remember that once when Grandmother was gone off to a religious convention, Mother asked each of us what we would most like to eat before the awesome Nervous Stomach took over our menus again. My father immediately said he would pick a large salad of watercress from the Rio Hondo and make a dressing of olive oil and wine vinegar—a double cock-snoot, since olive oil was an exotic smelly stuff kept only to rub on the navels of the new babies that seemed to arrive fairly often, and watercress grew along the banks of a stream that might well be . . . er . . . *used* by cows. When my turn came, I said, "Mashed potatoes and catsup." I forget exactly what went on next, except that Father was for letting me eat all I wanted of the crazy mixture and I never did get to. Ah, well . . . I loved watercress, too, and whatever forbidden fruits we bit into during that and similar gastric respites, and I did not need to stop dreaming.

My one deliberate challenge to myself was delicious. I was alone, which seems to be indicated for many such sensual rites. The potatoes were light, whipped to a firm cloud with rich hot milk, faintly yellow from ample butter. I put them in a big warmed bowl, made a dent about the size of a respectable coffee cup, and filled it to the brim with catsup from a large, full, *vulgar* bottle that stood beside my table mat where a wineglass would be at an ordinary, commonplace, everyday banquet. Mine was, as I have said, delicious. I would, as I have also said, gladly do it again if I were dared to. But I prefer to nourish myself with the knowledge that it is not impossible (potato chips), not too improbable (fresh beluga caviar). And now I am sharing it with a friend. I could not manage to serve forth to Mark Twain the "Sheep-head and croakers, from New Orleans," or the "Prairie hens, from Illinois," that he dreamed of in European boardinghouses ninety years ago, but mashed potatoes *with* catsup are ready to hand when he says the word.

A Recipe for Happy Hens

It is hard for me to write much less than a small book about the egg. If I could, I would probably start out with the opening sentence of one of my favorite kitchen possessions called most classically *Eggs*, and published in Boston in 1890: "The egg is one of the few things in the world original and positive in itself." I would then, after my own fashion, consider this beautiful object from almost every angle, mainly its wherefore.

An egg of course is meant to produce another potential egg producer, and that is why it is a living thing. Indeed, of all the foods we absorb in order to continue our own human existence, it is probably the most alive, just as wine is, in what we drink for various reasons connected with the same purpose. And like wine, an egg must be at its best when it is eaten, not a poor substitute for nitrogen, sulphur, phosphorus, all its parts. Some wines can submit to controlled pasteurization and emerge almost unhurt, especially if they are destined for quick and large consumption, and in the same way eggs can be regulated. The great difference here, though, is that an egg, because of its secret nature, can never be "pasteurized" and still remain as it was born, an intricate ovum, a small womb, with its own fetus and its protecting ovoid sea of albumen. The only way to pasteurize an egg is to render it sterile before it takes its mysterious form within the hen, and that is a sad story, according to a friend of mine.

He believes that he can tell the minute he breaks an egg, much less tastes it, if a rooster has been there too. He feels empathy, to put it mildly, for the hens raised commercially on little perches, high above the ground and far from Chanteclair. "Those pitiful chickens squatting there, all coopy, with their little old eggs rolling out on schedule according to the stuff they is fed, is in *misery*. They's sick, but they don't know it. A hen needs two things to be happy: a good rooster in with her and plenty of ground to scratch and to peck. These store-eggs without a rooster won't even beat up a good batter, and they is *not fit to fry!*"

Few of us are as sensitive to a hen's plight as this man, nor to the potency intrinsic to an egg's flavor, but as I continue to buy the best procurable eggs from the best possible sources in my present life, I admit fully that "they don't taste the way they used to." (What does?) In Whittier there was a tall, heavy old woman who came regularly to wash all our heads. She was a relic of the prairie days when water was scarce and "help" was plentiful, and although my mother had become used to California's gushing faucets she still clung to the vanishing fallacy that she really did not have time for attending to things like shampoos. We all liked Mrs. Ransome. (Her son was one of the first Whittier boys to go overseas in 1917, and Father taught us to sing to her, "Howya gonna keep him down on the farm, after he's seen Paree?" She liked it, and hugged us, and he later became a policeman.) She was quiet and strong-handed, and she also raised the best chickens in town. She kept us bountifully supplied with eggs, the biggest and brownest, and in the spring when they were dime-a-dozen she also gave us the dubious treat of having our scalps rubbed with their yolks, an old wives' trick which I still find disgusting to think on, but which like most such things probably has a firm and even scientific rightness somewhere.

What a chicken ate in those gone days was supposed to influence the flavor of its eggs, just as it will with a cow's milk, and once my mother disrupted Mrs. Ransome's whole agricultural pattern by insisting that her

breakfast tasted of garlic. (Mother was pregnant again, as I remember, and ate in her favorite position, in bed and from a tray, far from her madding crowd . . .) Mrs. Ransome grew most of her own food, and all the chickens' too, and she dug out every delicious scallion, onion, and leek from her plot, and my mother *still* tasted something wrong in her breakfast egg, until a lady from Philadelphia sniffed the little Wedgwood salt shaker and found that our loving but illiterate cook had wanted to give the poor lady something special on her tray, not ordinary salt from the kitchen canister but from a little jar at the back of the spice cupboard . . .

Today it would be impossible to suspect a fresh boughten egg of having one flavor instead of another. Eggs from the store all taste alike. It is too bad. And they all look very white, or in special cases and at higher prices a kind of Panchromatic Tan #2 developed for Beverly Hills "gourmets" and suchlike. I have not seen a *freckled* egg for too long to remember. It is reassuring, though, to continue to consider this miracle of reproduction, in a chancy and fragile world. Its shape is almost always perfect, after a few practice runs, and it keeps on being laid through peace and war, with basically slight dietetic vagaries except for a few purists like my friend.

An egg should be . . . SHOULD BE . . . fresh. But how is one to know the first subtle date, unless he has actually reached under warm feathers at the risk of a good protective peck and pulled out the fruit? Now, with refrigerating methods and computed chemical feeding and controlled hatching and all that, a graded government-inspected egg will remain edible for shameful lengths of time . . . and when in doubt, one can always float it gently in a bowl of water and see if it dances a little and bobs lazily toward the top. Then, in my lexicon, it is suspect or worse, although still all right, sometimes, for maneuvering into a dish less forthright than plain poached-or-boiled.

The quickest relationship between an egg and a man is when both are raw, the first perforce and the second from fatigue, weakness, or other hazards. One current remedy for such times is known colloquially as a Prairie Oyster, and an eggnog or a "flip" might also serve, as outlined in any good kitchen guide. I used to revive my faltering offspring with a formula less often printed, or perhaps never. I am afraid we never got around to naming it, but it is useful and good: a slice of dark bread, toasted or not, carefully spread with the yolk of one fresh egg and then patted generously with brown sugar and cut into little strips for little fingers. This would revive my girls as they grew, and growing is a hard job and needs plenty of encouragement. (I am past such hazards, but know that the same recipe, sprinkled generously with salt and freshly ground pepper instead of sugar, has worked timely miracles for me too . . .)

Many people have a skunner about raw eggs, but I think they could be persuaded by some artful arguments (especially if they do not *see* what goes on!), and meanwhile a very lightly cooked egg is the next alternative. Boiling and poaching are most merciful to our digestion, in the relative amounts of damage to their albumens and proteins and so on, which as they harden can gradually turn any decent egg into the gastric menace of a golf ball. It has been an ageless protest of invalids, dieticians, and even healthy eaters, that nobody knows how to boil an egg, and after a long time practicing I must admit that there seems to be a plot against us egg boilers at least. The season, the weather, the altitude, the state of the egg itself and, according to my friend, the hen that laid it, and even the water: they will conspire. In general, though, I feel fairly safe in putting fresh eggs at room temperature into cool water, bringing them rapidly to a full boil, and then letting them cool fleetingly under the tap as I ready them to serve, whether in eggcups in their shells, or cracked into bowls already warmed and buttered. Of course plenty of good hot fresh toast is essential to this operation.

As for poaching, I cheat. I own a pan which makes two round steamed eggs, not poached at all, and another one which makes six slightly triangular ones, not poached at all. It is a lazy compromise, but I condone it, not too successfully, by reminding myself that when I was a little girl I had to poach too many eggs in a huge iron skillet with vinegary water in it and a big skimmer and all that white floating off and surging around against the black pan and then the toast burning . . . It is like explaining that I do not go to church now because once I went to a school where we were in chapel on our knees five times every day and six on Sundays. Either argument is feeble, pusillanimous, and true in its way. The fact remains that I often use the egg steamers, and people like the results and so do I.

A delicate bypassing of this process is to make "soft eggs," which any good cookbook will explain. They are rather dramatic and oddly unexpected, especially for lunch on a hot day with other crisper things. They look hard-boiled when peeled and ready for serving . . . and then suddenly the center is tender, and delicious if one appreciates such things. The first of many times I ate them was from the buffet in Victor Hugo's restaurant in Los Angeles, when it was on Fifth or Sixth. This place was, for my family, the refuge of elegance from what my parents may sometimes have felt was a comparatively stark existence, and we basked in the wide-open windows in summer and were shyly aware of the soft-footed kind waiters, the muted voices of discreetly hungry dowagers, the silver bowls piled with lightly cooked shrimps and suchlike exotics . . . and

always a noble platter of *"oeufs mollets"* in aspic. At night, for birthdays
and when Kreisler was playing at the Philharmonic and all that, there
would be sweetbreads under glass bells, and a little orchestra sawing away
for our special pleasure, above our heads in a balcony not much bigger
than a bird's cage.

These soft eggs are often called, in classical cookbooks, a substitute for
the properly poached ones, and I like to think that even skilled cooks have
found them much easier to make look beautiful than any of us could ever
do in a shallow pan of fumey turgid water, all naked and raggedy as they
might become. Left in their shells while they cook, they can emerge almost as perfect as when they were rolled out. To be served hot, or cold as I
prefer them for aesthetic as well as nostalgic reasons, they are boiled for
six or seven minutes in their shells, chilled under cold running water, and
then gently cracked and peeled. I think there is something glamorous
about them, obviously. They can be served as a chilled garnish, or alone
with a good mayonnaise or vinaigrette, and all sorts of dainties alongside.
Once I ate them with caviar, lots of it, and plenty of black fresh pepper
and lemon juice. This, of course, is the sort of thing that can not happen
too often . . .

Fried eggs can be very good, but I almost never make them, feeling in-
secure in how people can best stomach them at an early morning hour. I
like the trusty method of breaking them into a hot and generously lubri-
cated skillet, clapping the top on it, and forgetting it at the back of the
stove until the cow is milked, figuratively. This method makes delicately
set and eminently digestible eggs, but classically it perhaps could not be
said that they have fried. Many people like them crisp on the edges, done
in sizzling fat . . . or turned over, or hard, or soft. I know one Swede who
almost resigned from his diplomatic post in Spain when eggs were served

to him fried in olive oil. I wish I could say that I also know a Spaniard in Stockholm who . . . When things reach this point in my own kitchen for an American or British breakfast, I remind my guests, the night before, that a reputable coffee shop opens at seven every morning, not more than a block from our home.

Scrambled eggs are another thing, and I am vain of my general success with them, although we usually eat them for lunch or a light supper instead of in the morning. My method is frankly derivative, and I like to recall that once I made a taciturn gastronomer laugh long and well in an attentively listening restaurant when he complimented me on my printed recipe and I said blandly, *"Grace à Brillat-Savarin!"* He did not know that female cooks could be humble.

"My" scrambled eggs should take about a half hour to prepare, and they are worth waiting for, it is generally agreed. I have gradually changed some of my methods to suit altitude, stove, all that. I used to start with a cold skillet, but by now my way is to warm a heavy one, melt some sweet butter in it and add some cream, and break the eggs into this gentle puddle. Then I mix them with a spoon, but never *beat* them, and let them warm with the pan, gradually pulling in the sides as they cook. When they are lightly blended and set, they are done, in large soft curds. Herbs or grated cheese can be put in with the eggs, halfway through the dreamy process. The trouble with this recipe is that few people will take the trouble . . . and it will not succeed if the cook is either hurried or harried.

Old Brillat-Savarin wrote several aphorisms about eating, and one of the most quoted is his ninth: "The discovery of a new dish does more for human happiness than the discovery of a star." My method for making his scrambled eggs is no more a discovery than were many of his own recipes. It is simply that I happened to be looking through the telescope instead of somebody else . . . and perhaps that I knew where to look, thanks to the amiable fellow's teaching!

It is interesting, in the face of the cold fact that there may be no such thing as a new dish, to find that the French lawyer admitted that his ninth aphorism was not his own at all, but that he heard a friend say it. With the same candor (and caution, for they *were* legal colleagues!), he never claimed as his inventions any of the recipes he outlined in *The Physiology of Taste*, but only made clear that some of them were his own methods for carrying out timeless patterns whose origins were lost in the smoke and steam of unknown and occasionally mythical kitchens. (. . . And I have read that the first way an egg was ever cooked enough to coddle its white and to warm it was to put it in a slingshot and whirl it through the air . . .)

In discussing *fondue*, which Brillat-Savarin learned to make to perfection during his exile in Switzerland, in such a deft way that he was noted for the rest of his life for serving it to his closest friends, he said forthrightly. "It is nothing more nor less than eggs scrambled with cheese, in certain proportions which time and experience have set." He then gave his recipe for it, with the perfunctory admission that "it was drawn from the papers of M. Trolliet, bailiff of Mondon, in the Canton of Berne," and with no further reference to the obvious fact that time and experience had indeed altered the Swiss formula.

At the risk of putting myself into such worthier company, I can say that probably not a single recipe I ever used has sprung virgin from my brain. It is true that I have read a great deal, and over many years, and that in self-excuse for this continuing pleasure I have even learned something from what I have read. By now I understand most of the basic principles of cooking in the same way that I know how to drive a car, almost by osmosis. It takes, with an ordinary person, a slow amalgam of experience and then time, surely, as the old man said, to learn the "certain proportions."

Roasting and boiling and baking have gone on for several thousands of years. It is the tools for them that have changed a little: controlled heat instead of open hearths, for instance. But the means are omnipresent for scrambling eggs, as long as hens continue their compulsive and neatly packaged reproduction, and the ends are age-old too, if eggs are indeed scrambled and then eaten at all. They can be ghastly or good, but the essentials (egg emptied into hot receptacle or one over heat) have not been eliminated by the most advanced kitchen equipment. It is how they get from the shell to the mouth that makes the most important aesthetic proof of progress, and "my" way comes fortunately from Brillat-Savarin and other more immediate friendships, and his came from his own friends and his surmises about how much an egg can stand before it will rebel. Neither method can be called a true discovery.

Soufflés are always trustworthy, I am told . . . as long as one can trust the guests to sit down when the soufflé says NOW. This takes a skilled diplomat at both stove and table, to assemble and pace the ingredients and the company. I know one such man, thank God, and without letting us realize it in the dining room he can make us ready at exactly the second for some delicate hot cloudy dessert he will produce, complete with its sauce. He is perhaps unique, although several good cooks in my world can perform miracles with the soufflé technique at the beginning or the middle of a meal. All of them know what they are doing. They have practiced, and read, and even gone to school. I have only read . . . and eaten! (As I consider some of these tacit betrayals of my own kitchen sloth, I think a book of them could be called *How to Be Lazy and Live*. I am a little embarrassed. I continue to be well fed.)

One of the best cooks I ever lived with, Madame Bonamour, gave me her recipe for a soufflé which she seemed to produce with her back turned to it, in case another dish was lacking at the last minute on her menu. It never failed . . . WITH HER. I think that the flour, the eggs, and the cheese she used in Dijon many decades ago had a different quality from what we can get here and now, and her whole slaphappy method is so un-orthodox that I shall give it in her own words and let curious cooks sniff out its ba-sic truths, using their own manuals: &

The nearest thing in my immediate repertory to a delicate airy hot dish, guar-anteed to fall if not eaten at once, is a cheese puff which I seem able to produce under extreme pressure with a dash and bravado unfailing up until now. I think I learned the trick from my mother, who was given to such shortcuts when the sup-ply of domestics ran out and our lunch needs must be served. It takes about a half hour, *Deus volente*. &

This, with my usual good luck, makes a crude but pleasant dish, depending for its own quality upon that of the ingredients. I cannot imagine making it with squeezy-

The Bonamour Cheese Soufflé

1 cup whole milk
25 grams flour
6 eggs
50 grams butter, melted
Salt, pepper
200 grams grated fresh Gruyère cheese

Mix milk and flour in casserole (ungreased). Separate eggs, and add 3 yolks to mixture, and the melted butter. Stir over slow flame until mixture begins to thicken. Add other 3 yolks, seasoning and then cheese gradually. Fold in beaten whites. Bake about 20 minutes in hot oven for moist soufflé, or slower and longer for dry one.

Edith's Cheese Puff

3 to 4 eggs
2 cups rich milk
Butter
6 to 8 slices stale bread
Sharp cheese, such as American Cheddar
*   or a mild Tillamook*
Salt, pepper, paprika

Beat eggs lightly in milk. Butter bread thickly and cut into pieces. Slice cheese and put some on each piece, in layers, seasoning well. Pour egg mixture slowly into dish, so that all is soaked. Top with more butter if wished. Bake in 400° oven for 30 minutes or until puffed and firm in middle. Serve at once .

fresh bread, for instance, and "slim" milk, and packaged sliced cheese. It needs honesty, to begin with.

 *Eggs Freda*

> 3 tablespoons butter or olive oil
> 6 ¼-inch slices precooked ham
> 1½ cups coarsely chopped parsley, chives,
>   marjoram, etc.
> 6 eggs
> Pepper

Melt the fat in a heavy skillet and brown the meat lightly on both sides. Put it on a platter or plates in a medium-hot oven. Add the chopped herbs to the fat and toss over very low heat until limp. Pat them into a smooth layer over the bottom of the pan, and break the eggs gently onto it. Cover closely, and allow eggs to set. When firm, turn each egg onto a slice of ham, herb side up. Pour any remaining fat over eggs, grind pepper over each, and serve with crisp toast.

There are many good tricks to be performed with eggs beaten gently in milk and then poured into casseroles upon everything from simmered herbs and vegetables to anchovies, or sweetened for custards, or put into pie shells. They depend upon the skill and ingenuity of the cook, as well as their makings. And endless books, both classical and nonsensical, list equally endless ways to play more tricks with them, from one end of a picnic or grand banquet to the other. Anyone can read, almost, and even cook! And now and then it is fun to think of dishes that one has never seen in print, much less concocted, like the strange one I ate for lunch at a Swedish country house once. It was a shallow casserole piled with thick slices of freshly cooked eggs, still warm, drenched as only the Scandinavians would do it with floods of melted butter. We ate it with bread from the oven. It was good, but I keep a somewhat aweful memory of it as beautiful to look at and overpoweringly suave and rich. I have never made it, just as I have never made since World War II a good invention mothered by the necessity of rationing . . . peculiar slices of tinned embalmed pinkish meats, elderly scraps of precious bacon fat. This recipe was named for a neighbor who had good friends who now and then slipped her a few eggs, which she would bring along. I would go into the hills where I lived when I could *live* and not merely subsist in Hollywood, and gather herbs. Needless to say, the recipe printed here is a merciful translation from ours, which tasted delicious in 1942: &

When I was little, my mother occasionally produced, with help, the only form of "croquette" I ever saw in our house, and since I myself do not use deep fat for frying, for dietary as well as logistical reasons, they were therefore the only croquettes ever, and the most delicious. I do not know where our cooks kept the fry kettle hidden, but it never appeared except when Grandmother, archenemy of all oils and human richnesses, was not aboard the lugger. (Once a friend from Mississippi came to stay with me, and when she asked where my frah-kell was, and I told her the bald truth that it did not exist, she began to pack her bags . . .) A kitchen wench aged from eighteen to eighty-five always made up Mother's concoction, which God knows was simple enough, and then Mother wandered out during the afternoon to pull the pan of mixture from the icebox and pat dozens of little croquettes into shape, with fine crumbs. I liked watching her, in the dim quiet kitchen. She had lovely arms, and the name of the little balls was exotic, and I knew that they would be delectable. I believe that they were served in our house in a tomato sauce, but charity pulls the veil there and it seems to me that they could well stand alone. Obviously I do not make them, but I have studied many recipes for them, and my mother's is the simplest: &

This is a recipe whose making was more important than the eating . . .

 Edith's Egg Croquettes

2 cups thick Béchamel
4 hard-cooked eggs, chopped
3 tablespoons chopped chives or scallions
Seasoning to taste
Fine crumbs
1 egg, lightly beaten with
2 tablespoons water
More crumbs

Mix white sauce with eggs and chives, season with salt and pepper and a little nutmeg if desired, and spread in pan. Chill for an hour or more, and then shape and dip in crumbs. Dip lightly in egg mixture and again in plain crumbs. Chill again, rectify the shapes, and dip once more in crumbs before frying in deep hot fat.

such a pretty kitchen ritual! But certainly the unfamiliar crispness of the little cakes was a voluptuous enjoyment to us after the daily bland boiled texture of Grandmother's required menus.

Such basically simple things can well live with us, from cradle to grave, and just lately a venerable man called to ask if I knew how to make a buttercup. Of course I said not, being both worldly and wily (not to mention womanly!). The recipe was from his childhood, but I knew that it was in fact as old as both of us times ten: Put an eggcup into a saucepan of boiling water, and then put a nugget of sweet butter into the cup and break a fresh egg onto the melted butter and cover the whole until it is set! Shades of Mrs. Isabella Beeton's nursery counsels, and Mrs. Marion Harland's! Shades of one of my own favorite restoratives!

The secret of all such plain fare is that the ingredients be fresh and lightly cooked. It is a cliché that somebody "is as tough as an overboiled egg," and it is at least a truism that the safest way to eat an egg and know precisely what one is eating is to take it from its own shell. There used to be a syndicated Sunday feature in the Los Angeles *Times*, along with the Katzenjammer Kids and Mutt and Jeff, with a bluff hearty unfeeling lovable lout named Warren and the writer, his tiny princess-bride-wife called Helen, who appreciated the finer things all the time and laughed merrily at her mate's weekly blunders. I read this continued saga with passion. Helen and Warren traveled a lot but always returned to their cat Pussy Purr-Mew, and Helen was very suspicious of the quality and honesty of food that bluff hearty unfeeling Warren would order for her tiny-winy hungers in out-of-the-way places like London, Paris, and Berlin. When in doubt, which was mostly, she asked for a soft-boiled egg *in the shell*. That way, she said firmly, *one knows*.

I miss Helen and Warren. I miss good brown eggs, especially the freckled ones. I manage to survive with recurring pleasure, however, on the perfect snow-white ovoids rolling out day and night from those unhappy hens, lorn for love and deprived of pecking and scratching. And while I eat with one hand I can always read with the other . . . when I am alone, that is! Here is one quotation that has long pleased me, from an article printed in 1865 in the *Atlantic Monthly*: "The relation of a hen to a dozen fair, white, pure eggs, and the relation of those eggs to puddings and custards, and the twenty-five cents which they can have for the asking, make even an ungainly hen, like many heroines in novels, not beautiful but interesting."

This reassures me, or at least stimulates me a little. I like to think that once there were fair white pure eggs selling for that price, and then I resent as a female the impugnment of the hen as ungainly, even though I do not like hens as such. I am scared of them when they are nesting and repelled by their stupidity on the run. They can be viciously cruel. And I never saw a custard or pudding I thought more than clinically interesting. But it is good that eggs can inspire such vicarious nourishment, even on paper! *Omne vivum ex ovo!*

🙠 | The Trouble with Tripe

THE MAIN TROUBLE WITH TRIPE is that in my present dwelling place, a small town in Northern California, I could count on one hand the people who would eat it with me. What is more, its careful slow preparation is not something I feel like doing for a meal by myself at this stage of the game, or even several stages. It is one of the things that call for a big pot and plenty of hungry people.

Not even my children really liked it, although studiously conditioned reflexes forced them to taste it in various guises and countries and to give fair judgment, which in their case was NO.

Friends tell me that they hate tripe because they, in turn, were forced to eat it when young or saw too much of it in fraternity boardinghouses as an "economy meat": reasons like that.

I could claim a childhood trauma if I needed to, and I admit that I did not face a dish of tripe from my grandmother's death until I was a good decade from it. In modern lingo, tripe-wise I lay fallow. The old lady, gastronomical dictator appointed by her own vision of Righteous Christian Living, a Nervous Stomach, and the fact that she more than generously shared the expenses of our exploding household, for some reason approved of eating the inner linings of an ox's first and second bellies.

In *Larousse Gastronomique*, where tripe is classified as "Offal," there is news for Grandmother. (She would dismiss it as foreign nonsense, of course.) "Rich in gelatine, tripe needs prolonged cooking," says the culinary scripture, "and is not easy to digest, so that it has no place in the diet of the dyspeptic [or] sufferers from gout." I sense that my dam was practicing upon herself and us a kind of sympathetic medicine to request that tripe be prepared and served (to be brave, eat a lion's heart; to remain shy and timid, eat violets in a salad, and so on . . .). Oxen are reputedly serene and docile, and she had a digestive system that ranked her among the leaders in Battle Creek's regular army of malnourished missionaries and would have honored her with a front seat at any late-Victorian spa in farther waters, like Vichy or Baden-Baden. The reasoning, perhaps: since an ox has not one but two pieces of equipment for his continuous ruminative consumption of the grains and grasses known also to be salubrious for man, why would partaking of some of his actual stomach not help Mrs. Holbrook's own unhappy organ?

Ergo.

Q.E.D.

Ecco.

Which we did and were, but apparently not enough to give me the same stubborn dislike for tripe that most of my friends claim. My grandmother unwittingly enjoyed perfect digestion, thanks to her constant attention to it, and it is no more than her due reward if she believed that her hypersensitive innards would and could assimilate this delicate honeycomb of animal muscle, with gastric gratitude if not pleasure. She did not believe in the latter anyway, as part of a true and upright life, and as for the hinted danger of gout, only gentlemen had that, in her days of rigid divisions of the sexual hazards of existence.

When I was little, there was only one way to serve tripe fit to eat, *i.e.*, fit for Grandmother to eat. It was seldom prepared when my mother was feeling fit enough herself to maintain some control over the menus, but when she was low in our private pecking order we ate it fairly often. My

father, quietly and successfully determined to remain cock of the roost with dignity, always found it commendable, or at least edible. The recipe for it, if I felt sturdy enough to give it in correct form, would start with boiling the rubbery reticulum in pieces, draining it too casually, and dousing it with something called White Sauce which was and will remain · in the same class as my grandmother's Boiled Dressing. The dish was at best a faintly odorous and watery challenge to one's innate sense of the fitness of things.

I recognize that such experiences can lead to cynicism, or the analyst's couch. In my own case, they seem mainly to have stiffened my wish to prove them mistaken, and I am now a happy if occasionally frustrated tripe eater.

I had a good beginning, the second time around (really a kind of ghost laying), at Crespin in Dijon. The small restaurant is gone now, but for a long time it served some of the simplest and lustiest meals I have ever eaten, especially on market days for the wine people who came in from all that part of Burgundy to talk about casks, corks, sulphates.

There were always snails at Crespin, of course, except in exceptionally hot weather, and in the cool months oysters out on the sidewalk in kelpy baskets, and all downed by the dozens. There was the classical green salad to scour the maw, and always a good plain tart of seasonal fruits if one could still face it. I remember some cheeses in the winter. And then there were sealed casseroles of *tripes à la mode de Caen véritable*.

Those casseroles, for two or six or eight people, seemed to possess the inexpressible cachet of a numbered duck at the Tour d'Argent, or a small perfect octahedral diamond from Kimberley. They were unsealed at the table. The vapor hissed out, and the whole dish seethed. Plates were too hot to touch bare-handed, to keep the sauce from turning as gluey as a good ox would need it to be (at a temperature more suited to his own digestion). It was served with soup spoons as well as knives and forks, and plenty of crusty bread lay alongside. It was a fine experience.

Crespin, with its hoary monstrous old oyster opener always there on the wintery sidewalk, his hands the most scarred I have ever seen and still perhaps the surest in the way he handled the Portugaises, the green Marennes, upon their dank beds of fresh seaweed . . . Crespin and the old man and even the ruddy marketers are gone, except on my own mind's palate.

The last time I went there, I was alone. It was a strange feeling at first. I was in Dijon late in the 1950s, to go again to the Foire Gastronomique. The town was jumping, quasi-hysterical, injected with a mysterious supercharge of medieval pomp and Madison-Avenue-via-Paris commercialism. I went to several banquets where ornate symbols were pinned and bestowed, with dignitaries several levels above me in the ferocious protocol of eating and drinking, and then I went by myself to the restaurant I wanted to be in once more.

In the small, low room there was a great hum and fume, like market day but even better, and every table but one was occupied by large, red-faced, happy, loud Burgundians. *My* table was empty, and it seemed indicated by the gods that I had come to sit at it. I had sat there many times before, and never would again. It was a little apart but not obtrusively so, up a step like the fantastic banquet boards still cluttered and heavy at the official feastings, but pleasantly enclosed on three sides, with the white window curtains at my back. If I had not come, a potted plant would have been set neatly in my place, I know. I felt pleased to be there instead, and as usual I was awed by my continuing good luck in life, especially now and then.

I think I ate a few snails, to stay in the picture. (The old scarred oysterman was not there, it being early November and very warm . . .) Then, although after all the banquets I felt about as hungry as a sated moth, I ordered a small and ritual casserole of tripes.

They were as good as they had ever been some decades or centuries ago on my private calendar. They hissed and sizzled with delicate authority. Nobody paid any attention to my introspective and alcoved sensuality, and the general noise beat with provincial lustiness in the packed room, and an accordionist I had last seen in Marseille slid in from the frenzied streets and added to the wildness, somewhat hopelessly. When he saw me digging into my little pot of tripe, he nodded, recognizing me as a fellow wanderer. I asked him if he would have a drink, as he twiddled out near-logical tunes on the instrument he wore like a child on his belly. He looked full at me and said, "Sometime a *pastis* at the Old Port." I have not yet met him there again, but it is almost doubtless that I shall.

I could not know that the next time I returned, lemminglike, to the dank old town, Crespin and the white curtains and all of it would be gone, but it is. It is too bad to explain.

The classical recipes for preparing tripe can be found in any good cookbook, which someone who has read this far will already know and be able to consult. I myself like the French methods, but there are excellent ones in almost every culture which permit the use of this type of animal meat. Here is a good one which is fresh to the taste, adapted from the "Trippa alla Petronius" served currently in a London restaurant called Tiberio:

This is a comparatively quick recipe (the true *tripes à la mode de Caen* may take at least twelve hours of baking), and it is very simple, which explains why it is sought after in a posh Mayfair restaurant where the clients may feel jaded. I think that the fresh herbs give it special quality, but perhaps it could be successfully tinkered with if they proved to be unprocurable. Fortunately this is seldom the case with parsley. If dried basil had to be used, one to two tablespoonfuls should be soaked in one and a half instead of one cup of wine and then drained, and I would be tempted to go a step further and use a light dry red instead of the Tiberio's white. All this would, I fear, make the whole dish more "ordinary."

While I am about it, I might as well discuss why it is much easier to make things with tripe now than it was a hundred or so years ago, or when I myself was little. I do this in a missionary spirit, convinced that they can be very good to eat and should be less shunned in our country. In these days tripe is almost always taken through its first tedious cleansings in special rooms, at the wholesale butchers' factories. My friend Remo, "meatman and mentor," says somewhat cryptically that the stuff is subjected to enormous pressure, which I assume means with steam. It is then trimmed to a uniform niceness, wrapped in bundles rather like large pallid grape leaves, and delivered fresh or quick-frozen to the markets where there is any demand for it.

✧ Tripe Petronius

*3 pounds tripe, previously boiled until
    tender
4 medium-sized carrots*
3 sticks of celery ⎱ *chopped very fine*
3 large onions ⎰
¾ cup butter
4 tablespoons tomato puree
1 glass (6 to 8 ounces) dry white wine
½ glass olive oil
2 cloves of garlic, minced
½ cup chopped fresh parsley
½ cup chopped fresh basil

Drain tripe and cut into 1-inch squares. Gently brown the three vegetables in the butter. Add tomato puree and wine, and stir until sauce thickens. Add tripe and simmer slowly for 1 hour.

In separate skillet warm olive oil, and add garlic, parsley, and basil, taking care not to overheat. Cook slowly about 5 minutes, mix quickly into tripe, and serve.

Once the cook takes over from the butcher, this modern treatment makes it possible to prepare tripe for any dish in an hour or a little more, by washing it well and then simmering it in ample water flavored to taste with carrots, onion, celery, herbs. When tender but not too soft it is drained, and then AVANTI, EN AVANT, FORWARD! Here is the older method, perhaps to shame some of us into trying our luck for a change, recommended in 1867 by the expatriate Pierre Blot, in his *Hand-Book of Practical Cookery, for Ladies and Professional Cooks. Containing the Whole Science and Art of Preparing Human Food*:

TRIPE

How to clean and prepare. Scrape and wash it well several times in boiling water, changing the water every time, then put in very cold water for about twelve hours, changing the water two or three times; place it in a pan, cover it with cold water; season with parsley, chives, onions, one or two cloves of garlic, cloves, salt, and pepper; boil gently five hours, take out and drain.

When I was a child I felt a somewhat macabre interest in watching our cook go into this old routine. It started in a washtub, with much sloshing with big scrub brushes and whackings at the slippery ivory-white rubber. Then I am sure that baking soda was put into a couple of the several changes of water, making things foam in an evil way . . . I suppose a battle with some of the digestive juices my grandmother counted on? For the last cool soaking, handfuls of salt were thrown in, or so it now seems to me. But I am downright sure that in our house there was no fancy nonsense of herbs and suchlike in the final slow boiling. Plain fare with a good white sauce, that is what we were served. "Eat what's set before you, and be thankful for it," was the gastronomical motto that quivered always in the air above our table while Grandmother sat there, and with a certain amount of philosophical acceptance it can be a good one, the whole chancy way.

Here, then, are a few more things it is easy to be thankful for, made of what I myself, although raised by an Anglophiliac mother, cannot easily think of as "offal." I like them all, at the right time, but even they are limited in their safety with some diners. They are my own deviations from the basic themes found in any good cookbook.

Before I give them, though, I feel like discussing a recurrent problem in conditioned reflexes in my own and others' kitchens. Both the Oxford dictionary and Webster's agree that "offal" usually means refuse, rubbish, garbage, carrion, and several other revolting things. This is unfortunate for people who read and speak English and American . . . a semantical barrier, made even more impregnable by the Victorian influence of squeamish ancestors, ladies like my grandmother, taught to avert their faces from "foreign messes" which might contain unmentionable animal parts meant by their Creator for reproduction or elimination but not for the proper Anglo-Saxon table. Even now, in England, the word "offal" is used semiprofessionally (like "entrails" and "variety meats" in the United States), and housewives prefer the more discreet and even euphorious term "livers and lights." This is a cozy blanket indeed, for correctly a liver is nothing but a liver, and the lights are plain *lungs* to a butcher.

In America there is so little demand for lungs, not to mention brains, hearts, kidneys, sweetbreads, and even livers, that they are often hard to find except in ethnic pockets of big cities or in upper-class restaurants, and when they can be bought in small elegant shops or supermarkets they are usually referred to almost furtively as "innards." I am told that doctors prescribing antigout diets call them, even more circumspectly, "miscellaneous soft meats." (I know one publisher who wishes that he could print every cookbook with perforated pages, so that the chapters on such a revolting subject might be pulled out at will and burned with sure disgust . . .)

In the American edition of *Larousse Gastronomique*, in direct contrast to this general aversion, some thirty-nine columns are devoted to the preparing of "offal," and I, perhaps as the devil's advocate, think it may be salubrious to list the subjects of their recipes. In Beef there are white meats (feet, belly or tripe, and brains), and red (lights, heart, liver, tongue, kidneys, marrow, and tail). In Mutton and Lamb there are kidneys, tongue, brains, feet, the pluck (which includes heart, liver, lungs, stomach), and the fry, as we call it in America, which some Westerners also know as "mountain oysters" and the French less ambiguously call *animelles*. Pork supplies kidneys, liver, brains, trotters, head, blood, and the entrails for encasing sausages. Veal (or Calf) has lights, heart, liver, head, sweetbreads, marrow, trotters, kidneys, and a fold of the peritoneum called mesentery which is not sold in America and which sounds like a delicate kind of tripe in any recipe of French cooking calling for *fraise de veau*.

Of course there are several of these butchered titbits that I have only read about, but my curious nose sniffs vicarious pleasure in their descriptions. Many of them I have never prepared myself but have enjoyed in European homes and restaurants of every class. Kidneys are of course socially accepted in England, although I have been led to believe, mostly from novels, that liver or tripe with onions is low on the scale. Economically I could question this judgment, of the first dish at least, for it is delicious when well prepared with good materials, and *not cheap*. Sweetbreads, which can be either the pancreas or the thymus gland of a calf or lamb, have for centuries been acceptable for high-class cooking, and therefore are often out of reach of diners in the lower brackets. They were an occasional treat when I was a little girl . . . one of our innumerable ways of proving that when Grandmother Cat was away, the mice led by her quietly sensual daughter would play, mostly around the dining room table. Later, as a student in France, I often ate the poor man's substitute, brains, and I still like them, especially prepared most simply with black butter.

So, in public and private kitchens, and in fat days and lean, I have tasted almost every part of cow, sheep, and pig, and probably without knowing it, of other animals. (I have never eaten sheep's eyes, a delicacy in some countries, and although I have recipes for preparing them, I shan't give them here . . .) I have eaten a Mountain Oyster Fry of lambs' testicles flown down from Montana, and they were prepared just as real oysters in a Hangtown, breaded and dipped quickly into deep hot fat and then folded into scrambled eggs, with crisp bacon alongside. A Hangtown Fry is said to be God's Great Breakfast after a long night of prancing and sousing, at least around San Francisco. In the same way, but at both ends of the game, mountain oysters, in a fry or not, are solemnly believed to be an aphrodisiac and a restorative. I like them but have never sought them out either at a fixed hour or for a fixed purpose, other than plain pleasurable hunger.

As for some of the things like palate and muzzle, even *Larousse* admits that they are no longer fashionable in France. I doubt that I have ever tasted the first, but I remember from several decades ago that a cold hors d'oeuvre of thinly sliced muzzle vinaigrette was considered somewhat low-class by the omnivorous students of Dijon. I myself found it very

good, rather tart and gristly, and gladly ate it when a few of us treated ourselves to a ten-franc dinner together (the franc was then pegged at twenty-
five to the dollar). The others dove into the
radishes and pickled onions and celery root
and salami that were served generously, always, before the correspondingly meager
main course. (And in my calorie-conscious
homeland I find it a fine trick to keep hungry people from eating too much of what
they are conditioned to think of as "food," if
I serve chilled marinated vegetables or another light interesting first course and *then*
what they presuppose they have come to
table for. They eat more slowly. They eat
more vegetables, if served as a separate first
course and not a routine accompaniment to
the main dish. They eat less, after the first
appeasement. At the end a piece of fruit
looks *right* to them, rather than a preten-
tious substitute for the chocolate meringue pie they have been taught to
expect. And they sleep better. And the next morning, the bathroom scale
reads more prettily. Yes, the French have a word for it . . . *abat-faim!*)

 ## Elsa's Summer Tongue
(good for cold lunches and sandwiches)

1 fresh beef tongue
1 cup white wine vinegar and ½ cup broth
    OR
1½ cups dry white wine
½ cup brown sugar
4 to 5 bay leaves
4 to 5 peppercorns

*Cover tongue with cold water for an hour, drain, and
curl into pressure cooker on rack. Add liquid, sugar,
and spices to about ½ the depth of the meat. Bring to
high pressure and then reduce at once to lowest for
about 1½ hours. Skin while hot, and trim thick end.
Put back into juice until cool.*

Any dependable kitchen manual will give the basic rules for preparing
tongue, and they hold for most animals eaten by two-legged people. Usually a fresh beef tongue is used. The cooking must be slow and long. The
cooked tongue, when tender, is peeled while hot and then either put back
in its juices to cool or seasoned, browned, and simmered with herbs and
vegetables to be served hot in different fashions. Any way at all, it takes

little attention, and is a delicious dish . . . *if one likes it.* (One longtime friend finds his own tongue swelling and folding back ominously into his throat at the mere thought of eating a piece of one, or even looking at it. I feel sorry.) Cooking can be done in a Dutch oven, a pot, a kettle . . . or in a pressure cooker, as in this simple recipe which my family has always liked, from a lady it has always loved: &

Veal kidneys are another meat I like to serve, but with age and experience I am chary of doing so, because of the dietary strictures of my guests. The meat should be cooked very fast, which makes its whole preparation an easy act for people who still like to play with chafing dishes as something besides warmers for cocktail sausages. There are two schools about preparing kidneys for their final dash into butter and sherry and onto the plates: the first slices them thin, after removing the fat and skin, and goes on from there; the second tries to remove all taint of kidneyishness by plunging the slices three separate times into cold water which is then brought almost to the boil. I find this last ritual nonsensical, for the meat is bound to turn hard and lose its character . . . which is of course the prime purpose of such a procedure with people who loathe kidneys anyway. Why bother to go through all this to get rid of a detested flavor and aroma? Why not eat something else?

As for the rest of cooking cut-up kidneys, it is wise to have everything ready to hand, whether at stove or on sideboard, exactly as with many Chinese dishes . . . &

 *Mallorcan Kidneys*

1 pair veal kidneys
2 tablespoons butter or fine olive oil
1 sweet onion, minced
Pepper, salt
½ cup sherry, dry or (in Spain) sweet
Watercress, coarsely chopped

Wash and cut kidneys into pieces. Melt butter, brown onion lightly, and add meat. Season, stir, and add sherry. Simmer 4 to 5 minutes. Make bed of cress, pour kidneys and sauce into it, and serve at once with hot toast.

This does indeed sound Oriental, with the contrast of the fresh cool green leaves and their bite, and the richly aromatic meat and sauce. And it is very easy. Another more elaborate way, which like many good recipes can be played with to infinity, is:

 Kidneys Ali-Bab

4 veal kidneys

¼ pound sweet butter

¼ cup brandy

1 cup thinly sliced fresh mushrooms

Salt, pepper, dash of cayenne

½ cup dry sherry

1 cup thick cream

Remove fat from kidneys and slice them very thin. Brown fast in sizzling butter, and then flame with brandy. When flame is out, add mushrooms and seasoning, stir well, add sherry, and cover closely. Simmer 4 to 5 minutes. Add cream, bring to bubble, and serve at once with (or on) crisp toast or hot rice. (Ali-Bab says that ½ teaspoon horseradish sauce can be added with the cream.)

Obviously this recipe attempts a certain compromise with the basic function of kidneys, or at least a masking of its olfactory reminder, by the use of both brandy and sherry, with cayenne somewhere too, and then the added bounty of a suggestion of horseradish as optional! Who fools whom?

A direct contrast to such delicious flim-flam is the way kidneys have been roasted for centuries by simple people. They skewer the fat-encased nuggets and toast them slowly over a hot fire until most of the grease has fallen down into the blaze, and then split them open and eat the savory meat . . . and often the crisp envelope too. A more refined way of doing much the same primitive thing is to find a butcher willing and able to provide what are called kidney chops, of either veal or mutton. They are easier to buy in England than in the United States, where mutton is not liked because of its definite odor and taste. (I know of one fine San Francisco restaurant that used to buy racks of mutton, parboil them briefly, and keep them on hand for making extra-large chops for its fastidious clients . . . no rank hint of lanolin and wet wool, and servings of Texan

proportions! Now they would go begging . . .) Mutton, because of our national queasiness, is thus hard to find, but occasionally a whole lamb will
be cut by a butcher charging fabulous sums, on order of course, so that
two or even four thick chops from each carcass will encase a half or whole
of the animal's two organs.

My meat-mentor Remo tells me that there are a couple of reasons why
we rarely see such a cut of meat: Americans don't know what to do with it
and would usually not do it if they could, and current meat inspection
laws require the officer to tear out the kidney from its natural nest of fat
bones, to see if it looks like a *nice* kidney. So be it . . . but if ever such a
cut comes my way, I seize it, season it with plenty of salt and ground pepper, and broil it very fast, to eat with cold or grilled tomatoes and more
pepper. It is an interesting experience. The meat is pink on the inside,
and juicy, and the kidney is not tough, and the tomato picks up and teases
and cavorts with the high flavors (although perhaps a good squeeze of
lemon on the finished chop would do as well in the off-season?). It seems
strange to me that I cannot come upon a recipe for this dish, which I have
eaten in England and here too, and which Remo tells me is called
bluntly a kidney chop by a handful of eccentrics like me . . .

According to him, this same small crowd calls brains brains, in a
butcher shop, whereas nobody else even recognizes them. This is a
shame. It is true that I never ate brains when I was a child, and by now it
is much too late to ask why they were not in my mother's category of such
secret pleasures as sweetbreads. They are comparatively easy to buy, especially if one lives in a "foreign" section of a town or district, and recipes
for them are not hidden, even in stylish cookbooks. They must be properly cooked before using, of course, and then cooled and played with ac-

cording to the cook's desire. Myself, I do not like them combined with eggs, a fairly common method, for the textures are too much alike and the tastes too similarly bland and mild. They should be *definite*, in shape and flavor. They can be prepared according to any recipe for sweetbreads and are delicious with a crisp coating, as when breaded and fried, and they respond well to tart marinades and the challenge of wines, herbs, spices. Here are two ways for proving some of this:

 Calves' Brains with Green Peas

> *1 pair brains*
> *½ cup white wine vinegar or lemon juice*
> *3 tablespoons butter*
> *Salt*
> *¼ cup minced fresh parsley*
> *Fresh peas, cooked, seasoned, buttered*
>
> *Blanch and prepare brains according to basic rules found in any good cookbook. Drain, and sprinkle with 2 tablespoons of vinegar or lemon juice. Let stand ½ hour. Melt butter, dry and salt brains, fry golden brown. Place on hot dish, add parsley to pan, heat well, and remove from fire while adding rest of vinegar or lemon. Shake well, pour over brains, and serve at once with hot peas.*

This excellent if somewhat finicky recipe has taken shape over many years, and as I remember, its first cook suggested a garnish of thick slices of fried tomatoes on rounds of fresh toast spread with anchovy butter. (Lucky peasants!) This sounds like a confusion of flavors but is very good as a hearty main dish . . . as it is also with grilled lambs' kidneys, which like lamb itself seem to be happy with the flavor of anchovy lurking somewhere.

And so, with bold knife and fork, eat well of forbidden fruits! The trouble with them is that some people . . .

Marinated Brains, Peasant Style

MARINADE:

2 to 3 tablespoons melted butter

1 tablespoon flour

2 tablespoons lemon juice or white wine vinegar

1 tablespoon finely chopped shallots or scallions

1 tablespoon minced fresh parsley

½ teaspoon dry mustard

Pinch of dried thyme, sage, marjoram, to taste

Salt, pepper

1 cup dry white wine

Mix well, simmer 6 to 7 minutes over low flame, stirring constantly, and cool.

2 to 3 calves' brains, blanched and cooled

3 tablespoons butter

3 egg yolks

¼ cup finely minced fresh parsley

Pour cooled marinade over brains, and let stand for about 2 hours. Drain, and strain the marinade into a saucepan. Brown the brains well in butter, add half the marinade, and simmer gently for 10 minutes. Place meat on very hot platter and put into low oven. Heat marinade to below simmer, and add egg yolks one by one, beating well with each addition and taking care not to let sauce boil. Strain over hot brains, and dust with parsley. Serve at once.

The Downward Path

WHAT IS SAUCE FOR THE GOOSE is not always the same thing for the gander, and can even finish him off, in one way or another. Once, for me, a potential romance came to a quiet finale when I misjudged the persuasion of an accompaniment to a leg of lamb which I thought would make any further appraising unnecessary. I still believe that the sauce itself was perfection, and that my prospective table mate did not live up to his carefully nurtured promise.

He and three staunch companions, obviously believing in the safety of numbers, came for a weekend of gastronomical frolic to my ranch in the dry rocky hills near Hemet, in California, to gauge me as a possible asset to their dedicated interest in *la bonne table*. They were cultural light-miles away from their home base in San Francisco . . . or perhaps I should say home plate, for they were skilled trenchermen and eminent in the several clubs in the City which, in those days before "gourmet" became a ridiculous term, were temples to food and wine. They arrived laden with ripe cheeses, prosciutto, little round tins of truffles both black and white, flat loaves of sourdough bread from the Wharf, all in case of a probable dearth of viands in my wilderness. They were protective of my intended victim, and of course themselves.

I, meanwhile, had prepared for their first meal a quietly artful rebuttal, in case that was what they were asking for. They were used to several wines and several courses. During my own limit of three very simple sections of dinner we would drink two unknown light beers, one from a

small brewery near Anaheim which somehow had survived Prohibition
and one from lower California. There was plenty of a respectable dry
champagne from Northern California chilling as needed, and of course
there was stronger stuff for any lapse from their studied alcoholic grace.

First, as I remember, we would eat chilled marinated green beans and
tomato, with a little anchovy somewhere to tease the palate for the meat
to follow, for it would be lamb. And after the meat, which I fully intended
to be superb, we would eat a refreshing compote of summer fruits, and
then some of the cheeses the three musketeers had brought along with
their fine d'Artagnan.

The lamb, a curry, was to be eaten with plenty of its sauce and white
Indian rice, already rubbed and ready to be steamed dry and pearly. Since
the whole course around its dish would be subtle, the classical condiments were limited, and correctly bland and suave: toasted almonds in
slivers, currants poached fat in dry vermouth, a green-peach chutney. I
took all this in an easy but serious stride, knowing that in some way it was
to change my life.

It is almost embarrassing to admit, so many lives later, that I cannot
find a recipe for the dish I spent two days preparing and have often made
since then. I know I did not invent it. Its principle is to half-roast a
chicken or piece of young meat like veal or lamb, meanwhile preparing a
strong and ample court-bouillon, and then drown the meat in the soup
and simmer it gently until tender but not overdone. Then the broth is
strained and made into a thin sauce, with flour and the usual adjusting of
salt and so on, and a moderate amount of the best procurable curry powder. The meat is dropped once more into the deep pot of deceptively
gentle gravy and is left overnight in its bath. About an hour before it is to
be served, it is brought once more to a thorough simmer, in what has be-

come an insidiously pungent sauce. (If for personal reasons of aesthetics one wished to change the rather insipid color of this brew, I suppose turmeric would be the answer, although I know of it only from books . . .) To serve, the meat is carved and placed nicely either on a bed of hot cooked rice, or on a platter with the rice served apart, and is doused modestly with some of the sauce. The rest of this is served separately, in a generous bowl.

For me, the meat has always been unusually succulent, and the interesting thing about the whole leisurely and comparatively undemanding process is that the flavor of curry, always delicate in spite of its increasing warmth, permeates the whole dish instead of remaining as a kind of mask or coating, a wild conglomeration of textures whose basic natures are completely hidden.

That time in Hemet I felt alarmingly complacent, if not even somewhat triumphant. Before the gentlemen arrived for their picaresque outing, I tasted the thin sauce several times as it waited in its deep pot around and over the leg of lamb, and I found it correctly sophisticated. It was light but tricky, almost illusive in its impact, and with a very fortunate consistency which was the obvious result of my skill at the stove. Irresistible seemed the word.

The four men arrived on time, relaxed and laden with the goodies which subconsciously served for them as survival kits. Eventually all but the chosen one, aloof and discreetly predatory as always, roamed up to the high lookout in the hills to see if the sun would sink again in the right place. They carried rattlesnake sticks, and some correctly chilled champagne, for emergencies.

My suitor, anxious to play his part for them and perhaps for me, put-

tered here and there about the kitchen and the big studio where we
would dine, checking to see if I had put the right glasses in the right
places and if the icebox was properly cold. It was mildly annoying to my
vanity to be quizzed so thoroughly and silently, but I told myself that I
should grow used to such things. His trained nose told him that curry had
been used somewhere lately, and he looked slightly let down at the plain-
ness of the three bowls of condiments he found under a napkin. I smiled
happily: his exquisite palate would understand them, once he tasted the
lamb, for I knew it would be among the most cunning dishes he had ever
been served, in his decades as a well-publicized but honest disciple of the
Tenth Muse.

Gradually I found myself irked by his snoopiness, after several more
peerings into cupboards and drawers. It is possible at this point that I expected him to seize his few unchaperoned moments to make some sort of
attack, no matter how covert, on my availability. By the time he hit his
real target, the deep pot of delicate curry simmering, ready for its final
drama, I was simmering in rhythm, and when he picked up a big spoon,
lifted the lid, and without a by-your-leave cooled and sipped at some of
the sauce, murmuring a perfunctory you-don't-mind-do-you, I did mind.

He sipped again.

"This won't do at all, my dear," he said gently, pityingly. "This won't
do. Alex and Bob and Armitage . . . well, you know who they are. This
is . . . do you call this a curry? I am sorry. Truly. But we still have time."

I remember how I leaned hard on the edge of the pine table. I felt
boneless with disappointment. This man, this high priest of hedonism as
practiced in a city where I thought I would like to live as one of the hand-
maidens if not even a subpriestess, this near-god, did not recognize the

deliberate confrontation with a subtlety committed to honor him. He was impervious to the insidious magic of the lengthy preparation of it, and the deep gentle ring of it on his vaunted palate. Feet of clay . . . Operation Feet of Clay, I said resignedly.

I said, "You mean there is time to do something?" I did not believe any of it. "There is only an hour or so. I have been making this for two days. It is really quite . . . that is, when we taste the meat . . ."

"Quickly," he commanded, like a surgeon who is stopped on a highway to attend a violent accident. "The curry powder. Veeraswami, of course. Some hot white wine. Dry. Anything. Hurry, for God's sake. They'll be horrified by this. They'll be starved."

And so on, and I watched my muddied idol, the man I had dreamed might eat across from me in my old age or at least sip pabulum somewhere with me in some kind of mutual rhythm, mix a thick paste of raw curry powder which was not from London, stir it almost brutally into the beautiful suave sauce I had concocted, and push the leg of lamb impatiently about in the darkening pool of juice.

When Alex and Bob and Armitage thundered down the hill, and we had tidied ourselves in our various ways (they wearing cravats from a far-off dining club in my honor), and when the usual preprandial rituals had been observed and the first course tossed off, we ate the juicy slices of lamb and the excellent rice, all covered with a real tongue-torch of "curry sauce," almost a tear-bringer. I was complimented on the unexpected succulence of the meat, which one of the gentlemen observed had caught a tiny flavor of curry even in its faintly pink interior, for some odd reason. (Lambs are very sensitive, I thought sardonically. Then I took a closer look at him, as a possible successor in my line of *gastronomes manqués*, but it was a short-lived interest . . .)

The condiments were of course pitiably inadequate in the face of such a blazing assault, and everyone was courteously silent about them, almost abashed: a three-boy curry to men used to a twelve-boy or, for visiting Boston nabobs, an occasional twenty-one boy! In a kindly way, my choice of light beers was commended.

I played my role as a well-meaning but untutored country exlass, and I felt disappointed and lonely. I had been a goose. Alex and Bob and Armitage could take their white-plumed gander home again, unmenaced. But I knew and I still know that the sauce that first lapped gently against the sides of that piece of meat, so tender, so carefully embalmed, was a gem of great worth, something unexpected in the sea of highly flavored disguises and maskings in our prejudiced careless gastronomy.

Perhaps those men lost more than I did, or perhaps we should leave well enough alone . . . forget sauces entirely? I think not. They are a fine challenge, when treated with respect, even at the risk of blasted expectations of future dalliance in digestive, sexual, and related realms.

In my own case, I learned a great deal about other people's natures as well as mine in this one earnest attempt to combine business with pleasure, and even more about the importance of resolute honesty, when my potential swain reacted as he did to that presumptuous sampling. I know now that I should have said, "Put that spoon down! Close that pot! Please, I mean. I have made a beautiful sly smooth curry such as you fat cats from the Golden Gate have never tasted. You will of course understand it, for you are serious and noted gourmets. So go away. Please, I mean. Stop snooping and *trust* me."

By then, of course . . . from that first betrayal to the final fiery denouement when we sat desperately gulping lager . . . it was clear that the three trenchermen would herd their leader homeward, still unfettered, all of them well fed and safe. I myself felt a delicious relief. Men and women being what they are, I might try again, but the next time I would use provisions other than an artful concoction of broths and spices called a sauce.

Anyone who owns a reputable cookbook will have the classical formulas for one within reach, with formidable lists of variations on the two basics, brown and white. In *Larousse Gastronomique* there are six of the former and eight of the latter, with a minimum listing of recipes for about 135 compounds of the brown and 145 of the white bases. There are only 42 cold sauces, with many of them using mayonnaise as a base, and then there are eight fundamental sauces to be served with desserts. Alexis Soyer in his *Gastronomic Regenerator*, which stood on every reputable library table and pantry shelf in England in the mid-1800s, gave about a hundred recipes, including a few garnishes and tips about preparing cockscombs and such. And in America, a century later, a trusted ally like *The Joy of Cooking* listed some 150 sauces, hot and cold, for meats, fish, salads, and so forth, and more than 70 for desserts, when the redoubtable Mrs. Rombauer and her daughter Mrs. Becker made another of several revisions of the family masterpiece.

Larousse defines a sauce as a liquid seasoning for food. The modesty of this dictum is almost as subtle as Escoffier's great rule for cooking: *Fais Simple*. I think it should be discussed and pondered seriously and at some length, by every teacher and student of gastronomy, for too many cooks, in every possible category of skill, are tempted by the intricacies of their trade to forget that a sauce must enhance the flavors and textures of a dish, and not mask them.

It is true that both accident and invention have produced most of the variations on the brown-white-thick-thin-cold-hot bases of procedure. It is also true that many of us, even real connoisseurs, often judge a dish and its cook by the sauce, and this is dangerous. I think that when I cannot tell, and tell clearly and at once, that I am eating beef instead of veal, or frozen crab meat instead of fresh, or liverwurst instead of *pâté de fois gras*, because of the masking of their true flavors and textures, I am being cheated shamefully. I am being insulted.

The other end of the stick, of course, is to eschew all sauces. This is a pity, if one has an active palate. It is like never drinking any but one grade of wine, no matter how commendable, and from only one wine district. There can be no scale of comparison, but in gastronomy as in many other fields the old saw that comparison is odious is a flat lie. Taste buds accustomed to the honest impact of one or two modest wines drunk with the daily fare will rouse themselves triumphantly when an occasional glass of really fine vintage stuff washes around them and will return to tomorrow's carafe of Chablis Village or California jug Burgundy with new vigor.

In the same way, nothing can be better for everyday good fare than a plainly grilled lamb chop or slice of roast beef. But now and then a complication is delicious: lamb cutlets served *à la Rouennaise*, for instance, sautéed and rich with pureed chicken livers and apple brandy, or *tournedos* cut from a filet mignon and prepared *Henri IV*, heady with truffles and artichoke hearts and Béarnaise sauce and Madeira and demiglace and . . . why not? If one's own *foie* is a little too *gras* for the actual engagement in such a battle of the senses, the mere reading of reputable cookbooks offers an easy escape into vicarious tasting, and the more classical they are, the more honest they will be in their direct approach to the intricacies they expound. In other words, one armchair banquet outlined by an Escoffier will be better than ten orgies described by his deviate disciples in magazines and ten-pound glossy tomes.

It would be foolish of me, or perhaps merely pretentious, to bother any reader with the basic rules for brown and white sauces, for mayonnaise, and so on. Here, though, are a few recipes which have evolved from a respectful inventiveness in my own self-taught kitchen practices, and further dalliance with most of them might prove interesting and amusing. ⅊

⅊ A Sauce for Vegetables

6 tablespoons butter
1½ tablespoons lemon juice
6 tablespoons dry white wine
Dash of tabasco, if desired

Heat all ingredients gently. When barely bubbling, pour over hot cooked cauliflower, hot artichokes, asparagus, small carrots, etc.

⅊ A Sauce for Fish

1 tablespoon minced shallot, chives,
  or green onion
1 tablespoon minced fresh parsley
2 tablespoons butter
Salt, pepper, to taste
1 cup dry white wine
½ cup commercial sour cream

Heat first two ingredients until golden in butter. Season. Add wine and simmer 1 minute. Stir in cream, and pour over broiled or poached fish.

This last recipe with its double threat is technically a "butter" rather than a sauce, although it qualifies for the *Larousse* definition by turning into a liquid as soon as it touches the hot meat. It is in honorable company, and an occasional look at the butters listed in any good cookbook will widen even an expert's horizon.

Several things we call sauces are not so considered, by the kitchen purists. Tabasco, for instance, is definitely a condiment, and so are the catsups and, I assume, the bottled standbys like Worcestershire and all their siblings. I am conditioned to think of them as what their labels say, and I like to have them on hand, although I suspect them of some knavery as well as being tricky to use with constant finesse. A good case in point, perhaps, is Kitchen Bouquet, which of course

is not actually a sauce but a last-ditch ally (for me, anyway) in case something takes on an abominable grayish tinge. A *minute* dollop of this dangerous juice can pick it up aesthetically
without any damage to its wished-for savor,
I believe.

⅋ *A Sauce for Steak*

4 teaspoons prepared mustard
2 or 3 drops tabasco sauce
Scant teaspoon salt
2 tablespoons butter

*Cream all together. Make 3 or 4 gashes in thick rare
steak, fill quickly with dressing, and serve at once.
A good variation, to be used the same way with thick
lamb or mutton chops, is to use half mustard and half
anchovy paste, and omit the salt.*

Perhaps this admission is one I should
not make, in the same class with keeping
"minit" rice on hand and instant coffee.
And pound cake and even biscuit mix. (In
this area the level of sheepishness is a personal thing, and I am quite bland about using canned unsweetened applesauce, and
beef and chicken stocks, and vertically
packed green beans in cans and so on,
which my mother and certainly my grandmother would have spurned
flatly. I still feel apologetic about several other time-and-life savers, thanks
to my ancestors' stern influence, which plainly was not all genetic.)

A kitchen essential, for at least my past several decades, is soy sauce.
Like all the other bottled extracts of mysterious and sometimes unmentionable fermentations and muddlings, it must be used with respect.
When so treated, it is much more than the routine little glass carafe on
the table in a chop suey parlor and can work its own magic if the food is
in need of more than cursory assistance. It is strongly linked with
Worcestershire in this first-aid category, and I think both of them stem
from the Roman *garum*. The recipe for garum is said to be a mystery,
but I can quote it from an earnest search in ancient cookery-bookery.
This version dates from about 400 B.C., and its product is mentioned in
at least half of the recipes given for meat and fish dishes by the great

stylish cooks like Apicius, although its roots probably go many centuries further back into Oriental gastronomy:

ℰ A Chinese Barbecue Sauce

6 teaspoons dry mustard
Dry white wine
½ cup orange marmalade, bitter if possible
4 tablespoons soy sauce

Mix thoroughly into stiff paste and coat meat according to cooking schedule, or use as marinade, thinned with more wine.

Place in a vessel all the insides of fish, both large and small. Salt them well, and expose them to the air until they are completely rotted. Drain off the liquid that seeps from them, and it will be garum.

What we buy as soy sauce is certainly not as fishy as Worcestershire, which is reputed to contain its fair share of anchovies, although its label does not note their state of decomposition. The English sauce, interestingly enough, contains soy! I myself keep on hand, by the gallon can, a medium-weight malty sauce which I can buy in a Japanese store in San Francisco, neither as light nor as heavy and dark with molasses and caramel as I could find in Chinatown. It is a compromise, like some Japanese arts in other fields.

The first time I ever used soy sauce for anything but seasoning, I obeyed the instructions of a Eurasian friend when I had been presented with several fresh fish which I could not cook at once. I painted them quickly with the thin brown stuff and put them trustingly into the icebox, to cook one and even three days later, prepared exactly as if they were still a few hours out of the water. They were fine. They tasted almost newly dead and there was absolutely no hint of soy sauce. The icebox smelled like a lettuce bed at dawn. My friend had not betrayed us. (This is an excellent trick with chops and steaks, too.)

Here is another good way to use soy, in what should perhaps be called the Modified Neoclassic Manner: ℰ

During World War II it used to be much easier than it is now, given the shift in exports from torn Europe to torn Asia, to buy oyster sauce.

This is a very good invention, surely as old as garum, and one eminently suited to replace even such staples as the so-called English sauces, most of which seem to have been developed by French cooks like Soyer and Escoffier. For a person with plenty of oysters to spare, which I have never been, here is an honest Yankee recipe based, almost surely, on one from China:

This "receipt" is from Marion Harland's *Common Sense in the Household*, and for the people with a Curious Nose here is its Oriental ancestor:

This recipe makes a thickish and grayish-brownish liquid, depending of course on the color of the soy sauce, which in China can be light or dark, thick or thin, delicate or heavy. Oddly enough, oyster sauces do not taste of oysters, but are fine with meats, fish, and vegetables, as a coating, a marinade, an addition. They will keep indefinitely in a cool place, well corked, and will add a surprising subtle smoothness to many other sauces. I like them.

While I am sniffing behind the Bamboo Curtain, I think it is worth mentioning one thing about Chinese cooking which is a direct contradic-

 Oyster Catsup

1 quart shucked oysters
1 cup vinegar
1 cup sherry
1 tablespoon salt
1 teaspoon cayenne pepper
1 teaspoon mace

Chop the oysters and boil in their own liquor with vinegar, skimming as needed. Boil 3 minutes, strain through a fine cloth, and return to heat, adding the wine and seasoning. Boil 15 minutes, let cool, and bottle for use, sealing corks.

 Oyster Sauce

12 oysters
1 cup oyster liquid
3 tablespoons dark soy sauce

Mince oysters and bring in their liquid to a boil, then simmer 20 minutes. Strain well, add soy sauce, and store in tightly capped jar in cool place.

tion of a tradition in classical French procedure, acknowledged its gastro-nomical peer. I believe that in France an honest chef will make each of his basic sauces according to a rigid formula, so that no matter what dis-guises he may add later, a knowing diner will recognize the origin. In China there is a Master Sauce, which is either used up or brought to a boil once a week or so, depending on the business and the weather. It starts with the juices of any dish of poultry or meat, which are kept apart from the dish itself and saved in a jar or pot. Other gravies are added as they evolve, from no matter what other dishes. This increasingly rich amalgam is stretched out now and then with wine or soy sauce or some salt, depending on the needs of the cook, much as heeltaps of good wine are poured into a vinegar jug which boasts a good hard-working "mother." Such a procedure is shocking to a French cook and of course can be lethal in the hands of anyone without a conscience or a palate. But it is traditional in high cookery in the Far East, and has been for several thou-sand years. It is a proof of the main difference, perhaps, between the two great cuisines: the Chinese is improvisational and without waste, and the French is precise and basically unchanging.

In this sense, our gradually shaping gastronomical pattern in America is more like the Oriental, in that we are pliant and are adapting our eth-nic backgrounds to the current supplies of food. "Casseroles" are a prime example of this sometimes ghastly ingenuity, and sauces are an-other. Something that was learned sixty years ago in a mountain village in the Ticino turns up in a patio in Napa Valley, twisted out of shape but still recognizable and still good. What we can do to the original recipe for a pesto from Genoa, for instance, should not happen, per-haps, but often does, and very edibly. Here is a reasonable facsimile of the basic recipe, with two or three variations which I often use: ✑

 This is an uncompromising recipe, and to be made honestly it needs
fresh basil. Since it lasts well, the trick is to
make it in batches while the basil patch is

 Pesto alla Genovese

flourishing! It can become almost a compulsive adjunct to good Italian cooking,
eaten in equal parts with butter with freshly
cooked spaghetti or added to thick vegetable
soups.

 And to be honest about my dishonesty,
I can make a good pesto with dried basil
leaves which I have soaked for an hour or so
in dry vermouth and then pressed dry, and
almond and even walnut meats instead of
the traditional pinenuts. This confession

3 to 5 cloves garlic, minced
¾ cup fresh basil leaves, chopped
½ cup dry grated Parmesan and/or
  Romano cheese
½ cup pinenuts
Olive oil

*Pound all ingredients except olive oil into smooth
paste. Add olive oil very gradually to paste, to make
smooth thick sauce. Store in icebox, sealing with film
of olive oil.*

will perhaps shatter my already tottering reputation as a disciple of
Gastronomea, but I am not deeply shamed by it, for my Quasi-Pseudo-
Almosts have nurtured and even pleased some firm classicists.

 About blenders, in the case of making a pesto, no matter how tricky
and traitorous I am about its ingredients, I prefer to use a mortar and
pestle, since I am used to several sizes of them in my own kitchen and
I probably get some atavistic pleasure from their primitive functioning.
Blending a pesto makes it more homogenous in texture, and to me somewhat less interesting, than I can do with the mortar between my knees.
The same is true with other sauces, like the age-old and currently popular
guacamole made of avocados. Me, I enjoy the slower method and find
the somewhat rougher texture pleasing. But blenders are almost as

� A Green Sauce

1 cup fresh parsley (and any fresh
    herbs available)
1 large sweet onion
2 cloves garlic
¼ cup wine vinegar
½ cup olive oil

*Chop herbs, onion, and garlic, and blend roughly
with liquids. Serve at once with grilled meats, frijoles,
chili con carne . . . or use as starter for gazpacho.*

✐ A Hot-Cold Green Sauce

¼ cup butter
¼ cup olive oil
1 to 2 cloves garlic, chopped
½ cup finely minced parsley and
    fresh herbs to taste
Grated dry Romano and/or Parmesan
    cheese

*Melt butter gently with oil and add garlic, never
letting it brown. Add chopped or roughly blended
herbs. Stir well and cool. Beat in enough cheese to
make smooth paste.*

omnipresent as death and taxes, and here
are a couple of things I make, which have
evolved from what somebody's great-aunt
showed me or a trusted friend suggested: ✐

This recipe does not have either nut
meats or cheese in it and is a far cry from a
true pesto. Here is one that goes back a little
to that classic: ✐

In my town a sauce called Genovese,
with more nostalgia than truth, is made
much in this way, but with fresh basil instead of parsley, and finely grated Monterey
Jack cheese instead of the dry Italian ones. A
platter of freshly boiled spaghetti, a bowl of this
sauce to be tossed about and served on every
plate, and one is to be envied . . .

Another way to cheat on this basic theme
of pesto is to use a generous handful of
chopped young spinach leaves instead of the
reputable basil and the disreputable parsley.
Still another is to buy a can of it, which so far I
have found disappointing, although I like what
I keep in my own icebox, no matter how
sneaky I have been about its basic structure.

This knavery extends into the whole realm
of sauces, once a cook breaks with tradition
and honorable protocol. It is a downward path,

strewn with lamentable lapses and, in many cases, a contradictory mounting of interest and amusement. There is, for instance, a sauce which I
have never found in any French cookbook,
at least not so named: *à la neige*, although it
is actually a cold *mousseline*. It was first
served to me in Dijon, when I was perhaps
twenty and the new asparagus was being
sent down from Paris in elegant baskets to
the rich or to the foolishly *gourmand* like
my landlady. She described the sauce which
we ate with the large pale succulent spears,
always served freshly drained and tepid from
the first and only cooking, as a mixture of
mayonnaise and whipped *crème double*. I have gradually evolved a recipe
which is not as delicate as hers, but very good with asparagus, cold
shrimps or salmon, and several other dainty dishes: ℰ

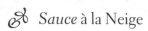

Sauce à la Neige

1 cup heavy cream
1 cup good mayonnaise
Juice of 1 small lemon
1 tablespoon prepared hot fine
    mustard (Dijon)

*Whip cream. Mix mayonnaise, lemon juice, and
mustard, and fold into cream. Chill well.*

There are, of course, infinite variations on the use of an honorable
mayonnaise in sauces to be served with cold fish, lobster, shrimps . . .
If one adds tomato puree and minced green pepper it becomes a kind
of *Andalouse*, and with chopped almonds and minced seeded cucumbers it is something else again, but still very good with salmon. And so
it goes.

There are two tricks with a basic mayonnaise, one hot and one cold,
which are interesting to me. One is with a hollandaise, which any good
cookbook tells even idiots how to concoct, not always with results guar-
anteed. Like most of them, it is still thought to be foolproof by the
woman who taught it to me. She lived alone, after a life of fastidious

and elegant dining, and here is her method, for one generous serving: ✑
Perhaps not many people still have little brown custard cups, but I do,

✑ Madge Dresser's Hollandaise for One

1 fresh egg yolk
¼ cup butter (scant)
Dash red pepper
1 teaspoon fresh lemon juice

Mix gently in little brown custard cup. Place in pan of hot but never bubbling water, while cooking meal. Stir occasionally as it thickens.

✑ Rouille Provençale

2 fat garlic cloves
2 small hot red chilles
1 thick slice bread, crust removed
Water, or broth from the fish the sauce will accompany
½ cup good olive oil (or more)

Mash garlic and peppers thoroughly in mortar. Soak the bread in water or fish broth, press dry, and mix well into mortar with pestle. Gradually add olive oil and work into paste, adding a little broth by teaspoonfuls. The mixture should be reddish and thick.

and this is a refined sauce, no matter how unorthodox. Even thinking about it strengthens my faith in human dignity. If one solitary old lady would make it now and then, so shall I!

The other variation on the mayonnaise theme has two robust little melodies in it (there are many others, in many lands, but these are my own pets). One is for the sauce for a Provençal aïoli, and the other, from the same region, is for a *rouille*, a very strong mixture made without egg yolks and therefore a kind of stepchild in classic gastronomy. It is served often with bouillabaisse, and while it is hot enough to spin the handles on a bank vault it can be an exciting addition to any fish stew, if approached with discretion. A touch of it in other sauces is good, with any fish at all. ✑

A truer mayonnaise, very regional and seldom made or served correctly north of Avignon, is called *aïoli*, to accompany the full meal of that name which is often eaten on Fridays in homes and restaurants in the south of France. This gastronomical caper can be simple or even grandiose in a crude way, with dishes modest or rich, from plain boiled potatoes and a few crisp raw vegetables to accompany the

boiled salt cod, to sliced pot roast and boiled chicken, to the full parade of an *aïoli garni* for Christmas Eve or the visit of Great-Uncle Marius: freshly cooked snails, sliced ham, little potatoes in their jackets, carrots and green beans and artichoke hearts quickly blanched and reheated, peeled hard-boiled eggs, little boiled squid, a dish here and there as the season and the cook dictate of mussels in oil or chick-peas, or sliced green peppers and onions and celery. The focus for all this, though, must be on two plates: the boiled cod and the stiff sturdy sauce.

 *Aïoli Sauce*

> *2 fat garlic cloves per person*
> *2 to 3 egg yolks, depending on size*
> *Pinch of salt*
> *1 scant pint good honest olive oil*
> *1 tablespoon (?) lemon juice*

Reduce peeled garlic to fine paste in mortar, add egg yolks and salt, and blend completely. Start adding oil slowly and blending with pestle or wooden spoon. Gradually the aïoli will thicken until really stiff. Add the lemon juice in cautious amount at the end.

This sauce is best made fresh, I think, and as usual I prefer it done in a mortar and not a blender. Somewhat surprisingly there is a recipe for it in Mrs. Rombauer's preeminently Yankee *Joys*, but for one of the few times in my long admiration of her I do not think it is worth trying to follow, and in case people do not have a good classic or regional French cookbook to hand, I give the following standard formula, which can of course fail as inexplicably as any other sauce made with oil or butter and eggs. If this one separates, or curdles, the acknowledged antidote is to stir it slowly into one fresh egg yolk in a clean bowl. And one good Provençal cook advises adding a scant teaspoonful of tepid water two or three times as the mixture seems to become too thick, to stop this possible calamity . . . a few drops now and then, upon the heated brow or brink . . . ℰ

Elizabeth David, an Englishwoman who has written with sensitive depth about foods and flavors of gastronomical planets other than her own, says wisely that this sauce should be made without fear of the amount of garlic, startling to Anglo-Saxon palates, for if it is skipped the mixture will prove heavy and cloyingly rich.

When I lived in Aix-en-Provence a *grand aïoli* was considered a pretty devastating festival, gastrically at least, and this wine and that one would be recommended to offset its rigors, and often serious students of regional cooking would interrupt their research in the middle of a meal for a quick salubrious toss-down of local *marc*. In general, though, the main menace is an overindulgence in the sauce rather than in all its accompaniments, and if one is psychosomatically ill-adjusted to a plain robust meal, accompanied firmly by the flavor of garlic, the whole thing should be tucked into gastronomical Siberia. It is a winter dish, always served at noon in French families, and in truth there are very few people here in California with whom I would risk it. But it is as natural and good as rain on the roof or peas in the pod . . . if one is hungry for it.

A Proverbial Matter

MEAT AS SUCH IS A GASTRONOMICAL CLICHÉ, perhaps because it has been a part of human nourishment even longer than the proverbs about it, from "One man's meat is another man's poison" to the lesser quoted but equally obvious "God sends meat and the devil sends cooks."

It seems to me that no single part of our so-called daily diet has been treated with more studied carelessness, mixed with an almost hysterical dependence, and this is why I myself feel freed from any compulsion to eat it unless it be of fine quality and in cunning preparations. As a cook, I always risk playing the devil's advocate, but I confess that most meat, sent to nourish us for one reason or another by one force or another, is mistreated to the point of inedibility almost everywhere from top to bottom of our kitchen world. It may be that it is best when most simply grilled or roasted, as prehistoric men discovered soon after they learned to make fire their sometime servant, and as we still try to prove on our backyard barbecue equipment. In any era, it must be healthy firm meat, to be suitable for the innate caveman in us.

The longer it has run on the hoof, before the arrow or lasso hits it, the longer it must wait before it is cooked, to relax tense muscles and calm down. Quiet pasturage, canny feeding, not too much capering about in seasonal excitements: these will make for tender and flavorful flesh in almost any snared animal. African tribesmen and Argentinian and Texan ranchers have their own tricks, but probably the most tempting for four-legged and even human consideration are played in Japan. There, in

Matsuzaka, the famous animals are stall-fed and plied with beer to make them hungrier. They are massaged by hand every day, to distribute the resulting fat evenly in their flesh, so that when it is served it is both lean and rich. In winter there are large hot water bottles to keep the stalls cozy, and in summer fragrant joss sticks burn to stop mosquitoes from interrupting the quiet beery munchings. It sounds like a good life, in a cowish way, and despite contradictions from several other meat-raising countries, Matsuzaka beef is considered with gastronomical awe.

I have never tasted it. And as for Awe itself, when faced with a piece of charred animal flesh my emotion has to be tempered with either voracity or plain clinical interest. I felt the latter a little while ago, when I was invited to a long Sunday luncheon in the garden of a stylish restaurant in southern France. A bonneted cook and two assistants carved from sizzling carcasses of lambs hung by their heels before a wall of glowing charcoal as high as a little house. The French are deservedly reputed to be canny, so instead of losing all the juices as they dripped from the meat (which happens when it is laid flat as we do on our barbecues, from the early Spanish days in California until tomorrow night in the Murgatroyds' patio), pans below the slowly turning bodies caught every drop. Some of it was swabbed up again by the two panting helpers, but some of it was also brought to table just as it had materialized, pungent with fresh herbs, to be spooned over the rough slices of meat and the small fresh white beans served with it. It was probably the most delicious lamb I have ever tasted. And I felt innately bored by the chichi that seems necessary, at least in that region and at that season, in order to serve a simple thing like roasted (grilled in this case) lamb with fresh white beans (*agneau rôti aux haricots blancs frais*). Fountains splashed. Flowers bloomed to the sound of a strolling musician. Bentleys and Ferraris purred to a stop on the road. A specially bottled local rosé was almost excellent, and the chef and all the others did their best, and somehow my interest remained clinical. It was my loss, not theirs.

The fact remains that I think lamb, and mutton too, can be fine fare. Mutton tastes better in England than in America, except perhaps in a few chophouses in great cities. However, I detest the British habit of serving it with mint sauce, to cover its taste of raunchy wool. I used to have to pick mint leaves for a last-minute macerating with vinegar and sugar, a horrid douse, during my years as a part-time child of my English "aunt," while my mother was procreating, and I have a bad taste about it, being adverse to subterfuge.

Pork is a tender and sweet meat when treated with respect. For instance, there is an eminently good way to put nicely fried chops of it between many layers of thinly sliced potatoes and onions, with plenty of dry white wine and seasoning. I add some bay leaves and nutmeg, and cover the whole tightly until all is tender in a moderate oven. It makes a fine smell in the house, and pleases people in winter.

Of course bacon and its porkish allies are part of our national cuisine. I bow to them. I like them to be cooked slowly and well drained, to be crisp when that is indicated, and not to be omnipresent at Gentile breakfasts. This holds for sausages, the tiny to medium ones served dark and appetizing from morning until night in Germanic and Anglo-Saxon countries. They should be treated with care, once having been bought from an honest maker, and then presented as an important part or adjunct of a good meal instead of as a casual or dutiful garnish. They are good on top of a Minorcan stew or hot *ratatouille*, or laid generously on stuffed baked potatoes or alongside gently scrambled eggs. They are good from a chafing dish, on the end of what I once carelessly called a "toothpick" to a

clerk who with tact changed it to "cocktail stick" on my bill. To cook
them, I make sure they are at room temperature, prick each one with a
sharp chopstick or other supposedly nonlethal instrument, and cover
them in a shallow skillet with cold water. As soon as it comes to a full boil,

I drain the pallid ugly-looking morsels and, in the same skillet, cover
them with either a light beer or a mixture of half water and half red or
white wine, and let them simmer until almost all the liquid is gone, turning them as they tell me to. They will be prettily glazed.

The best little sausages I ever ate were in Nuremberg, otherwise more
sadly infamous. They were made of beef, not pork. Between two flying
buttresses of the great church (now gone) was a tiny restaurant called the
Bratwurstglöcklein, and there Albrecht Dürer had probably sat, which is
why I did too, convinced that we both ate the same kind of hot small tender little sausages on the same bitter-cold days, and drank the coolly
warming floods of thin white wine.

As for beef itself, from Matsuzaka or perhaps Gardnerville, Nevada, it
is like sex and politics, a form of religion here to stay . . . at least as long as
people can raise enough cattle to provide themselves with the red meat
considered essential in their diets. Most of them feel fortunate to be able to
sit down as often as possible to a grilled steak, rare or "blue," and a baked
potato split open in its foil wrapper and deeply doused with a sauce of
some kind of pasteurized cheese, commercial sour cream, and plenty of
monosodium glutamate. As to my own approach to the general necessity
for beef in our nourishment, I think the best way to get it is to go to an
honest farmer (or to Nevada), buy a half or whole carcass and have it cut
into the right morsels, and then store it. What I buy lately in the Bay area
seems to have been irradiated, infrarayed, pumped full of mysterious coag-
ulants and preservatives. I would be willing to testify to this uncooperative

and indeed unpatriotic statement. I have bought the best procurable cuts
and have treated them like princes, and they have made a fool of me.
I swear that if I wanted to go to the infinite bother of asking for a chemical
analysis of some of my recent humiliating dishes, the respectfully cooked
meat would be found to have traces of God knows what substances in it.
I am therefore waiting for the kind men in plain clothes who carry off sub-
versives, and meanwhile making a few good things like stews, wherein
I hope to outwit them. (The tough but flavorful meat cut up for stews
seems less prone to petrification than more elegant parts of a carcass . . .)

Stews are a fine invention, and not a new one. Any household that
does not know how to construct a good old *ragoût* is to be pitied. When
I make one, I do it generously, to have plenty left. It tastes even better on
the second day. The third day it is still highly commendable, if it has
been made with fine fresh things and treated sensibly from the start. Any
honorable cookbook, from Larousse to the latest Whizzo-Presto Manual,
holds a few good recipes, which should be reread occasionally to refresh
the mind, and most cooks worth their salt and vinegar will gladly divulge
their own inherited or acquired "secrets."

One man I know insists upon a first almost black browning of the
cubes of beef, done with plenty of sugar. This gives the final product,
hours later, a handsome color which less dedicated people might achieve
with a last cautious addition of Kitchen Bouquet. Another friend who delights in remaking the simplest things as they have seldom been simple
before, thus spending much thought and many extra hours upon them,
prepares the meat for a stew in one large piece, which is well browned
and then covered with broth or water and some wine and simmered
about a half hour to the pound. It is left in its juices overnight. The next
day it is meticulously carved into one-inch cubes, with all fat and gristle

removed. The juices are the foundation for a generous gravy, in which blanched vegetables like carrots, onions, small potatoes and little turnips, celery, and slim green beans are heated and then allowed to marry for an hour or more. The meat is added for a quicker alliance at the end . . . enough time to make the whole thing logical. The result is as delicate as any decently hearty stew would dare be, with each ingredient keeping its own identity.

I myself seem to concoct a stew by osmosis, and therefore one is sometimes better than another, but I find them edible and consistently interesting. Usually I cook them to please my eaters, so that if the nononion member of the group will be present I use a judicious amount of garlic and leave out the offender. I like tomatoes but can skip them when I know I should, for other peoples' dietary or emotional reasons. Sometimes a stew, simple or complex, is good without potatoes. On the other hand, one made "white" instead of "brown," such as an Irish stew, is usually thickened only by potatoes and is relatively artless. Brown stews, or white, can rise as high as the highest haute cuisine, and unhappily sink as low as the most infamous prison's depths.

Veal, the pale child of ruddy beef, may at will be delicious, and fit meat for the eager cook to play with, because of its delicate flavor and texture and its beneficent acceptance of subtleties. I like the way it is roasted on a spit, braced with wild herbs, in Provence . . . a long sprig of fresh rosemary tied to its length, here and there. I have seen more herbs thrown on the coals beneath, somewhat as fennel is blazed under a *loup*, the wolfish sea bass, at its last minutes on the grill.

Chickens too are best roasted on the spit, at least when they have started out as real little good chickens and must not begin their private versions of suttee as long-dead, overchilled, drained, and flabby wrecks. The best one I ever ate was in an apartment as high as one could climb, above the Cours, Mirabeau in Aix-en-Provence. Frantic July tourist cars sent up a filtered sound and smell through the tall plane trees below the windows. In the eighteenth-century kitchen, well modernized (there was a brace of electric iceboxes on the hearth of the huge chimney), two little pullets turned almost silently on an electric spit under an infrared grill, but my hostess still came every ten minutes, as she would have done several hundred years before, to pat them with hot butter and their own juices. They were roasted in the classical manner, which is still the best and which is almost never tasted in its full fine simplicity. Sometimes in delicatessens and supermarkets one sees chickens sizzling and revolving slowly, and even sending forth fairly good smells, but they turn out to be coated with patented mixtures of chili powder and faked smoke flavor, to imitate barbecuing as it is commonly thought of in America. It is strange that people continue to ignore, or forget, the simplest method of grilling or roasting, on spit or in oven. There is good advice on all sides: Escoffier, Child, Rombauer. Heed it, lovers of plain ways and uncomplicated living! Unite, slaves of the steam kettle and the shakers of meat tenderizer and MSG! Read, and be rewarded! Eat two bites of a properly roasted chicken, and L*A*F*F* (at all the rest)!

The rest can be very good indeed. Its variations are limitless. Fortunately, so seem to be the recipes for them. I think a chicken hash, for example, is one of life's minor blessings, when made with intelligence and good material. I do not care much for the overbattered "Southern fried" chicken which should rightly be one of our national prides, but Arkansas Addie knew how to do it consummately, and for my father's seventy-fifth birthday she fried seventy-five drumsticks, because he had sometimes remarked mildly after carving at table that his favorite morsel

was the leg but that it never came to him, thanks to his courteous custom of asking each of us which part we would most like, before he served himself. Father was amused in a remote way by the imposing pyramid of crisp golden legs, which a mixed group of his admirers pounced on and gnawed more or less delicately from their fingers, but by that time in his life people interested him more than food, and although the number of perfectly fried drumsticks went down in our history as a minor culinary triumph, it was the cold dry champagne that flowed more easily through his probable ennui.

We ate little game at home, mostly because my father Rex would not shoot things. Once in about 1913 he went with Charlie Fay, a dashing friend, to hunt in Antelope Valley, now almost a Los Angeles suburb, but he returned sickened by the dreadful experience of seeing other hunters club down the trusting dainty beasts with their gun butts, and even with bottles and stones. He often carried a rifle when we drove through Laguna Canyon to the beach at night, because of the large cats, perhaps pumas or little mountain lions, we would see. But I never heard him fire it. He raised pigeons for several years at the ranch. He felt that they had a deep sense of parenthood as well as marital fidelity, as in his own case, and he deliberately spaced the nestings so that rarely would there be more than two edible squabs at a time, which would then be meticulously plucked and given to ailing friends, undoubtedly so that he would not have to watch us devouring his other fledglings.

Rex seemed to feel less identification with rabbits, and we ate a lot of his barnyard products. I always liked to, and I still do. Once he played a little joke on an aunt, who was believed by my mother to be somewhat flighty and who said firmly at the table that rabbit was disgusting and in fact unfit for self-respecting Christians and/or nice people. While she

stayed with us one spring, it was served many times, usually fried as knowingly as Addie ever fried chicken, and when Aunt Bess said that never had
she tasted more delicious drumsticks, nobody smiled as Father served her
with another and another. "Any idiot could see that the front leg of a rabbit has a definite bend in it," my mother scoffed later, for she did not love
Aunt Bess for marrying her favorite brother. "She plays a good game of
poker now and then," was my father's answer, and whenever we had fried
rabbit, usually on a Sunday, he was especially careful to save at least three
drumsticks for our anatomically ignorant but *gourmande* visitor, and we
never even tittered.

Once I went against all classical and even logical rules in cooking
game, which had been sent to me in California by our huntin'-shootin'-
and-fishin' cousins in South Dakota. The birds arrived frozen, and I
could not distinguish pheasants from ducks, much less a female from a
male and an adolescent from an oldster. I laid them all out in a big pan
to thaw, higgledy-piggledy, side by side and tail to top. I thought I left
the oven door open to make a mild draft, and set it at low-low, and I
went away for several hours. Some Helping Hand apparently passed and
closed the door and turned the heat up to a cautious 325°, and by the
time I got home the house was wafty with a fine perfume, and the game,
whatever it may once have been, was the most delicious amalgam of
perhaps pheasant and possibly duck that could be eaten by mortal man.
There had been no seasoning on the stone-hard little shriveled carcasses.
They had never been basted or turned. But they grew crisp, plump, and
succulent. They seemed to be reborn for a time, waiting with a quiet
sizzle for us to be amazed. (A friend once had this happen to her with a
fine leg of lamb . . .)

The innate horror of cannibalism is one I have never pondered seri-

ously, for my own application at least. This is probably because I would rather not eat meat than eat it for itself, even if it meant a slow and perhaps not too painful death to abstain. Two of my close acquaintances have died of starvation lately, diagnosed as deliberate malnourishment in one case, and they were far from miserable in their last sieges with life. Once I read, in an article about the Mbuti pygmies, that if they are indeed cannibals, which they deny, it would be an in-group matter. The writer added, "As an outsider, I wouldn't be worth eating." I feel the same way. There are cultural as well as gastronomical limits to one's innate and nonconditioned appetites.

In my files and in my thoughts, there are too many recipes about cooking our ever-present staple to stand review and selection. It is a fine thing that, for those who have read this far in my noncookbook, there are further fields . . . and let the devil take his hindmost ally, for neglecting what God may have sent to eat!

Having Fallen into Place

IF THERE IS SOMETHING THAT PLEASES and satisfies, it will fall into place in any welcoming life. A person lives in a room or sometimes a house, almost always with a cookstove and objects of respect and enjoyment, to make real an otherwise empty meaningless subsistence and give warmth. Often a dulled thick water tumbler will make anything in it taste better. That is because its shape and heft are right, whether it came from Ireland in a great-grandmother's trunk or from a shoddy rummage shop last week. This truism holds for everything we need to exist with. For me, vegetables are one of the pleasing allies in my personal war with survival. I like them. They please and satisfy me, and that is perhaps more than my just due: they have fallen into place for me.

A SURPRISING NUMBER OF YEARS AGO, or so it now seems to me, I wrote about a "vegetable love." I was quoting from some of W. S. Gilbert's lyrics in *Patience*, and he in turn was probably referring to someone more or less like Oscar Wilde, whose influence upon scattered young Englishmen in the 1880s had caused them to gaze soulfully into the eyes of "a bashful young potato, or a not too French French bean," instead of a two-legged maiden's. I was young and brash enough to dismiss this not uncommon phenomenon by a naïve and perhaps slightly libidinous hint that if one could *eat*, with proper pleasure, potatoes and beans and their like, there would be little danger of one's more carnal passions turning vegetable. By now I can only shudder with embarrassed regret at such a proposition, the while I have leaned more and more on my own well-being's dependence upon things that grow from the soil. I look better, at least in my own eyes, and I feel and think better, if I eat a lot of them.

This is of course not true of everyone. Perhaps it is a question of metabolism. One good friend of mine, a forest ranger who is also a fine kitchen gardener for his family, says firmly that he will never set teeth into anything that grows on tree, bush, vine, or root. He can and does live healthily on meat, eggs, and starches and an occasional enormous salad of tender leaves . . . and plenty of Scotch whiskey when he is not on duty. And there are many other people, apparently able to function as productive citizens, who survive on diets which seem to be right for their own needs. (I knew one woman who lived excitingly for about twenty years on strong tea and hard-boiled eggs. *Then* she died.) I doubt that I myself would feel well for long, without vegetables and fruits. I tried it once, for about eight months, and the lurking results were expensive.

To anyone of my pronounced leanings, vegetables are a physical pleasure to buy and clean and prepare, and then cook and serve forth. I love their colors, and odors, and the feel of them. Undoubtedly this is part of my enjoyment of them as my main nourishment when I am alone, and when I can cook for friends. I also like the people who grow and sell vegetables. Gardeners and greengrocers seem a little *fresher* than plain shopkeepers with their shelves of cans and cornflakes, and basically more attractive than either butchers or druggists.

I feel that I am fairly deft about using a pressure cooker, one kitchen tool which needs as much concentration as wielding a cleaver or boning a duck, except that perhaps it is even more dangerous. It involves live steam and should never be used by a person taking tranquilizers or alcohol for his own reasons, or one with a fever or the deep blues. When such a weapon is handled carefully, it can do many useful tricks, and depending upon the quality of its contents will turn out exactly what I am using it for, such as a good lusty broth or delicate zucchini to chop gently with plenty of butter. In other words, I like it for fast cooking of a few things staple in our family diet, and leave to the brides the Porcupine Meatballs Deluxe and the Instant Brown Betty the free recipe booklet always details. Once I tried stewing "a hen of doubtful age" according to directions, and it made one of the best broths I ever ate, and the meat too was good in a vaguely entitled hash, but in general I stay with vegetables in all their forms, and use the potent invention only when I too am at my best.

I think it is plain by now that I like lightly cooked foods and ones unmasked by lazy or sly cooks. Sometimes they are best raw: plain salads, mushrooms, celery, green peppers, even baby artichokes. Sometimes, blanched in plenty of boiling water and then chilled, they are delectable, and often the quickly cooked fresh things are delicious tossed over heat and served at once in any manner the cook has decided. Occasionally vegetables should be cooked fast in almost no water, and a classic example of this is *petits pois à la française*, with a basic formula of peas and lettuce and green onions and butter but also as many versions as there are good cooks. (I have made them with frozen peas and Los Angeles lettuce! Eminently edible, if a candid substitute for better days and better weathers!)

I think one reason vegetables are held in such disrepute by perhaps 70 percent of Americans is the Victorian influence upon our grandmothers, who in the prairie days and in Massachusetts and Oregon clung almost frantically to occasional directives from Mrs. Beeton in London, and even the Queen herself, to protect their families from the outlandish influences of Indians, Spaniards, Russians, and possibly Eski-

mos who might intrude upon their Anglo-Saxon prerogatives as invaders. In my copy of Marion Harland's *Common Sense in the Household*, which I use as a kind of arbiter of its times because it shaped my grandmother's culinary directives, the overcooking of fresh vegetables was daringly deplored, but the writer still recommended a concoction of cold chopped cabbage boiled at least forty-five minutes, mixed with butter, seasoning, and cream, and fried in a cake with a couple of beaten eggs until ready to turn out. "This is a breakfast-dish," she said. And Miss Parloa's *New Cook Book* from Boston stated firmly that while shelled green peas might need only forty minutes at a hard boil, spinach, cabbage, and carrots would require from one to two hours, and corn an hour (fresh from the garden and on the cob!).

In Mrs. Beeton's *Household Management*, which was originally published in 1861, honest-to-God vegetables seemed to figure most importantly in soups, although directions for the picking and cleaning of them by gardeners and scullery maids were ample. She liked to concoct "nourishing broths" from them, for less well-fed people than her readers, and very sustaining they were, in the main! She knew what she was talking about: the water in which clean fresh vegetables have been cooked, no matter how lightly, has strengthened and refreshed many a sick body, in her day as now.

The higher the kitchen in society, the higher the cost, of course, and while Mrs. Beeton wrote for housewives coping with an industrial revolution in which more and more land was being covered by urban sprawl, and more and more farmers and their daughters were forsaking the fields and kitchens for the factories, Queen Victoria and her court lived in an outrageously bilious atmosphere of long slow simmerings and waste. Juices and infusions and scraps that Mrs. Beeton and Mrs. Harland and even I would have saved were tossed out, and the emasculated remains were served to Her Majesty's courtiers so completely coated by rich disguises that one could never know whether he had eaten a turnip or a truffle. Here, to be specific for a bit of fun, is one recipe from a book called *The Modern Cook*, written by the Queen's "Chief Cook and Maître d'Hôtel," Charles Elmé Francatelli, in 1846 (which gave it exactly the right time to awe and influence people like my grandmother as she headed across the Mississippi some twenty years later):

ENDIVE, WITH CREAM

Pick off all the outer leaves, leaving only the white; trim the roots, and wash the endive in several waters, carefully removing any insects that may be concealed in the inner folds of the leaves. Put large stewpan half filled with water on a brisk fire, and when it boils, throw in the endives, with a handful of salt, and allow them to continue boiling fast until they become quite tender; drain them in a collander, immerse them in plenty of cold water, then squeeze all the moisture from them, and place them on a sieve. Next take each head of endive separately, cut off the root, and again look over the leaves, spreading them on the table with the point of a knife; when this is completed, chop them very fine, and pass them through a coarse wire sieve. Then place them in a stewpan with a quarter of a pound of fresh butter, a little grated nutmeg, and salt; stir this over the fire for ten minutes, add half a pint of double cream, a gravy-spoonful of pounded sugar; keep the endives boiling on a stove-fire until sufficiently reduced so as to be able to pile them on a dish when sending to table; garnish round with *croutons* or *fleurons*, and serve.

Croutons were "sippets of bread of various shapes and sizes, fried in clarified butter," and although Francatelli does not list fleurons under

either that word or "Garnishes," as far as I can tell, *Larousse Gastronomique* confirms my almost atavistic impression that they are "small flaky pastry motifs," even today. As for the dish itself, it is perhaps best left upon the ghostly table or sideboard where the Queen's maître d'hôtel dutifully watched over it. (Once in my childhood we had a cook who made fleurons, dainty little crescents and stars of the finest pastry, to transform a plain old beef hash into faëry. I think her name was Ora, and she was the maddest of all our crew, and on one Sunday-off she cut her mother and then herself into neat ribbons with her treasured "French" knife. Before that, though, she gave us perhaps our most elegant taste of haute cuisine, and one night I was sent from the table for letting out a loud unseemly moan of delight when she brought in something especially beautiful, perhaps plain old beef hash with fleurons . . .)

It is impossible for me to give a *quick* look at Francatelli's menus, because I zigzag and snoop and cheat the clock, but a fairly ruthless rundown of his "Entremets" fails to turn up creamed endives, in one year of listings. Perhaps the dish was served with an entrée, although "dressed vegetables," which this almost certainly must have been called, usually came at the end of the second and last course of a meal at court, with the sweets. In January, for instance, for sixteen people, the first course would be made up of two soups, two fishes, two removes (capon *à la Toulouse* and rump of beef *à la jardinière*), and six entrées. The second and lighter course would start with two roasts, of pheasants and snipes. Next would come two removes: an apricot soufflé and cheese fritters. Then would be served eight entremets: lobster salad, mushrooms *au gratin*, kirschenwasser jelly, chocolate cream, pears *à la Condé*, little molded cakes filled with a vanilla cream, and potatoes *à la maître d'hôtel*, and Brussels sprouts sauté with butter. Surprisingly often, Victoria's chief cook placed sea kale among his entremets, all through the year. It is a leafy vegetable of the mustard family, prized for its stalks, and the Queen (or he) must have liked it. Whether or not, she got it often, along with the omnipresent Brussels sprouts and salsifies of a cuisine which Francatelli tried hard to keep both classically French and royally British.

An Englishman only slightly less encumbered with titles than Victoria, but apparently more critical gastronomically, was Sir A. Daniel Hall, K.C.B., LL.D., D.Sc., V.M.H. He may yet be living, and if so, I admiringly pray that his digestion still be good, and his opinion as firm as when he wrote, in 1941, "Many unjustified reproaches are made against English food and cookery, but they are unhappily true when addressed to our treatment of vegetables." This candid statement was printed at the head of his foreword to André Simon's *Concise Encyclopedia*, Section III, and he managed in an admirably short essay, which because of his good manners stayed just short of a diatribe, to laugh at private gardeners in love with the prizewinning gigantism of their broad beans and peas and marrows, to sound a warning to the market gardeners striving for weight and size per acre (". . . in war-time doubtless it is necessary to obtain a maximum of fodder . . ."), and to scold lazy and careless housewives for their wasteful ignorance in preparing and cooking "fashionless, unattractive fare" (such as the Queen once ate, in spite of the fleurons round about).

I like this man. "For years," he wrote, "the diet of all classes has been shifting toward more vegetables and less meat; medical science has caught up and justified the wisdom of this popular instinct." Yes, *sir*, Sir A. Daniel Hall, sir! I have never been sure of what class I belong to, although I know several I do not, but I am aware from everything I see

and read that more people eat more fodder all the time . . . and that
willy-nilly we seem to be growing taller, with better teeth and eyes if no
noticeable increase of the brain cells.

When I was very young, living in the Western wilds of a little town
which barely qualified as such in the census, all of us émigrés brought
our own gastric patterns with us: the Mexicans ate strange pancakes
made by patting corn dough thin, but we did not; the handful of Jews
in Whittier did not eat ham, but now and then we did; the barely larger
handful of Catholics, and we the tight little band of Episcopalians, did
not eat meat on Fridays, but it was said that the Quakers did. And people who had come from the Midwest stuck to their habit of eating root
vegetables during the winter, even though the new climate begged them
to plant good fresh things the year around. We ate turnips and potatoes a
lot, since Grandmother had lived in Iowa a long time. We seldom ate
cabbage: it did not agree with her Nervous Stomach, and small wonder,
since it was always cooked according to her mid-Victorian receipts and
would have made an elephant heave and hiccup. We ate carrots, always
in a "white sauce" in little dishes by our plates, and as soon as my grandmother died I headed for the raw ones and chewed at them after school
and even in the dark of night while I was growing, with what my English friend would call the wisdom of popular instinct.

I do not remember much about other vegetables until I went away to a
school which believed in ample fresh food for its potential childbearing
wives of brokers, presidents, and especially bishops. We drank floods of
good milk from the school's four-legged cows and ate hundreds of tons of
crisp well-cooked fodder each year, as we were prepared for our destinies.
The kitchen crew, bossed by Japanese but with Filipino waiters, seemed to
dote on tempting us, at frequent festivals called by the names of saints,

with carved radishes and olives, celery twisted into beautiful swirling orna-
ments, soufflés of spinach (how can even an Oriental cook make soufflés
to be served simultaneously to ten tables of ravenous virgins?), enormous
grilled mushrooms with curls of bacon in their sizzling middles (how can
a cook . . . ?).

Of course we ate other things, such as soup every night, and good fish
and meat, and amusing delicious desserts, especially on Sundays to bol-
ster our morale for several extra hours spent on our knees, but it is the
milk and the vegetables that I most remember. (There were floods of milk
at home too, but Grandmother still haunted the vegetable bin . . .) Now
and then a waiter would get into discreet trouble with one of the more
overt students and disappear, and in my junior year Harry, the butler for
countless decades, killed two assistants and committed hara-kiri, but in
general the little dark men flew about the dining room like calm doves,
with their eyes looking far away as they carried in hundreds of full platters
and bowls and carried out thousands of emptied plates.

Not long ago I read about the first voyage Sarah Bernhardt made to
the United States, on the S.S. *America* in 1880. On her birthday there
were many presents of course, for she was forever a bright star, and "then
came a delegation from the crew with a gigantic bouquet of what looked
to be genuine flowers but proved to be raw vegetables some genius of the
kitchen had carved. . . ." And later there was music from the orchestra.

I thought with a twist of the heart of another birthday at sea, when
once my small girls and I got on the wrong ship. It was the one we had
booked passage on, all right, leaving from Genoa to go through the Pan-
ama Canal and drop us in San Francisco in about thirty-two days, but it
was still wrong, from the delayed start. It was held up for almost two
weeks in Trieste before it returned to Genoa, because some dictator had

made some new pact or broken some old treaty with France or perhaps Italy, so that by the time it sneaked into our port we had spent almost every cent we had to get home on, for meals, hotels, treats, books, museums, cemeteries, sherbets, galleries, horse-drawn rides, teas, excursions, and various other means of sustaining without danger of suicidal boredom (nobody wanted to go home *anyway!*) a large pack of restless worried permanently hungry people: my sister Norah and her two little sons, Monique, the adolescent daughter of a trusting French friend, the three of us.

We finally went aboard, and before a night had passed, Norah and I knew that we were on a new version of Traven's "death ship," a creaking filthy rejected Liberty bought for scrap by Italy after the war, to transport mysterious goods from port to port . . . sometimes fighting cocks for Cuba, sometimes stolen horses for Cádiz. This time we carried drums and huge bottles of acids somewhat casually piled on the forward deck, and fake-marble images of the Virgin Mary and Joseph to be unloaded in Central American ports. We made plans to skip ship in Barcelona, go at once to our consul and wire for money, and try again on another freighter, a disastrously expensive move but obviously essential to our children's well-being. It was then we discovered that our passports were locked in the captain's safe and would not be relinquished to us until we got to California, and that we would never be allowed ashore except on Sundays, when consulates were closed. Our dogged adaptations to this edict were interesting, a kind of Prairie Mother syndrome which seemed only to grow more powerful as we found, after we had cleared the last Spanish port, that below our decks were a frightening number of Yugoslav refugees who began to creep out, thin and foully dirty, to lie in the increasingly dead sunlight of our slow crossing. (They slipped overboard in the nights as we lay at anchor for almost a week, for unexplained reasons, in La Guayra under Caracas: people without passports, half-starved or sick, swimming toward a dubious freedom.) The captain told us not to go down to that deck, but gradually our children infiltrated, and secret waves and smiles came up to Norah and me as we looked with Anglo-Saxon impassivity and cracking hearts at the mute teeming people, so dignified in the terrible heat. One old woman managed to make from her handkerchief a little cross-stitched doll dress for my younger girl, who did not own or want a doll.

The crew of this strange lost vessel, we gradually learned, was made up of legally condemned Italians who had been given their choice of forced labor on land or a lesser number of years at sea, on such vessels as ours. They were of all ages under sixty, and of every criminal bent, from murder and sodomy to stealing a loaf of bread. We lived almost intimately with them, and in the main they were decent and kind to us as they served us in the tiny sweltering messroom and swabbed out our cabins. (Mine, shared with Monique and my daughters, was still labeled SIX GUNNERS above its louvered door, and the shower used by the twelve so-called passengers, as apart from the hundred or so human beings packed belowdecks, was marked OFFICERS.) The men who served us had very strong smells, of course, and occasionally they looked quite wild in a carefully contained way. The cabins stayed fairly tidy, if not clean, and the food stayed almost edible, but everything, and all of us too, became stale and rotten as the sun beat down and we crept from one tiny port to another in the Caribbean and up the Pacific coast, docking late at night and often sailing before dawn, if it was not a week later. We became apathetic about leaving the ship, since nothing would be open but the church on a Sunday, and we had no passports, and the crew *never* left, as far as we

could see. In La Union the whores pressed against the high barricade at the end of the little dock, and pushed their arms through it toward the men who leaned from the portholes of our ship, and the men pushed their arms out into the thick air toward the girls, and they called and wept together.

There is too much more to say here, but it will suffice that the food became very bad and limited, because the voyage lasted almost seventy days instead of a month, and we never took on any stores because of some law left over from Mussolini, and what was on board had been old by the time the poor old tub picked up her human cargo in Trieste and headed back for Genoa. We ate frozen pork chops and fairly good pasta: for the noon meal and the smaller evening meal that is what we ate or what was served, in rough seas and slick, in fog off the Canaries and heavy heat the rest of the days. So we actually ate pasta. There were two wines on board, a red and a white which changed noticeably as we got to the bottoms of the kegs, but which I made sure we all drank, watered or not. The water itself became turgid and of a menacing yellow, but Norah and I lined up our children every morning and had them down one small glass of it, each with a good tot of the brandy which was highly dosed with quinine and purgatives in case the crew got hold of it in a mutinous mood: more than one good straight swig would send them retching to the rails. I think this therapy was what kept all of us from succumbing to complaining innards, and if any of the five young people should become an alcoholic because of it, I might possibly sue the foreign power?

And from this floating dunghill of lassitude, corruption, dirt, and whatever evil I have ever recognized as such, came a little miracle, the day my older girl, Anne, was twelve.

I have a picture of it, a snapshot I took through a porthole. It is shocking, but also beautiful. I know now, looking at it, that the four children were happy people, there with the desperate crew and the affrayed sick refugees, on the wretched overloaded little ship. Their faces shine. They are thin, with circles under their excited laughing eyes, and their hair is lank. Watching them, my sister and I knew that her boys and my girls, and Monique too, were underfed and grayish of skin, with strange eruptions in odd places on their sweating little bodies. But that day was a festival! It was meant for people exactly twelve and under, and a little table had been pulled out on the upper deck, with four chairs, by a hand who had never smiled before then. Monique, not yet sixteen, was classed as an adult female with Norah and me, and the three of us peeked through portholes as the slouching stinking men who cleaned our cabins and waited on table carried out a most astonishing birthday cake and placed it before Anne, who was shuddering with suspense and elation and God knows what other emotions within her pallid dirty skin.

The cake was not made of dough and sweet icing, as the children sensed at once with great understanding, but was a kind of circular monument about eight inches tall, braced around a pan of some sort, of sliced and peeled vegetables: carrots, beets, radishes, a few limp stalks of chicory and endive. Everything was faded and basically repulsive, not crisp and "carved by some genius of the kitchen," so that there seemed no wish to eat it, even if one had been starved or cruel enough to destroy its pattern. The children were as if struck dumb at first, and then they became quite emotional with thanks, and several crewmen came up to look at the cake and shake hands and laugh a little, and go below again. (There was no music from the ship's orchestra.)

It was a most astonishing thing to happen in any life, no matter how short or long. Where had those few tired vegetables been kept hidden?

How had they stayed out of the soup pot for the refugees? Why had they not been stolen or devoured? There they were, as the death ship slid over the oily seas off Costa Rica, and some of the men could smile and the four children could accept a beautiful gesture . . . vegetable love, perhaps.

WISHFUL THINKING MAKES ME FEEL almost broody about the way I like to treat the things that grow on vine and bush and under the sod, so despised by my friend the forest ranger and perhaps many otherwise balanced people whom I have not yet met. How can I let this chance escape me, to tell the way Mr. Kan taught me to cook asparagus, three times three? Why should I not risk a publisher's ennui by taking a quick skip through the alphabet, surely an innocent trick, and giving a hint, a sketch, a mere suggestion of an ABC of vegetables? P stands for potatoes and for peas, and one more word about their charms and virtues cannot be amiss? A writing cook and a cooking writer must be bold, at the desk as well as the stove . . .

It will be obvious that my vegetable love has something casual about it, the occasionally dangerous result of any such intimacy. Many people take all kitchen work very seriously, especially if they do not like it or have an aversion to one of its aspects or demands, and vegetables are often first on such subconscious lists. Great pains are taken to prepare and then serve them so that they can be choked down as healthful, or nibbled as garnishes, and I simply do not have enough time in my life to spend any of it on some of the finicky methods I read about with clinical amazement. In one good guide, for instance, the directive for preparing a globe artichoke is something like this: break off the stem, trim the base, and take off the small leaves. Slice off one inch of the top with a knife, and then trim all the leaves with scissors to make a hivelike shape. Wash. Tie a thick slice of fresh lemon on the bottom. Boil in a large kettle, which must not be either aluminum or iron, filled with salted water. Cover the artichokes with a double layer of cheesecloth. And so forth. *Mercy!* The method is of course correct, and I have eaten the results and they are commendable, but I like runty artichokes, the kind most greengrocers do not sell, and I have used a large aluminum soup kettle for some thirty years to cook them in, and I would feel silly tying bandages of lemon onto them. Now and then I put a cut lemon into the water, or a douse of olive oil, or perhaps a couple of cut cloves of garlic . . . it seems to depend on the weather.

And I almost never peel asparagus, because if it is large enough to make that seem advisable I don't buy it anyway. (I would in France, where it can be more than an inch thick and still good, but the kind I get in California for a few spring weeks is too delicious and thin to tamper with.) And I never skin peppers, because the dishes I make with them are crude to begin with. I have a friend who always roasts and peels them, especially for a fine hors d'oeuvre, and I admire her for it and admit that I am a slob in comparison. As for tomatoes, I prefer to leave them in their skins, except for a sauce or soup or stew in which the pieces of surprisingly tough peel will roll into mean little sticks, not pretty or good. Otherwise I think tomato skins are part of the whole somewhat brutal smell and texture of most dishes I use them in, much as the papery pink or yellow skin of little new potatoes can add a special quality to eating them whole. They crackle, almost as if one could and would bite through an amazing new kind of egg in its shell.

ARTICHOKES, then: best when small, cut from the beautiful fernlike

bushes as soon as possible before cooking in rapidly boiling water. Hot, and always well drained, of course, they are good with melted sweet butter and lemon juice. Cold, a vinaigrette is more pleasing than a mayonnaise, to me at least. If they are little enough, there is no fretting with the pesky "choke," and one can forgo pulling off all the leaves and simply take a good bite or two of the heart end. This is perhaps overly informal, but delicious when possible. As for the giants usually sold in American markets, they are comparatively tough and boring after experience with the small ones of different shapes and colors to be bought around the Mediterranean, and along the California coast where there are Italian gardeners who save them for special people (and themselves) and ship the overblown ones to the wholesalers. Here is a good trick for the big ones, fine among *friends*, because somewhat messy to eat: Blanch them and remove the outer leaves and chokes. Set in a shallow pan, spreading the outer leaves enough to pack their bases and the hearts with a highly flavored forcemeat. (Here some people tie each vegetable together, but I just push them firmly side by side . . .) Douse generously with olive oil, and bake in a slow oven for four or five hours. This is best cold, I think, with a coarse red wine and plenty of French or sourdough bread for general mopping of plates and fingers. Depending upon the herbs one uses, the dish can taste "Greek" or "Italian" or "Provençal" or simply *good*, and it is a firm refutation of the otherwise correct assumption that wine is killed by the highly metallic vegetable.

ASPARAGUS: the thin green stalks of springtime are the best. And they are best cooked as Johnny Kan does them for a few days each year, in his restaurant on Grant Avenue in Chinatown. Once prepared, they can be served in many ways, and one of the best is with walnut meats and soy

sauce. They are fine chilled, in a vinaigrette. At home I like to season
them as soon as they are drained for the last time, drown them in hot buttery cream, and pour them over good toast,
the way we sometimes ate them when I was
a child.

BEANS: to please me they should be fresh
and young, almost newborn. In this fragile
and fleeting condition they still need to be
blanched for perfection, even if for two minutes, and then chilled in ice water. Then
they are ready for a thousand enjoyable
ends. (I can make commendable dishes
from canned or frozen beans, however, as
long as they are not suffering from some
form of acromegalia which demands too
much precooking and then too many disguises.) When I see good fresh ones in the
markets, I buy many pounds of them,

❧ Three Times Three Asparagus

*Break off tips of thin fresh green stalks, and
cut them diagonally about ¾ inches long
or snap them, as far as they will snap.
Discard the ends. Have plenty of boiling
water ready in a teakettle. Put the
asparagus into a pot, cover with some of the
water, and when it has reached a new boil,
keep it there for exactly 3 minutes. Drain
well, cover again with the boiling water,
and repeat the same maneuver. Do it once
more. This takes attention and a good clock
or timer. At the end of the third boiling the
vegetable should still be slightly crisp, fully
flavored, and very digestible.*

blanch them, and pack them vertically for the freezer. And now, even in
St. Helena, delicious youngsters are sneaking into the stores in the dead
of winter, when no local bean would grow. They are from below or over
or across some border. Happy us!

It is all right now and then, I agree, to toss them with almonds or otherwise to prettify them, but like asparagus they seem best left to a little butter
when hot, and in a vinaigrette when cold. It is like drinking a champagne
cocktail when one could as well, if the barman be honest, ask for a glass of
the good sparkly stuff unadorned by bitters, sugar, cherry, whatever . . .

THERE IS ANOTHER kind of bean which most surely does not come into this select alphabet of fresh vegetables, but it is a legume and I think I have a wonderful recipe for it, and I know that I can fake it occasionally from cans (*Mea culpa!*) with a trick I learned in a he-man magazine called *Stud* or *Him* or perhaps *Rod and Reel*: hot bacon drippings poured very discreetly and slowly over the top of the Boston-style beans in their pot, when they are brown and ready for the last half hour of baking. That is all. The anonymous writer added a homey touch by crediting his dear old mother with this treasure, and of course he detailed a twenty-four-hour process of soaking, baking in a slow oven, and so on, with which I agree fully when one starts correctly with the dried beans. Even with canned ones, always of the best procurable quality, a good hour must be allowed to let them marry with some chopped onion, mustard, and molasses one adds after a clinical taste or two before they go into the stove. And then that last magic touch of the hot bacon fat! Crisp. Delicious. Any good cookbook will tell a proper way to get that far, but never elsewhere have I heard of the *coup de graisse*.

BRUSSELS SPROUTS: I am not sure that it is legally possible to malign a person or thing by telling the truth, and everything I have heard against a Brussels sprout is usually true, too true. I still think the unfortunate little vegetable suffers from a malignant fate. It lives under a smelly cloud of its own making. I myself would prefer never to eat or even look at one, cooked as it is *common* to, with limp discolored pygmy cabbage as the result.

My first taste of Brussels sprouts was a gloomy one, which may be why I feel protective about them now. We had not been long in Whittier, and my father's new partner and his wife were coming to dinner, and I was to

eat with the grown-ups and then be excused. (Later my little sister and I
crept halfway down the stairs to take a look at the people in front of the
fire, and we were bewitched by the fact that the new man was tiny, with
dainty feet in black shiny pumps with bows, the kind we thought only
girls wore. And his. wife called him Harry as if it were spelled Hairy, al-
though he was bald.) Mother, in a subconscious bumble as always about
people who were going to stay for less than a month, did her best to make
the dinner interesting, and in an extravagant or desperate mood telephoned long distance to Jevne's, in Los Angeles, to have Brussels sprouts
sent out to Whittier on the noon "electric." Jevne's was according to some
people the most stylish grocery store west of Chicago, or at least Salt Lake
City, and it specialized in such exotics as imported barley sugar and
grenadine syrup and otherwise unavailable vegetables like Brussels
sprouts. Father brought the fastuous package home in midafternoon,
when the evening *News* was safely tucked into bed, and handed it to the
cook-of-the-moment, to boil the strange little cabbages until tender. She
did just that, baffled by their unfamiliarity, and when he took the lid off
the vegetable dish at dinner they were completely speckled with hundreds and probably thousands of tiny cooked bugs, too large and too plentiful to be called black pepper and too small to be actively revolting. He
put the lid back on, I suppose, and Mother carried the situation off in
some typically bland way, but the next day she bit her lip and almost cried
about it, and we did not eat Brussels sprouts again for many years, partly
because they were still not being grown in Southern California and partly
because of what was in a small way a traumatic family mishap. (Father's
partner turned out to be something of a disaster, too.)

It is probable that the next time I ate Brussels sprouts was in France, a
fat decade later, which is fortunate because they were cooked knowingly.

I was wildly hungry and happy in those days, and could and did eat not one horse but several, I am sure, along with everything else procurable at my landlady's, the student restaurants, the neighborhood foodshops, and for an occasional binge the three-starred Three Pheasants, where for exactly twenty-five francs or one whole dollar (there were also menus at eighteen and twenty-two francs) one could order the de luxe meal of something like eight courses, each one of which I devoured. I do not remember eating Brussels sprouts there, but if I did, they were well and cleverly masked, I would bet at least twenty-five old francs. They would be called *à la milanaise* or *à la polonaise*, or otherwise hidden in the rich flavors of veal stock, cream, brown butter, cheese, herbs . . .

Perhaps it is this continued effort to make something what it is not, in France, that can be almost as lamentable in bad hands as the predominantly Anglo-Saxon approach: boil hell out of a vegetable and then serve it only summarily drained and seasoned. Madame Bonamour, my landlady and unwitting mentor, made a good compromise, I would say: she cooked sprouts until barely tender and then drained and simmered them slowly in plenty of butter. Her main concession to their potential unpopularity was to boil two or three cloves of garlic in the water with them, in what I still feel was a futile effort to kill their smell. Old-fashioned manuals called things like *Helpful Household Hints* will back her up, and for cabbage and cauliflower too, but I do not.

My own approach to the problem of making Brussels sprouts gastronomically desirable is not as blindly dogged as it may sound, but it takes a little time to bring off. It results in a dish I seldom waste on casual diners, and perhaps it is best eaten as a full but simple supper, with plenty of hot toast and cold milk. I use only small firm buds. Each one must be rid of its outer curling leaves, and the stalk removed and the bottom gashed deftly in a shallow cross. The sprouts are then put into rapidly boiling water, with or without a clove of garlic (!), cooked in the uncovered kettle until barely tender, and then well drained. I spread them loosely on a cookie pan with plenty of butter, season them lightly, and in a mild oven (325°) bake them until they begin to turn brown, with a good shake now and then to swivel them in the butter. The process is tedious but pleasant. They become glistening like little nuts, with delicate soft centers. They might not be as good warmed over, although I have never had any left to experiment with when I have found the small hard ones in a local market. (I have tried my method with the frozen kind, with only fair success.)

Have I done anything here, I must ask myself, to protest that this vegetable need not be damned as a stinking soggy dwarf? I hope so, and meanwhile good kitchen guides continue to cope halfheartedly with all its possible and impossible disguises.

CABBAGE: needs to be treated with more respect than it usually gets, and then it can be delicate, digestible, and refreshing. The same is true of cauliflower and all the kissin' cousins of that family: a short stay in plenty of boiling water and a shorter drying off, and then into whatever dish awaits. There are exceptions. Just as a good churchgoing household can produce a dedicated gambler, so can sauerkraut evolve from a firm crisp head of innocent leaves . . . and if it is well made it need be no more a gastric menace than the freshly cooked vegetable. I would gladly eat a good *choucroute garnie*, anywhere but preferably in the back room at Lipp's, in Paris, since there it would be better than any I ever met in its homeland of Alsace. One must trust the local cook, however, with freshly prepared cabbage, and I do, since nobody has ever served it to me except myself, I do prepare it very well, and I am the local cook.

CARROTS: my preadolescent hunger for them has faded, and there is nothing I can say that has not been said better elsewhere about their usefulness in *mirepoix*, stocks, garnishes, and so on. I think they are shockingly horrid disguised as puddings, or shredded with raisins and crushed pineapple on lettuce leaves.

CELERY: essential in my kitchen, as background music in stocks and sauces, and cooked, and raw. It is like water chestnuts, cut fine into an omelet at the last minute, or in a salad of almost anything from chicken with mayonnaise to marinated green beans. It is good after simmering in a strong stock, and then drained and made into any reasonable variation of Celery Solari. It is important in much Oriental cooking, cut into thin diagonal strips and tossed in the wok at the judicious moment, to add texture and flavor. It is good cut the same way and marinated, to be mixed with sliced raw mushrooms and served as a crisp hors d'oeuvre for a summer or winter (or spring or fall) supper. Celery is a fine invention.

Here is one good recipe, basic enough to serve just as well for small parboiled onions or cauliflowerlets (or almost anything solid enough to get that far), which was never made except at Christmas when I was little. Its like is in any good American cookbook. It was always served by my mother at the other end of the long table from Father, the Carver of the Bird. There was a special dish for it, large and round and shallow, with tiny pink flowers in a border which was mercifully masked, and it arrived bubbling and golden and especially tempting because it had a usually forbidden *sauce* on it. &

This is of course a current approximation of what happened in the dim and possibly dank kitchen in Whittier, and then at the Ranch in the brighter one, but it always happened at Christmas, and here in St. Helena it still does. Thus is the sampler stitched, the tapestry woven.

CORN: and this is a delicate subject. I know a woman who is firmly condemned by her less sensuous and perhaps more sensible neighbors because she puts on the stove her biggest kettle of water and then hops into her car to drive several miles for a bushel basket of freshly picked corn and dashes back with it, to be husked at once by everybody within reach. The tender ears, which upon baring have the same indefinable perfume as ivory, are slid into the boiling water. The people prepare sweet butter and, according to their tastes, salt and pepper upon their warmed plates. The minute the water boils again, the ears are ready. The madwoman lifts them out on a long holey spoon as plates are carried past the kettle, and then everyone eats, rolling the corn around in the butter or nicely slicing off the kernels into the rich puddle. It is a fine way . . .

I myself do not bite into corn on the cob, because when I was not quite ten I had a few teeth knocked out by two fat boys sparking downhill on one bicycle, and I soon understood that it would be disastrously expensive for my parents to replace the hopefully permanent replacements. Perhaps in self-defense I have evolved several ways of making

✺ *Christmas Celery*

1 quart ½-inch slices of celery
Butter
2 cups Béchamel sauce (called white sauce in Iowa and Whittier)
1 cup grated mild American cheese (or Gruyère)
Crumbs, if wished

Parboil the celery lightly, preferably in a good stock for future use. Drain. Butter shallow baking dish generously. Mix celery with half of sauce, pour into dish, and sprinkle with half of cheese. Spread rest of sauce evenly over dish, sprinkle with rest of cheese, and with crumbs if wished, and put into a 400° oven until bubbling and lightly browned.

fresh corn a reasonable delight to other people whose chancy dental conditions might seem to preclude it. Gastrically it remains *verboten*, I understand, to people with hypersensitive guts, because of the little envelopes in which each kernel is contained. But I think that if corn is cooked almost in a flash, fresh as it can be, it is eminently digestible for most of us. It can be done as I have described, and then shaved quickly off the cobs and tossed with butter in a hot bowl or upon each addict's plate. It can be shaved from the cob while still milky and raw, and then stirred quickly into very hot butter in a skillet, heated fast, and removed from the stove to make its own creamy omelet. It works as well mixed with eggs beaten into milk and then poured into a buttered dish for a gentle baking. And here is the most delicious and delicate and mostly unattainable way I ever ate it, called Corn Oysters.

There are many recipes named that, but they have *flour* in them! This one comes from a Southern Lady who married one of my father's racier friends. She had put a note, giving her address and asking for a rendezvous or letter from "anyone interested," into an empty candy box on a railroad seat on a day coach between Atlanta and Memphis, and Harrison Turnbridge picked it up by chance and replied, and then for some thirty years they lived in the country near Whittier. She grew mignonette and herbs, and when she felt at her best, which was rarely, she would ask some of us to tea. She was always very tender toward me, but was said to throw things occasionally at the world in general. I fear that I may have been a little smug about my peculiarity, for she disliked my sister, but perhaps I can make up to both of them by recalling her recipe: ❧

I think Mrs. Turnbridge accompanied these subtle morsels with chicken and broiled tomatoes, and perhaps an "ambrosia" of orange slices and grated coconut, according to her girlhood pattern, but the way I best

remember them is on a rare Sunday in Laguna, when the men would go
up the canyon to the "summer stand" for corn and then shuck it, laughing and nipping at good bootleg bourbon,
and then Mrs. Turnbridge and my mother
and some other wives would score and grind
the kernels and put them to wait. Then we
would troop down the cliffs and along the
beautiful desolate beach, knowing that before too long we would be eating one-and-
onlies, too many to count. We would finally
climb back to the house. It took at least two
breeze-filled laughing women to help the
cook lift out the oysters from the sizzling
skillets and serve us, and everyone was
merry and at ease, quite different from in
Whittier, where on rare visits to Mrs. Turn-
bridge's remote ranch she would hand me one sprig of mignonette and
look with latent and hateful misery into my young eyes.

 *The One-and-Only Genuine
Unique Real Corn Oysters*

1 dozen ears corn
1 or 2 eggs
Salt and pepper
Hot fat

*Shuck ears and score each row of kernels. Cut from
cobs and put through fine food grinder, saving all the
milk. Let set for about 3 hours, or until milk is set into
custard. Beat eggs, using 2 if mixture is stiff, and add
with seasonings. Drop from spoon into hot fat, and
turn once when brown. Serve immediately.*

And so it can go, in any ABC: let D drop out (tiny dandelion leaves
make a fine salad . . .), and on to E, and for me, here anyway, E is for:

EGGPLANT: and too much to say about it, because it is a familiar in
my kitchen and in my culinary thinking. It is also very beautiful to look at
and touch. I cannot recall that I have ever eaten it without enjoyment.

Once, after my grandmother died and our cuisine turned heathenish,
we had a cook who fried crisp thick slices of it in crumbs and deep fat,
and the nearest I ever came to that again was in Paris in about 1935, in a
small restaurant with a Sicilian cook. The eggplants were the "long

purples" and were cut, unpeeled, to make a kind of fan from the stem end, and then dipped in a thin batter and deep-fried: a pretty and most delicious dish, one I would have liked to eat from my hand, leaf by leaf, if I had not been even shyer than usual at that stage of the game. Now and then, and here and now, I dip thick slices of what I can buy in the market, the large egg-shaped kind, in ample olive oil and then bake them on a cookie sheet, to serve plain or as a base for lamb or tomato slices. An even simpler version of this is to cut small eggplants in half, lengthwise, oil the cut sides generously, and broil until brown. Then they should bake at about 350° for an hour or so, until tender and shrunken. They are good sprinkled with fresh herbs and a little more oil, and either hot or cold, to be scooped from the shell by each diner.

A favorite food in our house is a kind of *ratatouille*. It smells fine during its long cooking, and it gets better over several days, so that I make it in the biggest casserole (which also serves for our occasional but always monumental *cassoulets*). When I first learned this dish, which of course varies with the supplies on hand, it was not called more than a stew, but by now fashionable restaurants along the Côte d'Azur and even in Paris find it canny to make a few "regional" plates, and myriad versions of it, mostly shabby ones, are called *ratatouilles* on their enormous menu sheets. Perhaps unfortunately, it keeps well!

There are some recipes that defy regimentation, and this for what we call a Minorcan stew is one of them. The best way to follow it is to assemble some fine fresh vegetables on a big table, put a large earthen pot and a cutting board with them, and sit down to contemplate their beautiful colors and sniff their overt summery smells. How big is the pot? It must hold enough layers of vegetables to have to be pushed down now and again, and it must have some kind of lid. What are the ingredients?

Eggplants, peeled or not and depending upon one's tastes, and/or zucchini, of course unpeeled, and onions, garlic, green peppers, red peppers if they are procurable, plenty of ripe peeled tomatoes, and some good olive oil: these are what make a Minorcan stew. Proportions are impossible to fix firmly, since everything changes in size and flavor, but perhaps there should be three parts of eggplant (and/or squash) to two of tomatoes and one each of the peppers and the onions/garlic. I really cannot say.

Everything is sliced, cubed, chopped, minced, and except for the tomatoes is put into the pot . . . thrown in, that is, for the rough treatment pushes down the mass. At the end, when there is less than no room, the tomatoes are cubed or sliced generously across the top, and the lid is pressed down ruthlessly. When it is taken off, a generous amount of olive oil must be trickled over the whole, to seep down. Then the lid is put on again. It may not quite fit, but it will soon drop into place. The whole goes into a mild (300°) oven for about as long as one wishes to leave it there, like five or six hours. It should be stirred up from the bottom with a long spoon every couple of hours. It will be very soupy for a time, and then is when it makes a delicious nourishing meal served generously over slices of toasted French bread, with plenty of grated dry cheese. Gradually it becomes more solid, as the air fills with rich waftings which make neighbors sniff and smile. When it reaches the right texture to be eaten as one wishes, even with a fork, the lid can stay off and fresh shelled shrimps be laid amply on the top, to turn white before they are stirred in . . . or small sausages already cooked well in beer or wine. Or it can simply be left in a turned-off oven, to be chilled later for probably the best so-called *ratatouille* ever eaten.

I learned to make it from a large strong woman in Dijon, a refugee not

political but economic from an island off Spain: there was not enough food to go around in her family, and she and her husband were the sturdies, so they got out. They ran a vegetable store with one little window and almost no space, and for the fresh stuff she would pop open a trapdoor and somehow get through it down a steep ladder and bring up cool cabbages or lettuces which they had bought before dawn at the Big Market. She taught me more than her stew, without knowing that I often pondered on how she washed her gleaming hair and stayed generally so sweet-smelling, when it was plain that both she and the lettuces must bathe at the public pump and sleep in the dark cellar or under the little counter. She cooked on a gas ring behind a curtain at the back of the store, and that is how I first came to ask her questions, because the stew had such a fine smell. She looked at me as if I were almost as ignorant as I was, and after my first lesson from her I bought a big casserole, which I still use, and got to work. I had two burners on my stove to her one. The stew is best made in an oven, but who had an oven? Not she, not I.

About MUSHROOMS: this is another quick jump, but in spite of my jauntiness I have half an eye on my editor, and suspect there may already be several too many letters in this self-indulgent alphabet. Mushrooms are friends of mine, although I am forbidden to pick them, through an odd happening in the Marché aux Champignons held once or twice a week during the season in Vevey, on the big square that slopes down to the Lake of Geneva. My husband and I became friends with a tall thin old woman who was one of the licensed pickers of dozens of different kinds of what the books call edible fungi. She taught me what I know about cooking them. And one cold day she looked me in the eye and said that I must never dare serve one I had gathered, never dare even pick one. She could tell, she said, by my nails, my earlobes, my skin. It would be death in the pot. This was a strange blow to me, although I think that I had never picked a mushroom in my life except to look at and smell. But I was supposed to resemble my father's mother, and she was almost legendary in her mushrooming. She even found black morels in Iowa! I myself had her way of sniffing out where mushrooms were growing (like a trained truffle-pig in Périgord?), and then my husband would gather them for us. The old woman looked proudly at him and said he was a safe one, with the real flair. I was dangerous. She spoke so fiercely that I heeded her without question, and still do, and depend upon a few friends I hope she would have approved and the markets where cultivated mushrooms are increasingly plentiful and good. I am glad she bothered to tell me. She was like a sybil, all wrapped in gray woolens, with a long red nose, and little piles of odd-shaped fungi on her portable market table.

Once my parents came to see us in Switzerland, and my mother and I went off on a short jaunt. We stopped for lunch in a village between Lausanne and Berne and ordered two *croûtes aux morilles* and some local white wine. Morels are justly more expensive than plain mushrooms from the woods, but it was a special spree . . . and they were so delicious that with only faint demur from Mother we ordered two more of the large pieces of toast drenched with hot cream and piled with black slices of the strange phallic growths that are almost but not quite as mysteriously tantalizing as truffles. I am sure we asked for more wine. I remember that the large café cat came in and sat cleaning his paws in full view of my mother, who prided herself on being unable even to swallow with one in the room. Finally she went into an elaborate and almost Jesuitical rationalization of the plain fact that she would like to eat another *croûte*, or perhaps one between us. The gist of her argument (against her mother's early training? Her damaged liver? Her lifelong war with her voluptuous nature?) was that she knew she would never taste such a beautiful thing again. It was that simple!

Of course, the last shared portion we could barely swallow, but it was worth surfeit to see my dear smothered lady there, so relaxed and filled with the subtle flavors of the wild morel, and the delicate cool wine, and the warm room with a dozing tomcat in it. And here is the way the sybil in Vevey told me to make a good *croûte*, whether or not the fungi be rare: &

⍣ Vevey Market Mushrooms
(or any)

1 quart fresh mushrooms

3 to 4 tablespoons sweet butter

1½ cups rich cream

Salt, pepper

¼ cup fresh lemon juice

       OR

½ cup dry white wine

1 tablespoon Worcestershire sauce,
      if wished

Thick slices of toasted and buttered
      French bread

Brush mushrooms, or rinse and dry quickly, and cut in halves or large pieces. Heat butter in skillet, add mushrooms, and move them about briskly. When they have made their juices and then reabsorbed them, add the cream and seasoning and stir until bubbling. Quickly add the lemon juice or wine (and the Worcestershire if wished), and pour at once over the toast. This is a fast job, well worth the attention it needs.

OKRA: another friend, and I am pleased to find it now in Western markets and to buy it frozen when I want to. Some people abhor it, except sliced discreetly into a gumbo, because it can be very slippery. Arkansas Addie taught me how to wash it and then slice off the stem end carefully, so as not to break through into the pod, and thus prevent most of this unpopular quality. She also showed me a delicious combination of tender green beans and okra: after the beans have been parboiled, drained, and seasoned and put back with plenty of butter to "set," the okra is parboiled lightly, and then laid on top of the kettle of beans for the last ten minutes of their cooking together. As soon as the okra can be pierced with a toothpick, the pot gets a few good shakes and perhaps some more butter and salt and pepper, and a surprisingly delicate dish is ready to be served.

The best okra I ever ate was when I was teaching in a black school in the South. I could have lived on it, I felt, but it was impossible to enjoy, even secretly, such a toothsome thing when on the other side of the wire screen in the dining room the students got none of it. (They had flies, but the teachers did not, comparatively speaking.) I could not sit there sensuously nibbling the crisp perfect pods, so hot and rich, while they ate from famishment the usual canned corn and ribs. The school was a haven for waifs picked up by its patriarchal founder, and that summer a prime example of what his Christian benevolence could pull from the gutter was one of the most beautiful Creoles I ever saw, a dreamy shattered man with the profile of Jelly Roll Morton, and the all-time shakes. He owned a white jacket, which he wore now and then the way diplomats put on their decorations for a visiting ambassador, and at noon dinner he sat by the teachers' door into the dining room, weaving and nodding in his chair, but adding a note of elegance with his fine decaying bones.

One day as I left the room he stopped me and said in a soft voice that if there was anything in the whole world that I wanted to eat, he could fix it for me better than anyone in the whole world. I felt flustered, for I was so hungry by then that it was innate, like having a hump on my back or fourteen toes, but how could I ask for some little lagniappe, with all those children watching me as I sat behind the wire screen? I evaded his dim gaze in its bright yellow eyeballs, and his controlled trembling, and I thanked him.

In a few days he told me again that he would like to cook something to please me, and in a kind of panic I said that I loved okra, which was in season then on the school farm and was being cut up in the canned corn

with the ribs. He cackled in a secretive way and dropped into an immediate doze in his chair. The next noon, when only the white academic head and I were left in the teachers' side, he wove in with a small platter of okra he had apparently fried while the cook's back was turned, and it was one of the rare times I ever saw my boss relax. Like two truant children we sat in unsuspected communion and plucked the crisp brown pods from the dish with our fingers and crunched silently on them, while the man who looked like Jelly Roll smiled gently and then snoozed off again, shaking and sweating. All the students had marched out from their side. A fan buzzed somewhere in the kitchen. I wondered how the vegetable had been cooked . . . perhaps blanched lightly, then dipped in a thin mixture of egg and flour, and fried for two minutes in hot deep fat? There were a couple of pieces left. The academic head stood up suddenly, said something in a bitter voice about how she was pleased to see that I appreciated the famous cooking of the Deep South, and clumped out past the sleeping majordomo. I decided to stay right there and eat the last crumbs of his dish, for like my mother with the *croûtes aux morilles* I knew that never again would I taste such a dainty mysterious thing, a kind of gastro-planetary conjunction. When I left, only four minutes late for my next class, the flies from the students' section were hitting furiously against the screens into our small exclusive ghetto, and the fan was off, and the strange cook slept on his stool like a corpse, if one can be in rigor mortis and still shake. I thanked him later but never again succumbed to his feverish blandishments; he had recognized me in spite of my white disguise, and I wanted to work there a little longer

ONIONS: they are as much a part of my cooking as eggs or brown sugar, but I have produced many meals without a trace of them, to lure a dear friend to my table. He believes firmly and perhaps with rightness

that they are poison to whatever it is that keeps him watching his diet
and therefore eminently solid and well. I bow to his dictum and my respect for it and him, and at the same time am mildly impressed by how
much I use onions in my daily and festival cooking when he is not
around. I like to make tarts of them, sliced thin and limped in butter
and then poured into a pie shell and covered with a custard. I like them
in rings, soaked in milk and drained, and added to salads of blanched
chilled vegetables. They are good fried with apples and tossed at the last
with little browned sausages. They are good glazed, for a garnish for pigeons or other game.

I use mild onions mostly, and I depend always upon what are called
green onions here and scallions in the East for a lift, discreet or brutal, to
salads, omelets, countless other kitchen messes. In the same family, leeks
are delicious, but I seldom buy them because they are ridiculously expensive in California, not at all "the poor man's endive" of Europe. Often I
substitute the slender delicate green ones for them. Garlic is of course essential to my private cooking, and happily I can lean on it with several
people like my nononion friend, who mysteriously will tolerate large
amounts of it. I do not like to find whole cloves of it in what I am eating.
Sometimes I impale a few on toothpicks and then fish them out when
they have given their desired impact. Oftener I mince or crush them, one
or several according to my plans, and when they are to go into a mixture
which must be browned I make sure that they never turn more than pale
golden before the rest is added, else they will be come acrid, an onerous
condition in any walk of vegetable or animal life.

PEAS: see BEANS; see anything I have written about freshness; see
CORN, for instance! And then I must add that I like frozen peas if they
are given intelligent attention, and I even like canned peas. Dried peas

can be delicious. The best way to eat fresh ones is to be alive on the right day, with the men picking and the women shelling, and everybody capering in the sweet early summer weather, and the big pot of water boiling, and the table set with little cool roasted chickens and pitchers of white wine. So . . . how often does this happen?

POTATOES: can be a once-in-a-while thing, too. Perhaps the most subtle I ever ate were in Sweden, when they were steamed quickly, right from the garden, on a bed of fresh dill, and then lifted out like fragile eggs and served on hot plates with more chopped dill and sweet butter. They were almost evanescent, like the upper or lower cheeks of baroque cherubs.

When I ate them I thought of a movie I saw when I was perhaps thirteen. It was a James Barrie revival, perhaps with Janet Gaynor, about a brave little child actress of possibly sixteen who cared for several younger child actors, all dressed as real people, almost. I envied her. They lived in a Dublin garret, very garrety and picturesque. They *were* brave, and bravely she served them a pathetic meal of nothing but limitless bowls of little potatoes boiled in their jackets, and a big pitcher of milk, and butter which they put on the praties as they held them on the ends of their silver forks. I laughed out loud, and so did my little sister, for that meal was our dream. And I still serve it. I still serve, quite without bravery or even bravado, a big bowl of new potatoes boiled in their skins, and plenty of sweet butter, and thanks to my unsuspected education in Switzerland where even the poor people seemed to feel quite brave with all that cheese lying around, a good slab of Gruyère at room temperature. A bite of salty buttered potato . . . a little piece of the cheese . . . a sip of milk or light white wine: what a jolly garret!

There are several thousand things to do with potatoes, as kitchen manuals will explain. I do not use the vegetable often here, except when I see some blushing small ones, because they have been shipped from too far away, or have lain too long in refrigerated sheds and wholesalers' bins. When I want a starch, I often substitute a pasta because of this uncertainty . . . or because I am lazy.

Once on Long Island I saw jewel-like tiny potatoes lying in a newly plowed field, in late August, and I pulled off my shoes and plunged out into the soft sandy dust and culled enough for a fine lunch. A car slowed down on the road, and I thought it might be the workers back from a break, or the police, but there was a great laugh and it drove on. Later I learned that I had embarrassed my hosts (who enjoyed the nutlike little culls before they felt any qualms). But the next August came an air-mailed box of "more of the same," and I have always wondered how and when other people got so knee-deep dirty to pick them for me, out in that elegant banlieue.

These little gems, and any young potatoes, should be rolled around briskly in cold water with a brush, plunged into ample and briskly boiling water, and drained as soon as they can be pierced with a chopstick or sharp fork. Then, to be what are correctly called *Shook* Potatoes in some of my ungrammatical but familiar circles, they should be put back at once into the hot kettle, and shaken until their delicate skins pop open and they become floury and light. Plenty of butter, freshly ground pepper, chopped herbs if one wishes, and there is a frabjous dish indeed. (I know one quasi-resident of those fleetingly generous fields of Long Island who delights to serve a large bowl of the little hot nuggets with a silver boat of melted butter, alongside a pound of fresh gray caviar. Ah, well.)

Big potatoes are good baked, when they are good potatoes. Big good baked potatoes are good stuffed. Stuffed big good baked potatoes are handy to know about, because they can be prepared in advance and then given a final fast bout in the oven. In many American restaurants they are served in foil wrappings, split open to let the steam escape and then plied with various mixtures of sour cream and herbs and cheese, always with a thick cut of grilled meat. I spurn these on principle, although occasionally at home I stuff freshly opened potatoes in somewhat the same manner, to please adolescents of all ages. For me, a plain baked potato is the most delicious one, of course with plenty of butter and fresh pepper. It is soothing and enough . . .

 Gnocchi di Zucca (Pumpkin Dumplings)

2 cups pumpkin pulp (canned will do well)
2 eggs slightly beaten
1 or 2 tablespoons flour
½ teaspoon baking powder
Nutmeg, salt, ½ clove mashed garlic if
   wished

Make a thin puree of the pumpkin, eggs, flour, and baking powder. Add spices, stir well. Let stand 1 hour. Stir again and drop by spoonfuls into rapidly boiling salted water. As soon as the dumplings rise, skim into a bowl of very cold water. Drain well when cool. To serve, heat in a casserole with plenty of butter.

PUMPKIN: the only reason I mention it is that I have a recipe for delicious little *gnocchi*, unexpected and pleasant. I ate them first in Lugano in the house of Signora Donati della Pietà, and although I have never enjoyed them anywhere else as much as there, I can recommend her approximate rule:

These are good with poultry or game, or pork, or alone with a salad for a simple meal, and they are nice to know about, because they are simple and can be made ahead of mealtime except for the last heating.

Otherwise and for other recipes, I would not care if I never tasted pumpkin in any form. Some of its cousins are edible, if baked slowly:

Danish squash, acorn squash, and the like. I prepare them for people I like, who happen to like them. The *gnocchi* are more interesting . . .

RUTABAGA: down with it.

SPINACH: I say it is better than broccoli and I certainly do not say the hell with it, like the little boy in the classic cartoon, and I know a lot of artful ways to cook it to please people, but it does not much tempt me personally.

Here is one thing everyone likes, which can be made step by step at the stove or speeded up in a blender. I think I evolved my method from a Venetian recipe. Occasionally a friend will follow my directions and then reproach me, because the tart was not as dry and easily picked up in the fingers at a country luncheon as she had found it here. This is always because nobody wants to believe that it should bake at least four hours or *longer* in a 250–275° oven. It should be almost dry, easily sliced, and as easily eaten either hot or cold. It makes good canapés, in small squares. It freezes well, too, and thus is a handy thing for an unexpected covey of guests, for it can be put, stiff as a paving block, into a moderately hot oven for a sensible few minutes, to be eaten at once. &

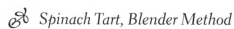 *Spinach Tart, Blender Method*

2 packages frozen chopped spinach,
> *thawed in bowl*
1 large mild onion, cut in chunks
2 cloves garlic
4 to 6 stalks celery in 1-inch pieces,
> *with leaves*
1 cup chopped herbs: parsley, etc.
Scant cup olive oil
4 to 6 eggs, slightly beaten
2+ cups coarsely grated cheese, mild
> *or nippy*
Salt, pepper, nutmeg, to taste
Dry crumbs
More olive oil

Coarsely blend thawed spinach and its juices, onion, garlic, and celery. Add herbs and oil and blend again quickly. Mix lightly with eggs, cheese, and seasoning. Spread about ¾ inch thick on generously oiled cookie pans. Sprinkle well with crumbs, drip more oil on surface, and bake for at least four hours in 250° oven (slightly higher if electric), until dry and somewhat crisp.

TOMATOES: and I love them, the love apples . . . The best way to eat them is in the garden, warm and pungent from the vine, so that one can suck unashamedly, and bend over if any of the juice escapes. The worst way, I feel fairly sure, is "stewed" as we occasionally had them when Grandmother ruled our gastric if not gastronomical roost. There in the little side dishes beside our plates would be a lumpy pinkish puddle of sogged bread, undoubtedly stale to begin with, boiled with tomatoes stripped of all their skin and seeds, so that they were almost without flavor. Fortunately the cook seldom made this mess, since almost all of it went back to the kitchen untasted, a basically depressing and wasteful comment, a real slap on any good culinary cheek. And I cannot remember ever eating them any other way, while Grandmother was alive. Later we grew them at the Ranch, in Gargantuan quantities, and every shape, and scarlet, deep red, yellow, and we ate them every way except stewed.

Between the warm fruit held in one's hand in a garden patch and the despondent slough of my beldam's unswerving treatment of them there are myriad delicious things to do. Perhaps one of the most refreshing, to serve in summer either before or with grilled meats, or by itself for a good luncheon, is slices of ripe firm tomatoes which have been well sprinkled with herbs and olive oil on a large platter, and left to ruminate for a few hours. Before serving, what juice they have freed should be tilted out of the dish into a cup, for the cook to drink privately: the tomatoes will have held on to most of the oil, and their liquid will have mingled just enough with the herbs, and altogether it is a fine little nip, very strengthening!

Stuffed baked tomatoes can be rather limp and mussy, and I would rather eat a stuffed green pepper. If there are firm red love apples which *demand* to be filled with some kind of forcemeat and then put in the oven, to serve hot or cold, it is a good idea to put a teaspoonful of dry rice in the bottom of each. An even better idea is to forget the whole thing, and follow any good recipe for Tomatoes Provençale. They are more fun.

One of the major surprises of my early womanhood was a remark my father made as we drove hell-for-leather from Whittier to San Francisco on some bit of family derring-do. We stopped at King City for a salad or a sandwich, in blistering heat. And it was there, in a café I could draw to-day, or go to if it still stood and if ever again I went to King City, which I shall try not to, that Rex said mildly about a bit of garnish on his plate, "Anyone who serves tomatoes without peeling them should be shot at dawn." I believe we walked out: it was too hot for eating, anyway, but what astounded me was that my father, who seldom made any comment about flavor or texture at the table or indeed in our presence, could have felt thus strongly all the time I was growing up under his eye, and was probably expressing myself firmly on a great many aspects of our daily meals . . . *politely* but firmly, and not at table. Many years later, when I went to keep house for him in his old age, I was careful never to serve tomatoes unless they had been meticulously flayed.

I use canned tomatoes a lot. Off-season, they give more zest to some dishes than the meaningless little "fresh" ones to be bought in cellophaned boxes. I especially like the canned pear-shaped fruit packed "Italian style." They can be drained of their juices and seeds, and stuffed with almost anything: a stiff mayonnaise of crab meat to eat cold, a forcemeat of crumbs and sliced olives and cheese to bake lightly and eat hot, or plain as a fine garnish to broiled lamp chops . . .

TRUFFLES: ah well, and ho hum. But they are fun to *read* about, and now and then a tiny tin drifts to the top of my Christmas stocking, and is tucked away. It is said that they are aphrodisiac, but I would not know. I do know that they are delicious, if not always "best," eaten raw, but I shall continue to smile happily on those perforce preserved. I cannot believe

what I have been told about soaking the fresh ones in cognac to make them more pungent, but it is true that a dry white wine will bring out the perfumes of even the canned ones, and leave a beautiful bit of dark juice to find its place elsewhere (in a sauce . . . or down the cook's omnivorous gullet?). I have also been told, by people who sniff out truffles the way some do Picassos, that the aficionados often carry with them a packet of Rosy Salt, which when they are presented with a scrubbed raw truffle they pinch like snuff between their thumb and forefinger of the left hand, and then sprinkle upon the strange earthy fungus. It might be very good on hard-boiled eggs, too, I say with jaunty frustration. It is made of three parts of salt, two of paprika, and one of cayenne pepper. Truffles, anyone? Eggs? Rosy Salt?

ZUCCHINI: yes. Here I am like the old lady at my table on a British liner, who handed the enormous breakfast menu card to our waiter with this one and apparently all-inclusive word. My only hesitation about the vegetable is that I have never eaten it respectfully prepared in England, and seldom in my homeland except at my own table. Around the Mediterranean I have never eaten it cooked in any way I would not be proud to serve myself, and one good gentleman cook has called it "a lavish gift from Italy to the United States, partly atoning for Al Capone and pizza." This is no place to detail the hows and whys, but even a casual look at a few current cookbooks about French, Italian, Spanish and Portuguese kitchen customs will make it clear that the tender little squashes should be picked when they are not more than three to five inches long, sometimes with their blossoms still shriveling umbilically at one end, and that they should be eaten at once. In England they are called vegetable marrows, a distressingly ponderous and connotative term for such a dainty thing. But there they are long heavy monsters, which after they have been photographed for the local Garden Club members for their imposing length and weight are peeled-chopped-boiled-minced-stuffed and otherwise affronted, as are their grudging consumers. In America they are occasionally served in a wet stew with bits of tomato and green pepper and onion . . . and are almost unfailingly pushed aside . . .

. . . except here! Here I can serve zucchini successfully, and with inner glee, to lifelong loathers of the stuff. I take a faintly vicious pleasure in this game, the way I once did in giving decaffeinized Kaffee Hag to my guests after dinner in Switzerland, and then gently leading them into scurrilous remarks about people who would do such a thing, while they praised me for my own potent brew.

Here is one way we eat tender sweet zucchini, which might not please in any other surroundings. At the end of a hard day it makes a most calming supper. It is good to take a quiet bath first, and then eat a big bowlful of the soothing pap, and go to bed. Sometimes it is nice afterward to pour a mugful of cold milk with a tot of rum in it, and put it beside the bed, and read an old Simenon while one sips and perhaps dozes . . . ❧

This is indeed an innocent dish, and it has salved many worldly wounds in my circle for a long time. It is not the kind of thing one offers

❧ Private Method Zucchini

8 to 10 small clean zucchini, without stem ends
4 or 5 summer or yellow squash, if wished
1 to 2 stalks celery, thinly sliced
Handful of chopped parsley
3 to 6 sliced scallions
OR
1 small chopped onion (optional)
Butter

Either barely cover all ingredients except butter with boiling water and cook rapidly until tender, or do them as prescribed in pressure cooker. Drain well, saving juices for something else. Return to kettle, mashing coarsely with big spoon and adding seasonings and butter to taste. Shake briskly. Serve in bowls with soup spoons, with or without bread or toast.

ℰ *Unstuffed Zucchini*

THE UNSTUFFING:

3 cloves garlic

¾ cup olive oil

2 green peppers in chunks

1 cup coarsely chopped parsley

4 eggs

1 teaspoon dry "Italian herb seasoning"

1 teaspoon salt

½ teaspoon pepper

2 cups grated Parmesan or other dry cheese

Dry bread crumbs to make thick paste

In blender, mix garlic and oil to thin paste. Gradually add peppers and parsley until coarsely blended. Add eggs and seasoning, blend once more, and pour into large bowl. Mix cheese well into liquid, and then enough dry crumbs to make thick paste. Let chill at least two hours. Taste to rectify seasoning, and stir once more.

THE VEGETABLE:

12 or more small firm zucchini

Olive oil

Blanch squash by plunging into boiling water, cooking rapidly until barely tender, and then plunging into cold water. Drain well, and split lengthwise, leaving tips on for added strength. Do not hollow, as is customary, but using a teaspoon and the fingers pack a thick layer of unstuffing on each half, and place close together in shallow baking pan. Drip olive oil amply over each piece, and bake about 1 hour, in 350° oven, or until lightly browned. Serve hot as vegetable, or well cooled as hors d'oeuvre.

to casual friends. It can of course be gussied with a good sprinkling of grated Parmesan, for instance, but it remains starkly simple, and a meal in itself for the Chosen Few.

A far cry from it is something I like to make for summer suppers, and even winter ones now that firm small zucchini come from out of the Mexican nowhere into the Californian and perhaps Eastern here. It is most easily made with a blender, partway, but a willing hand with the chopping is probably even better than a machine. The process is somewhat like constructing a bastard pesto, and then despoiling it. The results are admirable, either hot or cold. ℰ

AND WHAT OTHER CATEGORY of words can go from A to Z? Animals, perhaps: ALBATROSS to ZEBRA. Me, I have a lifelong vegetable love . . . long since fallen into place.

Nor Censure nor Disdain

"CASSEROLES" ARE, I THINK, an American Phenomenon, like Cokes and chewing gum, and by many traditionalists they are put somewhat disdainfully into the same category. On the other hand, they are probably well on their way around the world, not far behind the ubiquitous soft drink and pacifier, as more people live hastier lives everywhere.

Both Webster and Larousse agree that the correct definition of a casserole is an open-mouthed vessel in which foods may be baked and served. It can also be, in classical cooking, a mold made painstakingly of rice or mashed potato or pastry, baked and filled with vegetables or meats in various sauces. Webster says that *en casserole* can also refer to the food within one of these receptacles of earthenware or more edible starches, but it is in the American edition of the *Larousse Gastronomique* that the nearest approach is made to our national definition: "In U.S.A. a *casserole* defines a dish made of two or more elements . . . rice . . . spaghetti, etc., in combination with meat or fish plus a sauce or gravy, and often a variety of vegetables. This one-dish meal can be prepared in advance and cooked and served in a decorative *casserole* . . . very popular in homes where there are no servants. . . ."

And there it is, neatly summed up! We make them every day, and write books about them, and exchange recipes for our own latest family triumphs of Matter over Time, and manufacturers sell seasonal variations on the theme of oven-proof dishes decorated by famous artists, and electric timers in millions of kitchens are set every morning to guarantee that

the evening meal will be correctly crisp and bubbling by exactly 6:30 that
night, and basically it is a good evolution, a healthy institution, an interesting gastronomical compromise.

It is of course abused. Reputable cooking manuals like Mrs. Rombauer's *Joys* do not even list the word in their indexes, probably on the
assumption that any honest housewife *knows* that some foods can be
honorably assembled according to the supplies on hand and her own
discretion, and baked in an open deep-sided dish with some crumbs on
top, for at least two good reasons: she wants to use some small amounts
of meat or vegetables left from another meal, and she wants, while she is
in the kitchen in the morning, to prepare a meal to bake later. Another
excuse for making such a dish is that she has been asked to bring one to
feed ten members at the annual Potluck Get-Together of the Whist
Club Harmonizers. Still another is that she is going to serve a buffet
supper to ten of her husband's colleagues and their wives, and knows
from experience that her way of combining eggplant and oysters and
cheese is worth a raise in pay.

All three reasons are good, as long as the housewife is indeed honest.
Perhaps "ethical" is a stronger and better word, for there is nothing much
more unpleasant than a careless or stupid mish-mash of unrelated foods
hiding in what may be our national dish, and a cook who will serve one
should be drummed from the kitchen.

There are some basic rules about Casserole Cooking which should be
instinctive, but which can be *learned* by the most unskilled beginners.
Naturally they are guided by the cook's own quirks of taste, but they have
little to do with actual prejudices. The foods used should never in any
way be dubious in either looks or taste, as can happen unexpectedly to a
remnant left too long at the back of the icebox . . . or even overnight, un-

covered. One ingredient should dominate, so that the dish is plainly
made of chicken, or shrimps, or lamb. There should not be a pointless
mixture of flavors and textures, just to use up that cup of pimientos, that
saucer of cold steak, those two chicken wings, the sour cream left from
last night's cocktail party with perhaps some chopped clams in it, all
bound together with a bowl of leftover macaroni and two cans of cream-
of-something soup. (Oh! Sprinkle it with grated cheese. Put plenty of
paprika on top. Harry will be late, and ravenous after golf . . . he'll eat
anything on Wednesdays . . .)

A good casserole will have clear-cut textures as well as flavor, and tired
food can never stand up to the slow baking it should be given. The ingredients should be firm, if not completely fresh, and crispness can be added
with thinly sliced green pepper or water chestnuts, chopped nuts,
crumbled crisp ham or bacon, according to the cook's judgment. It is hard
to say which is the more displeasing: a casserole made of a dozen indistinguishable hints of exhausted flavors, or one that is noxious mushy pabulum resembling the predigested purees fed to helpless infants.

Obviously my ways of describing these basic rules are in my own
words, but I think any real casserole-cook would agree with them and me.
I myself believe that it is a good thing to have the backbone of the dish
fresh and firm, and then perhaps to make whatever holds it together (rice
or a form of pasta or perhaps potatoes) just before the whole is assembled.
This cannot always be done, of course, since such dishes are already a
part of our modern need to save time. Rice, if correctly cooked and
stored, will hold its texture for a few days, but most kinds of pasta do not
improve with age, and I have found that while I am preparing the other
ingredients for a dish to be served several hours later, I can make fresh
spaghetti or noodles or capellini for it, with much happier results than if I

use the remains of last night's starch. (In other words, it is best not to cook pasta with one canny eye on a leftover, although I do that with almost everything else!)

The books written about this kind of cooking are interesting, if sometimes a little hazardous for one's mental digestion. The most unfortunate and at the same time most common expression of enthusiasm for the new-old branch of kitchen art is: "*Anything* goes into a casserole." It is not necessary to say more about why I find this reasoning actively dangerous. Casseroles are here to stay for a long time, and they are, for good or ill, a part of our living patterns, and I think it is dastardly to reduce them to the botulistic mediocrity such statements condone.

Oddly enough, it is our own families who live in the greatest danger, for a casserole which will perhaps serve four or five can and most often is slapped together from good-to-shameful remnants from the icebox, whereas some truly worthy dishes are made from near-scratch for the Whist Club and the Business Buffet, with real care and thought. Perhaps that is why my own personal belief in combining leftovers and fresh ingredients seems valid, at least at home . . .

Increasingly there are such compromises with one's knowledge of good cooking and one's harried way of life, and a friend of mine with a large family has evolved her own formula for what she calls "casserole cooking"; three thick layers, first cooked starch at the bottom, then meat freshly and lightly cooked and cubed if possible, and then a juicy vegetable, preferably tomatoes. The whole is covered with grated cheese and crumbs, all having been generously buttered and seasoned, of course, and is cooked for half an hour or so, until it bubbles and sends out good whiffs. Her theory is that the juices must sink into the bottom layer. The result is pronounced eminently edible by her food-conscious crew. It is preeminently modern America, not neo- in any sense of that prefix.

Casseroles lend themselves all too easily to mass feeding, and many a schoolchild has been forever warped, gastronomically, by the two-by-two slab of stiff macaroni-tuna served him on Fridays in the cafeteria. Macaroni and tuna, prepared separately and then combined in light layers, *can* make a decent casserole marriage, I like to believe, although personally I list the strongly flavored canned fish with bananas and chocolate bars as something safely behind me, a childhood aberration. As for macaroni, it will remind me forever of the catered salad we served in boarding school to raise money for a new swimming pool.

This monstrosity is often to be found in delicatessens, a kind of *cold* "casserole," in the slant-sided glass counters where food is kept cool in large pans that look like unmentionable hospital equipment. My surmise is that the hollow bent pasta is cooked past the *al dente* stage but not to a glue, and is then cooled and tossed with a mayonnaise made of very old eggs. My interest in this salad is plainly clinical, but in 1927, when Lindbergh was loning it over the Atlantic, I was battening on the dish in Miss Harker's School. I loved it, and we never had it at home.

By now, somewhat more mercifully, macaroni is one of the standbys for our national hot casseroles: it does not deteriorate as fast as some of the other Italian-type pastes, and it feeds a lot of people with little effort, as I found when I was selling catered food to my schoolmates for exorbitant prices. A big pan of macaroni and cheese, plain or fancy, will provide a lot of tasty nourishment, as any experienced member of the Whist Club will agree . . . and when it is prepared with ham and tongue *alla milanese*, or with eggplant and mozzarella cheese, it can be a production stopper at the most sophisticated buffet confrontation. And I will still take any other kind of pasta ever invented, in or out of a casserole.

Although I subscribe frankly to the somewhat outdated ways of combining a few freshly cooked things soon before serving them or even at the table, I often make dishes ahead of mealtime, and from so-called leftovers, which I think meet all the requirements for our national "dish." It is family history that once when my father wanted to carve more meat for a guest, he begged him fervently, "Help me finish this, for God's sake, or she will make a casserole of it!" And she probably would have, for in times when I have combined going to an office and running a decently nourished household I have evolved many ways to cook more than will probably be needed for a meal, so that something will be left, to challenge what I prefer to think of as my inventiveness rather than my lazy penury. (It is fun.)

I "kept house" for my father for several years after my mother's death and before his, and I came to recognize, and then fairly skillfully to cheat, his conditioned opposition to leftovers. He was very snobbish about them, and about several other kinds of food. For instance, he once surprised me by spurning a tender and artful kind of patty of chopped beef which I had devised for him after he had a double set of choppers installed and found it difficult to chew the prime sirloin steaks he was used to. When I asked him why, he said that "hamburger meat" was for roadside stands and economy measures. "I realize that times are hard," he said bitterly, "but are we reduced to *scraps*, made of God knows what?" I then proved to him that I was buying his accustomed cuts of beef, boning them, and chopping them myself to make his little entrées, although of course I avoided my real reason for this dietary hazard. He ate the next one, but I could see that it was more with pity than pleasure, and I moved on to further disguises. He would accept superextravagant stews, in a tacit recognition that they were fairly easy to chew with his new machinery, but there

was always a reservation in his enjoyment, and I myself found a commendable *ragoût* demanding more time than I should give to it during
that chapter in my life.

Once, in an almost unconscious protest against the ingrained snob-
bishness of people in general and my father in particular, I bought a beef
heart. It was a young one, my slightly astonished butcher assured me. In
my cookbooks it was more often than not listed as an economy meat, and
I decided that I would make it into a luxury dish, to amuse myself at least.
I studied every method for attaining this goal, which from the first was labeled an impossibility if I had read between the lines. I combined the results of my research, and for what seemed several days as I look back on
them I turned, marinated, parboiled, skinned, soaked, and otherwise tried
to change the beef heart's muscular nature. There was a tedious roasting
at low heat, with too much attention demanded to baste the thing enough
to keep it from becoming thick leather on the outside.

I served it on a bed of watercress, with a sauceboat of its juices alongside, and a newly sharpened knife. My father, always the carver, attacked it
with only a quick glance at me on his right. My two little girls sat on his
left. We were deftly served, and according to family custom the children
got a puddle of the gravy in the pit my father made automatically in their
whipped potatoes. Then, of course, I was hoist on my own *cafard*, for nothing could be done about our cutting the slices he had so neatly sliced off.
He took the carving knife, made one thin bite for himself, chewed at it,
and then while we sat watching, he asked me gently, "Just what is this?" I
was damned if I would tell him, so I looked at the girls, who were aware of
all my preparations, and I countered by saying, without impudence, of
course, "Well now, Father, tell *me*." He put the carving tools back on the
handsome platter, so brown and green, and said, "Dinosaur." That is all:

DINOSAUR. And that was one of the times that happen rarely in human lives, when a wave of maniacal laughter, the kind that verges on tears or hysteria, engulfed all of us, and we lay back in our chairs from it, and then sighed, and then went howling off again. Finally we quieted, like the ocean after a storm, and we put the watercress behind our ears and ate all the whipped potatoes and decided that I had found the longest way in the world to make really delicious gravy. I have read that in Paris in 1848 or so, some gastronomers ate elephant meat from the prehistoric deep freeze of the Russian steppes, and once in Whittier, in about 1955, we ate dinosaur.

But I did not dare to make a casserole of its near-petrifaction. Time has drawn its kind veil, again, and I cannot remember what happened to the large dark boulder so cunningly prepared and served forth. Instead, I probably roasted or poached some little chickens the *next* day, and the next day made a casserole from *them*.

One good reason why few kitchen manuals, the reliables, the old Tried-and-Trues, bother to devote any space to such concoctions is that they are obviously dependent upon unpredictables like two cups of yesterday's chicken cut from the bone, or a good end of a grilled steak, or some excellent juice from something-or-other. In my own case, two days after I undoubtedly disposed of the piece of dinosaur, I most probably simmered the stripped chicken carcasses with a few herbs, dried or fresh, cooked some rice in the broth, browned some fresh or tinned mushrooms in butter, and put the rice, mushrooms, and chicken scraps together in layers in a casserole (referring to the dish!), with more rice on top and then some butter, to become crisp. This concoction would not want the ubiquitous addition of grated cheese, which often seems a kind of password to careless casserole cooks: anything will pass muster as long as it rests under a top layer of pseudo-Parmesan or cheddar.

A good cookbook, from *Larousse* to the latest honorable throwaway for a new refrigerator, will give infinite variations on the theme of slow cooking to mingle well-chosen flavors, which is what the whole thing comes down to. They will range in timing from three days for a real *cassoulet* and twenty-four hours for honest-to-Boston baked beans to thirty minutes for a tuna-rola (canned fish, condensed soup, cooked pasta . . .). These variations are ready to hand, in private and public libraries as well as in one's head. What I add here are simply personal footnotes, and will more than qualify in the classical rather than the locally popular sense, because they are made with some care, and from partly fresh materials, rather than leftovers. Often they are baked in wide pans or dishes not more than three inches deep, instead of in the higher oven-proof vessels which stores tell me are most popular. I find that this makes a crisper top when that is desirable, and the food is easier to serve to more than four or five people, especially at a buffet-type meal.

In our cultural way of thinking of dishes that can be prepared beforehand, even in the morning for an evening meal, it is obvious that nothing which might spoil should be used in them. This leaves out raw fish and raw fowl: they should be prepared and included in the Magic Pot as soon as possible before it assumes its final form and goes into the usually slow oven. If cooked fish and cooked chicken or other poultry are mixed with the ingredients for a reasonably long wait, real care must be taken to keep the whole thing safely chilled until the heat goes on. This is true too of the molluscs like oysters and mussels, and all the delicious cannibals of the deep, from Mexican prawns to Maine lobsters. They can be death in the pot. In the same way, frozen turkey or a like meat can bring pain and woe if it is allowed to grow warm and then wait too long. And veal and pork can too, I am told. Beware, beware!

But good old sturdy dependable beef, one of the modern housewife's best friends, can always make part of a casserole to count on, whether it be chopped or cubed from last night's roast or freshly browned in decent fat to add to the mixture of starches and vegetables, and then left to cook slowly at the right time. Lamb is honorable too, both cooked and fresh, especially if one first looks in an open-minded way at a couple of Armenian or Greek or Turkish cookbooks. Here is a recipe I like, on this last theme: ✍

✍ Lamb and Brown Rice Casserole

2 pound shoulder of lamb, without bones
¼ cup flour
¼ cup olive or salad oil
1 cup raw brown rice
1 large onion, thinly sliced
1 quart meat stock (or water), heated
½ teaspoon thyme
Salt, pepper

Cut lamb into 1-inch squares and dredge with flour. Heat oil in large skillet and brown meat well on all sides. Place rice in bottom of casserole. Cover with meat and onion. Rinse skillet well with stock and spices, and add to casserole. Cover tightly and bake for 2 hours or more at about 375°, checking now and then to add more liquid if necessary.

This is a typical casserole, a "typical casserole." Where did it spring from? Its variations are endless, depending upon what the cook finds, once meat, rice, and liquid are available. If cooked lamb is used, the time is cut in half (and so is some of the flavor). A cup of dry vermouth or two cups of dry wine or two cups of tomato juice can make part of the liquid. In the last case, basil is a good herb instead of thyme. Eggplant in season, and sliced green peppers, can be sautéed separately and added halfway along. A tin of anchovy fillets can be chopped and added ten minutes before serving. A quick mixture of yogurt and sour cream, mysterious with minced fresh mint, can be stirred into it just before serving. And so on and so on. It depends upon where one's great-grandmother was or was not born, perhaps?

A good standby for something that has to be prepared well in advance is ham, which is, to put it bluntly, already embalmed and therefore in

minimal danger of immediate decay. Here is an apparently pleasing dish
as far as I can surmise after decades of dependence on it, which can be
put together and then pulled out for last-
minute cooking: &

This dish is very good with another
"casserole" of noodles and butter and
crumbs, with or without sautéed mushrooms added at the last, all of which can be
cooked and assembled while the ham is in
the oven. Pickled fruit is good, alongside, or
a compote of fresh fruits and melons afterward.

In a book of this kind it seems impossible to keep divisions of food sternly separate. Salad dressings seem to fall into place
in a section purportedly meant for sauces,

& Baked Ham in Cream

6 ½-inch slices loaf-boiled ham
½ cup brown sugar
2 tablespoons paprika (or more)
½ pint heavy cream

*Cut each slice in half, sprinkle well with sugar and
paprika, and place together like a sandwich. Place in
shallow casserole, cover with rest of sugar and paprika,
and pour cream around slices. Cover and keep cool
until cooking time.*

*Bake in 350° oven for about 30 minutes, basting
often with cream.*

and here I could and I think should mention a casserole of pasta which
would more correctly be put into the chapter meant to discuss starches
and breads and all that. It is served often where I live. I am sure it has
evolved over at least three generations and ten times that many cultural
shifts, as the original Italian winemakers of Napa Valley settled into their
increasingly well-fed skins, and by now it is almost a staple, for which we
are always grateful.

It is a hearty dish, very good "warmed over," and if there are any bites
left they are fine stuffed into hollow tomatoes, or blanched green peppers,
for further slow baking. As far as I can trace it down, it first became known
as a local dependable after the turn of the century, served by a handsome
gentlewoman who ran a boardinghouse for unattached lawyers, news-

papermen, and suchlike. They were young, hungry, and articulate, if the remaining ones of them who now recall her genteel gastronomical delights are a fair sample, and I suspect that the traditional name for this dish, Zalaveri, is a crude pun on what happened in their mouths when they thought of the dish. The word does not exist anywhere but here. It is not in any Italian dictionary, or any regional cookbook. Several dialects are still spoken in families in my valley, and nobody will give parenthood to this poor little bastard. My theory remains unchallenged: it is a salivary excitant, *provided* one is young, hungry, and prone to punning.

St. Helena Zalaveri

1 large or 2 small onions
1 large or 2 small green peppers
6 tablespoons olive oil
1½ pounds lean ground beef
1 medium can tomatoes
1 #2 can cream-style corn (not whole-kernel and not fresh)
1 level tablespoon salt
1 level teaspoon black pepper
1 one-pound package noodles, large or small, lightly cooked (al dente)
2 cups Italian-style mushroom sauce (optional)

Chop onion and green pepper and sauté lightly in oil in heavy skillet. Add meat, and stir until seared. Add tomatoes, corn, and seasoning. Mix the drained noodles lightly with the whole, and pour into two medium-sized or one large oiled casserole. Pour the mushroom sauce evenly over them, or add some beef stock if they seem too dry. Cover, and bake in 350° oven for 45 minutes. Uncover for the last 10. Serve with grated cheese.

For some reason, according to local tradition, the cream-style corn is essential. So are the rather startling amounts of salt and pepper. The mushroom sauce is not, and as time marches on, the dish seems to be growing less "hearty." I have even eaten it made with leftover turkey, and excellent it was. But that peculiar touch of canned cream-style corn was there, to keep it a true Zalaveri, and Northern Italians have assured me it is a kosher requisite . . .

And here, for fun, is a forthright but still delicate little dish which can be prepared well ahead of time, if care is taken about keeping it properly chilled until the oven and the cook are ready. It is delicious with rice, which can be prepared in that last half hour or so:

Naturally dishes like this one, if they demand to be left in the icebox until cooking time, need an extra minute or so in the oven, or a sensible few minutes outside it, beforehand. (Common sense has long since dubbed this "common sense.") They may not be casseroles in the still indefinite meaning of the word in our hurried and servantless culture, but they are good to know about, and they are convenient, and that last is the prime requisite of a modern housewife. They need not be baked in elegant vessels, even if they are meant to be served at the table in what they cooked in, but of course any well-trained family, especially a hungry one, will come to respect and even admire a streamlined white pot decorated with cherries and butterflies as much as a dark brown stained fruity-looking glazed clay thing Great-Uncle Charles brought from China after he had paid his respect to the Dowager Empress . . .

In other words, it is what is in the pot that matters, and in order to matter it must be assembled, at no matter what speed or with what harried reasons, with balance and foresight. And then a casserole is, to paraphrase a sacrilegious quip, probably one of the greatest modern inventions since aspirin . . .

Sweetbreads Bonne Femme

Butter
½ pound fresh sliced mushrooms
½ cup chopped fresh parsley and green
    onion or chives
3 pairs sweetbreads, blanched and halved
Salt, black pepper, dash of cayenne
1 cup (or more) dry white wine
Juice of one lemon
1 cup veal or chicken stock
More butter
2 teaspoons flour

Butter casserole generously. Mix mushrooms with onions and herbs, and lay on bottom. Lay sweetbreads on bed, and season well. Barely cover with wine, and then sprinkle with lemon juice and add stock. Dot well with butter, and sprinkle with flour. Cover casserole and cook at 350° for ½ hour. Remove cover, cook 15 minutes.

One Way to Stay Young

A MAN I COUNT AMONG MY MOST trusted friends once said of a green salad, "I can recommend this dish to all who have confidence in me: salad refreshes without weakening, and comforts without irritating, and I have a habit of saying that it makes us younger." Jean Anthelme Brillat-Savarin was going into his seventies when he published this mild remark in 1825, a few months before his death, but he was and is one of the youngest people I ever met. It could not have been the salads alone . . . but surely his countrymen's habit of following a good dish with some leaves of green lettuces is one of the best ways to stay refreshed and comforted in our pattern of survival.

I much prefer it to a custom which is rapidly spreading into American culture from the West Coast, where I suspect it was a stepchild, spawned by homesick refugees, of the Italian way of eating a few fresh raw things before the pasta: the ubiquitous "tossed green salad" served automatically at the beginning of many restaurant meals, and perhaps more private ones. I suppose it is better to eat something from the overfilled bowls of chopped lettuces and radishes and so on, which are put before the diners while they wait for the rare grilled steak with stuffed baked potato to be slapped down, than it is to plunge right into that mechanical blast of proteins. At least it prepares the stomach, if not the tastebuds, for what will soon come sizzling from the infrared grill, and it would throw into chaos the whole routine of not only the waitresses but the kitchen to try to replace it with a small hors d'oeuvre, in an average eating place in America.

As one looks around a public dining room, and if one can see through the deliberately tactful gloom, it is as if above almost every head, at least of the males, a little banner floats, saying bravely: MIGHT AS WELL EAT SOME RABBIT FOOD WHILE THAT T-BONE-TENDERLOIN-FILET-MIGNON GETS CHARRED ON THE OUTSIDE AND BLOOD-RARE INSIDE, GOD DAMN IT. And the salads are badly concocted, badly mixed, and decorated with tasteless olives, rounds of overdeveloped radish, now and then a quarter of hard-boiled egg, or a scallion stuck almost sheepishly on one side. I know one place, quasi-Italian, where marinated garbanzos are to be discovered at the bottoms of the awkward little ice-cold bowls. I seek them out.

In general this silly business called "tossed green salad" constitutes what in France is called a hunger-killer, an *abat-faim*, to keep the customer sober enough to see the steak he has ordered, something in place of a couple more vodka martinis from the bar. The dreadful bowls can be assembled hours ahead of time, and pulled out of the salad reefer as needed by the waitresses, who will then douse them with "Russian-Thousand-Island-Roquefort" according to the customer's wish. (It is generally disastrous to say no to this rattle of choices and ask for plain vinegar and olive oil . . .)

In other words, I deplore the whole caper, and hope it is not creeping too firmly into what I still like to think of as the home kitchen in our country. A green salad, I firmly believe, should *follow* the main course of a meal, at noon or night, and should be made almost always and almost solely of fresh crisp garden lettuces tossed at the last with a plain vinaigrette. "I can recommend this dish to all," as my friend said some time ago, but I do not recommend it at any other place in a meal, in a way which may seem arbitrary . . . until one remembers that any other place would have been inconceivable to *him*!

There are salads which can and do come first, and even act as a whole

light meal, but the traditional green salad needs no masking, unless one
adds an herb now and then to carry along the flavor of the main dish. A
chicken cooked with tarragon might call for a touch of tarragon in the

delicate salad to follow, to refresh one's spirit and body afterward. Or one
can pull a country trick I learned long ago from Jeanne Bonamour, and
splash the last bit of juice from the meat platter into the salad which is to
follow a roast of beef or lamb or even chicken. Now and then with game,
a hunter's salad made of tender leaves of spinach and watercress can have
some pungent raw mushrooms grated into it . . . In general, though, a
simple green salad is best left simple and green.

The "made" salads which in France are rightly called *composées* can
be very interesting, and obviously I am able to discuss their possibilities
with less passion and more clinical detachment than I can the apparent
fate of a "tossed green" in our native pattern. I remain opinionated, however, and far from as mild as my mentor the old Frenchman would advise.

Almost any reputable cookbook, from Larousse to Rombauer or
Child, will give good ideas for "made" salads, and in between the masters
one can find innumerable formulas too dreadful to be printed twice, or
even once. I shall ignore the latter with a deep bow to the former, and
write about a few refreshing and comfortable dishes I like to make for my
own people, to please and in some cases fill them so that they will need
nothing more than a little cheese and fruit, or an amusing dessert occasionally, to feel that fate cannot harm them.

Almost surely I hang on, even subconsciously, to something I first
learned in Venice: blanched small fresh vegetables, lightly marinated or
served plain and cold with a sauce apart, are delicious, together or alone.
I often make some variation of this exercise, and it pleases us. One good
one is to prepare zucchini not more than four inches long, green string-
less beans, separate buds of a cauliflower, and perhaps small rosy potatoes

in their skins, and serve them in piles on a long board or fish platter, instead of tossed together in a big bowl as I remember them first. They should be blanched correctly, in the so-called French manner, by plunging them (of course cleaned and tidied) into a lot of boiling water, removing them with a skimmer when barely done, and plunging them again into very cold water and draining them as they chill and start to sink to the bottom. This procedure horrifies dieticians and home economists, who say with justification that it robs the vegetables of some of their valuable nutrients and even their flavors. I do not hold with the last condemnation, and for serving little garden things in my own fashion I often like them prepared in this heinous way. They look pretty and they are good, and that can be said for few of us human beings, even food experts!

For such a platter of delight as the one I have started to describe, I would marinate the beans, all laid lengthwise, in a strong vinaigrette if they were somewhat old and tired ("of a certain age," to be discreet . . .), and leave them alone and unadorned if they were of the almost unprocurable slim sweetness of beans that most people can pick only in their own gardens. After the neatly stacked beans on the long platter might come a snowy pile of the cauliflowerets, and then perhaps another pile of little potatoes cooked in their jackets (or small firm peeled tomatoes). Then there could be a neat stack of short firm zucchini, perhaps slit on one side and stuffed with a fillet of anchovy. (This last can stand alone as a fine hors d'oeuvre, with extra dressing made from the anchovy oil . . .) There would be one or two bowls of thin dressing: a plain one of wine vinegar and oil, especially if nothing had been stuffed or marinated, and another more pungent one with mashed anchovies and herbs . . . and occasionally a mayonnaise or mild *aïoli*. This is a handsome plate, and a fine one both winter and summer, depending upon one's supplies, to start an informal meal either large or small. It is *interesting*, and if boredom is one of the sure incitements to incipient ulcers, my platter is a fine antidote!

Another good one, which we call Italian because it is red, white, and green, is tossed lightly in a big bowl instead of being laid out on a platter: ❧

❧ An Italian Salad

> *3 pounds tender green beans*
> *1 cup vinaigrette dressing*
> *1 large or 2 small sweet onions*
> *1 pint milk*
> *1 can sliced pimientos*

Blanch the beans, drain well, and toss with marinade. Let stand at least one hour. Slice onion paper-thin, and soak in milk one hour. Drain and dry well, saving milk for other uses if wished. Put onions in cold bowl, add beans and their marinade, and pimientos. Mix lightly, and let stand at least one hour more, chilling well.

This is a pretty thing, and delicious before a plate of pasta, for instance . . . or roasted veal or lamb or chicken. Its possibilities are as endless as one's supplies, both outward and inner.

Potatoes are often used in salads, everywhere they grow, from Mexico to Morocco, and they are an adjunct to any self-respecting tray of hors d'oeuvres in small European restaurants where much nourishment may seem to be offered for a minimal sum . . . again an *abat-faim!* If the first course is plentiful and well seasoned, who will notice that the meat dish to follow it is somewhat meager?

Paul Reboux once listed the ingredients for a Moroccan salad which he recommended to further a beautiful woman's invitation to discuss polygamy: cooked potatoes cut into rounds, celery, tomatoes, sweet red peppers, dates, and bananas. The whole is doused with a kind of vinaigrette made of strong white wine, lemon juice, and sweet oil, thickened with pounded hard egg yolks . . . and except for the two fruits, it is almost exactly like an Ensalada Jardinera I learned to make in Mexico and often produce now, which substitutes shredded lettuce and cubed beets to be added at the last.

Almost everyone in the Western world has eaten some form of the potato salad most often encountered on picnics and at small-town potluck suppers, and even in delicatessens. It can be delicious. It should be well made, of course, as what should not? I doubt that my own life would be much affected if I never ate it again, but I like to make it now and then, and to think about it in terms of other people. Perhaps the strangest I ever ate was when I was teaching in Mississippi. It was very smooth and creamy, almost like a beaten puree, but cold and lightly seasoned. I have met only one other person who recognized my description, and he was born and raised in Iowa! And undoubtedly the most elegant potato salad I have ever eaten or made, in these restricted definitions, was my own somewhat irreverent adaptation of one of Escoffier's recipes. It has been a long time since I could boast of having a generous admirer who was also an importer of truffles, and, not by coincidence, it is exactly the same length of time since I have made this beautiful dish, but there is no reason not to dwell on it . . . and perhaps it like several other things might be amusing with fine black olives?

Salade Demi-Deuil, More or Less

5 to 7 peeled black truffles (1 medium can)
Their juice
1 cup dry white wine
6 to 8 potatoes
2 tablespoons mild prepared mustard
Salt, pepper
1 to 2 tablespoons good strong vinegar or lemon juice
1½ to 2 cups fresh rich cream
Tender salad greens (hearts)
Mild vinaigrette sauce
Paprika

Slice truffles very thin, and put with juice into white wine. Let stand one hour while potatoes boil in their jackets. Peel when done, and cut into generous bowl while still warm, in ½-inch cubes. While they are still tepid, mix mustard, seasoning, and vinegar, and add cream slowly, stirring all the time. Add this dressing and the truffles and wine to the potatoes, and mix carefully but well. Let cool for 4 to 6 hours, stirring once or twice with care not to break the truffle slices. Prepare generous bed of small leaves of salad greens which have been lightly coated with simple vinaigrette dressing, and turn out the salad onto this. Sprinkle with paprika if wished, and serve at once.

This is an invention of true elegance, because it is so simple in what is now a way of almost unattainable extravagance. It is pleasant to reflect upon, and I feel fairly certain that Escoffier would not censure me for my tampering, because of my obvious respect for both him and his dish.

When I was still innocent of truffles and their agents and attributes, there were other pleasures, and one of them was Elizabeth Klein. The only time we ever managed to keep a cook for very long was when she came to stay with us, for reasons known only to herself but probably strengthened by our blissful admiration of things she would make when she felt like it . . . like crullers . . . like tapioca pudding baked all night with a whole jar of apricot jam . . . like German hot potato salad . . . There are many good recipes for this last hearty dish, but I know that the way she used to make it was the best, and still is in my memory. It was served steaming for lunch in winter, on days surely starred with gold in my gastronomical calendar. Of course it was made of potatoes peeled and sliced while still too hot for any normal human being to handle (Elizabeth was definitely neurotic and left us finally to care for the Catholic priest, although she was a fanatically devout Lutheran . . .). Symmetrical morsels of salt pork or perhaps bacon were "tried" in a big skillet until done, and sliced onions were browned gently in the hot fat, and then into it, with great fumings, went vinegar and seasonings and last the potatoes. And then, and this was the magic part for us, chunks of iceberg lettuce were quickly cut into the hot mess, and it was turned into a bowl and served. This is probably the one good thing I shall ever say about the strangely meaningless round heads of hard lettuce which are scornfully called "Los Angeles" by San Franciscans, but those lukewarm limp rich lumps, buried as they were in steamy crumbly potatoes coated with delicious indigestible dressing, have kept me quietly loyal to such a wretched vegetable, and blindly so to the scrawny and perhaps exalted woman who was a good cook when she felt like it.

There is a salad which Russians have served to me as a Russian Salad, and which I like to make, and it contains not only whatever the garden or market can offer of fresh "summer" vegetables, but cubed boiled potatoes at will. Cucumbers of course, and radishes, green onions, tomatoes, all properly cleaned and cut into bits, are mixed lightly in a big bowl with the potatoes. In another bowl sour cream is whipped until light, and seasoned with lemon juice and plenty of paprika. The unflavored vegetables are put into little bowls, and the cream is poured over them. This is a refreshing change from our Western custom of marinating things and seasoning them, and it would be pleasant to eat in the garden of a *dacha* near Moscow, perhaps. Meanwhile we eat it in my backyard at the foot of Mount St. Helena, which was explored and named by the Russians!

Sour cream is a good kitchen friend in salads, and to help dieters I often mix it with plain yogurt . . . just as at the other end of the calorie stick I mix it with a rich mayonnaise! A classic salad can be made most happily, to serve for instance with cold salmon, of thinly sliced cucumbers tossed with a seasoned sour cream dressing made with chopped or finely slivered almonds, and this dressing made with cucumbers finely chopped instead of sliced is excellent with many fish and shrimps and lobster, half- and-half with mayonnaise for extra suavity.

Fortunately, some dishes have evolved too slowly over too many centuries for us to bother about their inventors. They have sprung from the materials available. It is a different thing in newer cultures like ours on the West Coast of America. Who first served a martini, if anyone really cares? Who first served a Caesar or Cesar or even Cicero salad? (I know of at least two people who have been actively repelled by the headwaiter's ritual of breaking barely coddled eggs over this mishmash at the last minute, in posh restaurants, and I myself feel a mild distaste at some of the "original" recipes I have read for such a hearty bowl of disguisements . . .) Who first prepared a Green Goddess? (Here the proprietary mayhem is almost as serious as with the Caesar, but I shall proceed blandly!)

 Green Goddess Dressing and Salad

> *8 to 10 fillets of anchovies*
> *½ small sweet onion*
> *10 to 12 parsley sprigs*
> *6 to 8 fresh tarragon leaves (or ¼ teaspoon dried)*
> *3 cups mayonnaise*
> *2 tablespoons tarragon vinegar*
> *2 tablespoons chopped chives*
> *1 clove garlic*
> *Chilled dry leaves of mixed salad greens*
>
> *Chop first four ingredients very fine. Mix with mayonnaise, thin slightly with vinegar, and add chives. To make salad, rub large cold serving bowl with cut garlic, half-fill with greens, and just before serving toss thoroughly with dressing.*

In rare cases one can still eat this last seductive dish in what I call its virgin state, in San Francisco where it is reputed to have been born, and as far as I know it is still purest at the old Palace where it probably *was* born. It is not as fashionable as it was some decades ago, but here is the recipe which is still followed honestly, given to me on a card signed simply "Chef." It is good made at home, too, to be served with generous amounts of very crisp but tender romaine, escarole, chicory, any sturdy garden leaves:

In spite of its richness, this makes a commendable salad to serve before a light meal of simply broiled chicken or fish, if one clings to the Western habit of eating a "green" salad first . . . and I cannot imagine eating a Green Goddess at any other place on a menu. I suspect that it is not widely known outside of California . . .

A dressing which has never recaptured for me the rich delight of its flavor in my childhood was one of my mother's inventions, I think. We ate it on special occasions, perhaps for birthdays or the first meal to welcome an honored visitor. It was made mostly of whipped cream and chili sauce, and any pickle buff will know that this latter heady concoction has nothing to do with the chili powder used in some Western cooking but is a trusted condiment made in American kitchens of a few generations ago, in quantities unheard of today. It is thicker and rougher in texture than a tomato catsup, and spicier in taste. I suspect that it is one of the things best made in large batches, and few people have either the supplies or the space for it now. Fortunately it can be bought in widemouthed bottles distributed by a reputable pickle provider with some fifty-six other products, and while his cannot match the bite of what I was reared on, it is handy on the shelf.

It seems strange that my mother managed to sneak this into our cuisine, when catsup itself was frowned upon as an expensive and unwholesome frippery by my grandmother . . . but at the risk of rambling a little from this discussion of salads I think I should give Edith's general formula here. I can excuse myself by remarking that her chili sauce adds a surprising fillip to a dull vinaigrette, for a change (this would be unorthodox but acceptable after any meat dish containing tomatoes?), and that it is excellent added to mayonnaise and/or sour cream, to be served with cold poached fish or chilled vegetables.

To make this commendable adjunct to the pantry, one needs three dozen large ripe tomatoes, two dozen red and green peppers, one dozen large white onions, and then three cups of very strong vinegar, one of dark brown sugar, and a scant one of salt! About three teaspoonfuls each of ginger, clove, and cinnamon are tied in a little bag, to keep the sauce bright red in color and not a dark brown. All the vegetables are peeled or seeded according to their needs, and put through a medium-coarse grinder, and then the whole soupy mixture with everything else added to it is boiled slowly for about three hours or until it is thickish, in a huge pot and with a long wooden spoon. (I still use the one from Whittier, and it is by now an indescribably fruity color, somewhere between royal purple and ancient mahogany.)

✆ *Edith's Avocado Cocktail (!)*

1 cup chilli sauce
½ cup mayonnaise, if wished
1 cup whipped cream
4 to 6 large firm avocados
1 cup lemon or lime juice
Shredded lettuce (optional)

Mix the first three ingredients, and chill. Peel and dice the avocados and shake gently in a large bowl with the fruit juice, until well coated. Chill for 2 to 3 hours. Drain. Mix lightly with the dressing, and pile in small chilled bowls or cups, on shredded lettuce if wished.

Of course this sauce is made in the summer, and last year I was startled to realize that there are still pickle flies, even though few people make pickles. They are large clumsy insects which appear mysteriously, at least in rural parts and small towns, when vinegar and spices are being boiled together and are sending out a fine smell. They knock themselves in an awkward angry way against the kitchen screens, now just as they did long ago, and then they disappear completely when the stuff is put into its jars. They are apparently satisfied, and able to exist somewhere until another addict starts his fumey brew. It is almost worth planning to make something like my mother's chili sauce a decade or so from next July, to see if the poor starved things can have survived . . .

And now for the hors d'oeuvre we used to think of as so stylish and special, and which depended for its very life upon my mother's concoction: ✆

I have read a lot of variations of this "cocktail" and its sauce, usually containing crab or lobster or even chicken, but I like Mother's best. It has real innocence.

By now in my life my friends know how I feel about people who cheat when they disclose their prized recipes, and leave out or distort one Secret Ingredient. I sneer at such puny knavery, compassionately at times but still sneering. Of course there are rare cases in which it may be justified, because of professional hazards, and I know of one famous restaurant, strangely enough located in central Nevada, where there is a flat if teasing refusal to tell how a most delicious salad of capellini, served on the buffet before dinner, can be made of cold pasta and still stay light and delicate. I respect such hardheaded caution . . . when I have to! . . . and keep hoping that some fine day my intricate surmises about the recipe will be confirmed by my friends the hosts and guardians. I *think* I know what they do, what their tricks are, but not yet have I succeeded in making more than a reasonable likeness of the peculiar little hors d'oeuvre. I suspect that the capellini is cooked *al dente*, then well rinsed in very cold water, and after thorough draining mixed lightly and sparingly with an herby vinaigrette and a modicum, a mere smidgeon, of sour cream. But . . .

In the same way I tried for several years to decide what gave a friend's plain green salad a special flavor, a kind of nuttiness or should I say nutness? She did not want to tell me, and since I am innately unable to beg for such favors, I went right along trying things that might be the secret: mixtures of nut *oils*, for instance. Finally she wrote to me before she closed her kitchen forever, saying that she felt foolish to have been so coy and that her "secret" was a tiny bit of good curry powder, perhaps one-sixteenth of a teaspoon to a cup of plain oil and vinegar dressing! Sure enough . . . except that hers still tastes better on my mind's tongue.

This is like Freda's secret ingredient, which she was never coy or secretive about and which I often use; it does not have quite the same delicate surprise about it, with me. She made salads of rather tough but delicious little greens from her garden, and just before they were tossed in a bowl with the vinaigrette, she sprinkled them with a few pinches of whole or lightly pounded sesame seeds, which had been toasted. (She kept them on hand in a little jar in the icebox, as do I.) One would hardly accuse a sesame seed (much less curry powder!) of being a secret, especially caught on a leaf of bitey escarole in a layer of oil and vinegar, but such can be the case, and I have proved it. Perhaps it is a question of the *sparing* use of a secret?

Here in America we are inclined to think of "made" salads as rather rich concoctions held together by variations of a thick dressing like mayonnaise, perhaps lightened by the judicious use of finely sliced celery and served on or with or near lettuce leaves, and usually involving chicken, lobster, potatoes . . . There are many kinds of such dishes, which I like to make because they taste fresh and are an interesting change for people who do not see me too often . . . and an agreeable form of monotony for those who do. Such salads can be either raw or cooked, depending on their natures, and delicate or robust depending upon what is to follow them.

One hors d'oeuvre we were always glad to see when we lived with a friend in Aix was her Greek Salad, although why it was called Greek I do not know, since it was not made in the classical way called *à la grecque*. It was raw fresh mushrooms sliced paper thin, and marinated for perhaps an hour in a vinaigrette very strong with fresh herbs. With a good bread crust to catch the last drops of the perfumed sauce, and a glass of cool rosé, it made a fine introduction to a meal, and it still does here in St. Helena, where a fungi-friend often shares his haul with me.

Another raw appetizer we ate in Aix, and which my children found too bitter but I liked very much, was the tiny artichokes which are usually called culls in the fields. They were about the size of a big walnut, and

following the wishes of the two Sicilians who lived with us were served
whole, then split lengthwise by each of us and sprinkled with lemon juice
and dipped in rough salt. We ate one or two
inches of the stem first, and then came to
the firm crisp little heart. In California I seldom see such small fruits or whatever they
are (thistles, perhaps?), except in fancy jars.
Here, though, is an amusing recipe for
cooked artichokes, which I too call Greek,
perhaps in confused honor of my landlady
and her guests. It can be made with the
frozen hearts, and beginning with that it is
so unorthodox as to be almost shocking.
Once prepared and tasted, I believe, it can
be the introduction to a very good menu which might include a kebab,
with a pilaf:

 Greek Artichokes

2 cups or 1 pound package artichoke
hearts
1 scant cup black currants
1 cup dry white wine or vermouth
½ cup vinaigrette
2 dashes tabasco sauce (optional)

Mix all in casserole, cook gently, covered, until
artichokes are tender, and let cool. Drain and chill,
and then drain again before serving.

   This reminds me a little of what is sometimes called a classic California dish but which can be eminently edible no matter where it first
turned up, usually named Celery Victor in the West, surely for some
homesick Italian chef. We used to eat it almost ritually at a good small
restaurant on Geary Street in San Francisco, where of course it was called
Celery Solari. (We went there always on our sprees from Southern California, because the food was limited in choice and carefully prepared, because several waiters loved us and we loved them, and because across the
street were two theaters, so that often Mr. Drew and his family of nephews
and nieces like the Barrymores, and even Trixie Friganza and *once* Tito
Schipa, might be at the next table, eating Celery Solari and eye-catchers
like Baked Alaska.) Here is the basic recipe for the salad, and it is a good

one to use, because it can be prepared well before serving, and the broth from it is a fine base for other stocks and sauces: &

 Celery Victor-Solari-Veneto

> *1 large head of celery*
> *Good broth, chicken or beef*
> *Simple vinaigrette with plenty of coarse*
> *black pepper*
> *Hard-cooked eggs, chopped*
> *Canned fillets of anchovy*
> *Canned pimiento in strips*
> *Coarsely ground black pepper*

Strip celery of outside leaves and split entire head lenthwise into two or four pieces. Simmer until tender in enough strong stock to cover. Let cool in broth. Drain, and arrange in flat casserole. Marinate well in a simple vinaigrette, turning several times. Chill, drain, and serve on platter or salad plates, sprinkled with chopped egg and garnished with crossed anchovies and a strip of pimiento . . . and plenty of coarse pepper.

At the Geary restaurant there were always three or four shelled crab claws, plump and fresh, alongside this cooked section of celery, and the whole thing tasted new and titillating, not heavy. I often prepare celery in this manner, for a salad in winter, and even from the can the sturdy vegetable will respond well to a quick heating and then cooling in a seasoned broth. Cooked thus to serve with other blanched vegetables it is a good thing, on a platter with one or two dressings, but I still think the best way to serve it is alone, flanked by succulent crab claws from the morning's catch . . . fruits of the sea.

There is one more salad I want to tell about, because it is so good and apparently so unexpected. It is definitely Mediterranean in its origins, but I can serve it before a meal from other parts of the gastronomical map. It makes a good hors d'oeuvre, or even a main luncheon dish with plenty of bread and wine and then a commendable cheese and some fruit afterward: &

Almost any good kitchen manual lists hundreds of concoctions, of various edibility and acceptability, under "Salads." These lists should be looked at now and then, if for no other reason than practice in how to repudiate most of them, but many such "made" dishes, especially if served as a single or first course, can be refreshing and delicious.

And I still believe that a tossed green salad should never be presented before the main course of even a simple meal. This is my cold blunt mean statement of fact as Fact represents me, a citizen of the kitchen. I think the position is clear?

ℬ *Une Salade de Provence*

2 large red peppers (or 1 cup canned
*   pimientos)*
2 large green peppers
2 cloves garlic, minced
¾ cup olive oil
1 to 2 cups mushrooms, sliced or button,
*   canned or fresh*
Salt, pepper
½ cup wine vinegar
1 can fillets of anchovy (optional)

Seed and slice peppers. Slowly heat garlic in oil until opaque. Add peppers, stir, and simmer, turning often. When limp, add mushrooms and brown a little on a quicker fire. Season well, add vinegar, and remove from heat. Chill for several hours. Stir before serving, and garnish with crossed anchovy fillets if desired.

Questionable Crumpets and Such

THE SMELL OF GOOD BREAD BAKING, like the sound of lightly flowing water, is indescribable in its evocation of innocence and delight. Inevitably, almost everyone with more than two words in his head or heart will try to use them to say how or why the smell and the sound are beautiful. Some of the worst poems in several languages, for instance, have been written about the ancient fountains of Aix-en-Provence or Rome, and few authors could or would point with pride to any description of the effects upon their souls of the whiff of a hot loaf lying on a kitchen table, without qualifying for dust-jacket blurbs. Suffice it to say, then, that in the truest and least dialectic way, good fresh bread and chuckling fountains are soul food.

Water is being used by modern architects to make happier the people who scurry like organized ants around the bases of monolithic office buildings in great cities. Unless the ants protest, in rare concerted resentment during a water shortage, spindly whitish spouts rise from rectangular basins, usually of black cement, and plash back into the pools colored by cigarette butts and sogged sandwich papers, and above the noise of traffic there is occasionally a tiny crashing sound of water upon water. It is lovely.

In much the same way, canny merchandisers pay home economists to invent formulas for packaged *bread* which, when toasted, will smell almost good, almost like bread. People then pay double prices for it: the process of removing all the nutritive values from the ingredients and adding them again is costly. In the most deliberately edible and expensive brands, nationally distributed of course so that they will taste the same in Minnesota and New Mexico, computerized "values" are so expensive and rare that to compensate for their inclusion the loaves have shrunk to the size of muffins, almost doll-like in comparison with the cheap varieties which boast of their extra length of squeezy-soft slices, designed to build longer and more brittle bones in frailer bodies for the good of the nation.

(Here it is plain that a frustrated poet who has been laughed out of writing about the fountains of Aix, and starved out of active participation in American bread eating, will still be able to combine hunger with words and become bitter and loquacious about at least one of our national calamities!)

As the level of mediocrity grows more firmly established in our minds, so that an increasing percentage of us will accept tasteless and indeed worthless bread as all we can expect, the art of baking has been taken over by artists on one hand, and crackpot health faddists on the other. Fortunately, most of my friends fall into one or both of these loose categories, and unforgettable loaves have been given to me. One was made into a turtle, with currants for eyes, dried then and glazed heavily and mounted on a piece of driftwood. It was to gaze at. Another, from a man who subsisted mainly on nuts and lived in a tree except during the rains, when he used my kitchen for personal and professional warmth, was called Bible Bread, to *eat*. It was as heavy as stone and almost as hard to chew, but very sustaining. It kept well, and was ugly, and its formula is gone with the wind . . . and the rain.

Somewhere in between these culinary extremes are many good breads, for the eye, the nose, and the belly. They have evolved from laboratories as well as man's quirky rebellion against the twisting of Nature. At

Cornell University, not too long ago to have lost importance, a bread was composed which was proved to be completely adequate to support healthy life, if nothing but it and good butter were eaten day in and day out. The researchers found, on the other hand, that animals fed solely on commercial bakery bread could not develop normally, and died young. Most reputable books about baking give recipes for variations of the Cornell or Triple-Rich Bread, but there is one easy trick for any interested cook: for bread, cookies, and cake, add in the bottom of each cup of flour to be used, one tablespoonful of soy flour and one of skim milk powder, and one teaspoonful of wheat germ. As even a beginner will know, this will change the texture and "lightness" somewhat, but certain adjustments can be made, always cheered on by the dream of feeding loved people a bit more of what they need, in nonpill form.

The very term "nonpill" will brighten the eye of a food faddist, no matter how erroneously, but no doubt more good than harm is done, at least in bread, by cooks who demand stone-ground flour, organically grown grains, wild honey. Our national protest, no matter how tiny, against ersatz nourishment, has of course been helped along by even more widespread alarm at our increasing waistlines, and one of the best-selling formulas for the staff of life, to be bought in packaged slices either near-white or near-brown, is distributed from a town conveniently named Hollywood but located in Florida. The connotation is immediate: a lissome starlet, blooming with inner health behind her sticklike façade, thanks not to bright-colored pills but to all she can eat of bread knowingly concocted from whole wheat and flaked or rolled wheat flours, yeast, molasses and caramel, salt and malt and honey, monoglyceride, yeast nutrients, sesame seeds, more flours made from whole rye, oats, soya, gluten, and barley, and then dehydrated powders made by a few more modern miracles from carrots, pumpkins, lettuces, artichokes, celery, cauliflower, parsley, cabbages, and of course iodine-rich kelp. To retard spoilage, which is a sly implication that all the ingredients are "natural," and therefore prone to natural decay, calcium propionate is added, as is the case with even low-caste loaves today, and as a final bow to tradition, water is included, and actually called by name. Plainly such a list of ingredients must guarantee *something* . . . like stardom or slimness or far-out transcendentalistic calm . . .

No matter how peculiar the formula, bread baked at home usually tastes and smells and is better than any I can buy. But I don't bake much, anymore. Even with a freezer and receptive friends handy, I tend to make too much of a good thing, when occasionally I succumb to the culinary rhythms of making bread. I also find the mixing and kneading a tiring process, especially when I am alone. I like to do it with someone else, to spell me. The whole game is an enjoyable and almost hypnotic kind of ballet, often without much talk needed, and the warm room and the primitive ritual lead to serenity.

Lately I have baked with a doctor friend who, to many people, is a real diet crank, a genuine crackpot, because he is unorthodox enough to preach and practice his theory that bad food can abet and often induce disease, while good food can alleviate and as often cure it. This is heinous in some eyes, and he has hung on to his professional rating in the national medical cabala by a thin and sometimes raveled thread, for several decades of spectacular success. He agrees with most other knowledgeable doctors that bread is essential in a healthy man's diet, especially if he leans toward the vegetarian rather than the high-protein side, and he agrees even more so with that wise handsome Victorian, Alexis Soyer, who a hundred or more years ago said that men who live by the sweat of their brow should eat only whole grains. My doctor breaks with Soyer's dictum that refined emasculated flours should be eaten only by "the effeminate and delicate": in certain types of cancer, for instance, he prescribes small amounts of bread rich in the surplus alkalinity rice flour will give it, whereas tuberculous patients will need the opposite aid of acidity.

Any good book about modern baking will give excellent hints about pans and all that, but here are a few which we have worked out for whole-grain flour breads:

> Teflon pans are easy and perhaps best, and need not be oiled.
>
> Pyrex or tin pans are good, and should be lightly oiled. (My friend uses apricot kernel oil, which is a personal and somewhat esoteric whim.)
>
> A 14-inch piece of broom handle, flattened a little at the stirring end, makes a fine mixer for the dough.
>
> The work table should be low, to add weight and strength to the hands in kneading. Very strong thorough kneading gives good texture to the loaves.
>
> Incubation: to encourage rising, turn oven to 350° for 2 to 3 minutes, and then off, and then let pans stand, uncovered, in the warmish oven with its door closed.
>
> When using active dry yeast, mix it immediately upon adding to the warm water, or it will cake.
>
> Old tired bath towels are fine for wrapping the loaves while they cool, unless one wants a hard crust.

And here is a basic bread recipe, which will make two large loaves or several smaller ones: 🚲

It is interesting that one is not at all aware, in this finished bread, of the slightly precious additions like nutmeg and chopped green grass! The baked loaf is delicious. It is also a little overpowering to anyone accus-

tomed to downing five or six slices of
Squeezy-Soft as a pusher for meat-
potatoes-gravy-green-salad-and-Jello. A
couple of slices could have him under the
table . . . and perhaps somewhat slimmer
and livelier, the next day.

Another doctor willing to devote his
life to theories based on the cold fact that
man must eat in order to live was Henry
Lindlahr, and his books about "natural di-
etetics" are still important to any students
of this premise, whether in or out of the
medical profession. He was an important
Scientific Food Nut, in other words, and
may well live down his fleeting fame as the
inventor of Serutan. He did not believe in
fermented doughs, as we know them in
breads like pumpernickel and the West
Coast sourdough, but he did give workable
recipes in his numerous books for sweet
and fruit-filled loaves. Instead of apricot
kernel oil, or plain old Mazola, he used

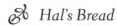 *Hal's Bread*

4 cups unbleached white flour

2 cups pastry whole wheat flour

1 cup brown rice flour

1 cup buckwheat flour

½ cup bran (the husks)

½ cup chopped green wheat grass (or plain
garden grass, alfalfa, parsley . . .)

½ teaspoon cinnamon

¼ teaspoon nutmeg

1 teaspoon dry "Italian herb flavoring"

2 cups warm water

1 cup warm water stirred at once with

2 (or 3) teaspoons active dry yeast

1 cup hot water stirred with

2 teaspoons blackstrap molasses and

1 teaspoon sweet butter or apricot kernel oil

Stir first nine ingredients together, thoroughly. Add 2
cups warm water, the water-yeast mixture, and then the
water-molasses-oil mixture, and stir with strong wooden
spoon or stick until well mixed. Turn out on floured
board or table, and have more flour (unbleached white)
on hand to help kneading and to keep the dough from sticking. Knead firmly and well, moistening the hands
occasionally. The dough will be done when homogeneous and still slightly sticky.

Cut roll of dough into 2 even parts, press into large Teflon or oiled glass or tin bread pans, and rub tops with water
to smooth. Incubate 40 minutes if 2 teaspoons of yeast have been used, 20 to 25 if 3 teaspoons, or until the dough rises
a scant inch above tops of pans. Bake in 350° oven for 45 minutes. The bread is done when it is loose in the pans. Turn
out on bath towel and wrap well to cool.

olive oil, which was rarer than hen's teeth to most of his Midwestern patients. (When I was a child, my grandmother from Ireland by way of Iowa saw to it that every time a new baby was born in the big brass bed upstairs, a two-ounce bottle of the exotic foreign stuff was available, as the Old Testament would recommend, to anoint the navel for a week or so. It was only my father's small double cruet of vinegar and oil, which he brought out when Grandmother was away and we could eat green salads, that made me realize that the delicious smell could be connected with food instead of fresh-laid siblings . . .)

Like my friend, and many other good cooks, Dr. Lindlahr agreed that yeast is the best and most interesting leaven to work with in the world, and that such "risers" as soda, baking powders, and even eggs are hard on some stomachs. He experimented tirelessly before he was satisfied: "We tried certain brands of so-called wheat flour . . . entirely lacking in bran, and, therefore, in the long run . . . entirely unsatisfactory. We then tried graham flour . . . the bread made from it was dry and straw-like in flavor. We found that the common (Bohemian) rye flour . . . suffered from the same disadvantages as the white. The German whole rye . . . tends to sour the contents of the digestive tract. We also tried various whole grain unfermented 'health breads' . . . coarse, unpalatable, tough and lumpy, [causing] detrimental effects on the digestive organs. In short . . . all the popular brands of flour . . . were lacking in some important constituents and were not as palatable and digestible as we desired. We then proceeded to try the golden mean." And here it is, guaranteed to satisfy "all demands as to pleasantness of flavor and perfect digestibility":

As a child of the Twentieth Century (barely), I am ignorant of what a bread mixer is, and as for how to make potato water, the Chicago Food Nut's *Vegetarian Cook Book* does not tell me, in spite of its strongly mid-

Victorian allure, and its 1921 publication date. I can remember that my dyspeptic grandmother drank floods of barley water and rice water, but never potato water, and I cannot find in her own copy of *Common Sense in the Household* a recipe for the last liquid, even under "The Sickroom" or "The Nursery." But in Mrs. Rorer's *Philadelphia Cook Book: A Manual of Home Economics*, 1886, I find what one perhaps needs, to make Health Bread #1: for a potato sponge for Milk Bread, pare two potatoes, put them in a saucepan with a quart of boiling water, and boil until very tender. Put one cup of flour into the bread bowl, pour one cup of the potato liquid into it, and beat quickly. Then mash the potatoes in the rest of the liquid through a collander into this batter, and beat again until smooth. When lukewarm, add the yeast and salt. Mix, cover, and stand in a warm place (72°F.) overnight. And this apparently makes a kind of sponge which the next day is worked into a dough of warm milk and flour. Ho hum.

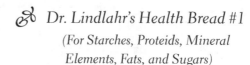

Dr. Lindlahr's Health Bread #1
(For Starches, Proteids, Mineral Elements, Fats, and Sugars)

4 tablespoons olive oil

4 tablespoons honey

1 tablespoon salt

4 cups boiling potato water

1 yeast cake

½ cup warm sweet milk

8 cups stone-ground whole wheat meal

2 cups rye meal

Put olive oil, honey, and salt in bread mixer and pour in the hot potato water. Let stand until lukewarm. Then add yeast dissolved in warm milk, and the whole wheat and rye flours. Mix 10 to 15 minutes, and let rise 6 to 8 hours in warm place. Knead thoroughly, shape into about 4 small loaves, and let rise about 20 minutes. Bake 45 minutes in a moderate oven. (The sponge can also be made from leavened dough which has been kept cold and sweet from the last baking.)

I have never made Dr. Lindlahr's bread, and feel increasingly disinclined to involve myself in trying, but neither have I made French bread, not to mention *croissants*, although I have probably eaten enough of both of them to make a delicious pile as high as the Tour Eiffel. I do know about two women, however, who possess Lindlahrian zeal and en-

ergy and who have triumphantly evolved sensible and trusted ways to turn out perfect (Parisian) loaves and crescents. Like countless readers of these ladies' books, I feel myself on almost a thee-and-thou footing with them, and would be hard put to it not to refer to them by their first names if I met them more than once in person. Julia Child, culinary arbiter of at least this much of our century, has recently worked for five solid months alongside her husband Paul (they are a two-oven family), and after some 200 bakings which used more than 250 pounds of flour (bleached American!), she has set down her perfected method, which she says makes better French bread than many bakers in France are producing. If Julia . . . I mean, if Mrs. Child says that, I believe it. I may never even try the recipe, but I accept it as infallible. The same is true of what Paula Peck brought forth, after trying once a week for eight years to make perfect croissants: I have read her recipe many times, with an almost masochistic interest, feeling quite sure that I might never attempt to follow it but still recognizing it as *right*. Mrs. Peck *is* right, as far as I can see with my jaded and carping eye, and whatever I read about in her guidebook to the art of baking, I can savor unquestioningly with my curious nose, my spiritual palate.

Perhaps I should feel more actively ashamed, that I am so torpid. Why do I sit back and let other people sweat to do my figuring and my inventing? I am a clod. When I bake at all, unless I am goaded by a madman like my doctor, I take shortcuts, and content myself with artless by-blows. *Mea culpa.* But people enjoy them once in a while, and that salves my conscience, at least temporarily and a little.

Technically, of course, biscuits as we know them in America, and muffins and sweetened breads with fruit in them, and coffee cakes and suchlike, are not bread. But they do need flour, and some of them need yeast instead of baking powders and eggs, and they do send out good smells. They take relatively little time, and they do not demand strong arms and hands for kneading. Certainly, however, they could never be thought of as the staff of life! (But bread such as we know it in our supermarkets would be a sorry thing to lean on. Better perhaps to forget it, and use starchy substitutes for an occasional cane or crutch. And thank God there are other good ones, like rice and kasha and dried beans and all the pasta shapes . . .)

I think that the most underhand trick I pull out of my fat bank of them, now and then, is what my family has long called Cheese Crumpets but which are perhaps more correctly a kind of scone. They are dishonest and gratifying, and here is the recipe, which I could well blush about, if it were not dependably pleasing for lunch, for instance, with a green salad and some fruit, fresh or in compote. ℬ

Of course the flavor and quality of the cheese are important in this rich invention. I have never used American types, or cheddar, but a mixture of Romano and Parmesan is good. And the bottoms of the little monsters (Serumpets? Cones? Scrones? Crumpets?) should be delectably high in calories. Like most things made with "mixes" (but why not make them of an honest-to-God biscuit dough?) they should be eaten at once. They do not respond to the stresses of Time, even in a freezer.

Other tricks can be pulled with packaged mixes, for hastily concocted

 *Questionable Crumpets*

½ cup mixed butter and olive oil
1 egg
1 cup rich milk or light cream
2 cups Bisquick
1 cup grated Parmesan or any other
*   light cheese*

Melt butter in olive oil in cookie pan. Add egg and cream to flour mixture, stir lightly, add cheese and mix again lightly. Drop like cookies onto pan, in what should be "more than ample" oil and butter. Bake at 425° about 15 minutes or until golden and done. Serve at once, without more butter. Can be large or small.

✣ Genoa Dill Bread

1 packet dry yeast (or 1 cake compressed)

½ cup warm water or milk

1 cup creamed cottage cheese

2 tablespoons white sugar

½ white onion, minced

    OR

1 heaping tablespoon dehydrated

    minced onion

1 tablespoon sweet butter

2 to 3 teaspoons dried dill weed, rubbed

    fine (seeds if preferred),

    OR

½ cup fresh chopped dill, to taste

1 teaspoon salt

¼ teaspoon soda

1 unbeaten egg

2½ cups (approximately) all-purpose flour

Soften yeast in warm water or milk. Mix cheese, sugar, onion, and butter, and keep warm. Add dill, salt, soda, and egg, the yeast mixture, and then enough flour to make a stiff dough, mixing thoroughly. Let rise in floured or oiled bowl for about an hour or until double in size, in a warm place. Break down, knead lightly, and form into one or two loaves. Bake in well-greased pans at 350 to 375° for 45 to 50 minutes.

pizzas for instance, or *pan bagna*, or any coverings where true biscuit dough would be classically desirable. And even premade boughten biscuits from a tube can be good, in a pinch: separated and dipped in melted butter and some chopped herbs, for instance, or in sugar and spices . . .

One of my sisters often made yeast breads as a sure therapy for the Blues, and leaned on a seductive and fairly quick loaf filled with the Nordic scent and flavor of dill. She tried in California and Nevada gardens to grow the herb, to use it both fresh and dried and in the seeds, but without much luck, and both she and I came back always to the reputable store-bought kind. Her recipe, which she said she clipped from a magazine and then played with, is dependable and good, and I think it would be interesting to make it with fresh or even dried parsley, chives, and why not tarragon, to eat on a picnic with cold roasted chicken? ✣

This bread is worth some slight bother, nothing compared to a real one's, and is delicious for as long as it lasts, warm, cold, or toasted.

Almost any honest bread makes good

toast, and can be used to the last scrap and crumb. It is essential for elegant titbits like the ones served for tea in novels and even real life now and then . . . rings of delicate white bread, always at least a day old, spread with sweet butter and cinnamon and sugar, or chopped watercress.

Probably the most improbable of all these tea-bites remembered from my childhood, but served cold and never toasted, were the nasturtium-leaf sandwiches at Mrs. Thayer's ranch, north of ours. Usually I played outside there, pretty much like a wild Indian, but now and then I would be invited with my mother to drink tea in the dim parlor . . . probably to learn a few manners, by which both ladies set commendable store. The little white morsels were almost as thin as the *croque-monsieurs* at the old Palace, probably put under a weight once made, and it seems that the tender leaves that lay between the blankets of sweet butter and fine white bread should be gathered with the dew on them. Ah, yes.

Most sandwiches are more direct. Some people feel that the Fourth Earl who named them should be garroted or roasted whole or perhaps drawn and quartered, mainly because of what has happened to a piece of hot meat between two slices of bread since he slid into notorious fame, probably at the gaming table where a quick snack was indicated, in 1792 or before. I hold with the general suspicion about such hurried and cursory feedings, whether in a London Club or a corner drugstore, since I myself have had to subsist on them, when caught unprepared in small towns from Maine to California, not to mention Nevada, Illinois, Mississippi . . . They can be indescribably bad. They can also, as any practical person knows, be the true opposite, given the right ingredients and the right time and place. Picnics can be right. So can a warm living room, and so can a small cold French railroad station at dawn, if one reaches down in the steamy gassy air toward a little buffet wagon trundling along the quay, and brings up a sandwich made of a fresh long roll with ham dangling out of it and good butter to hold it together.

Our family has combined the last two elements of protected hearth-side and touristic nostalgia to invent a Railroad Sandwich which, we feel with smug modesty, is perfection. The recipe would be almost scandalous to print in proper form, involving as it does certain elements of live human flesh, but I can sketch a commendable outline, I hope. For one Railroad Sandwich, always referred to by its full name with some reverence, buy a loaf of the best procurable "French" bread at least eighteen inches long to serve perhaps six people. Have on hand at least a half pound of sweet butter, not too cold to spread, and an equally generous pound or so of the highest quality of sliced boiled ham. A pot of mustard of the Dijon type is indicated to add an optional fillip. Slice the loaf from end to end in two solid pieces, and then carefully remove all you can of the inner crumbs. *All!* Spread the two hollow shells generously with butter, and with judicious smears of mustard if desired. Lay upon the lower half of the loaf plenty of ham slices, overlapping thickly. Tuck them in a little at the edges, but not too neatly: a fringe is picturesque to some people, and pleasantly reminiscent; to my family it is essential. Put the two halves firmly together, and wrap them loosely in plastic or foil or wax paper, and then a clean towel. Then, and this is the Secret Ingredient, call upon a serene onlooker (a broad or at least positive beam adds to the quick results, and here I do not refer to a facial grimace but to what in other dialects is called a behind-*derrière*-bum-ass-seat-etc.), to sit gently but firmly upon this loaf for at least twenty minutes. One of the best of our sitters over some twenty years of assistance was Bonnie Prince Charlie Newton, built like a blade of grass during those useful and far-gone years, but with

a curiously potent electricity between his little beam and the loaf, almost
like infrared cookery. He could make the noble sandwich flat without
squirming on it, and melt the butter and marry it to the mustard and the
crisp shattered crusts, better than anybody. Even without this charmer,
though, a Railroad can be a fine thing, cut upon rescue into thick oblique
slices and given the esoteric ingredients: first a long loaf of French bread,
then . . . then . . .

Of course it is usually possible to fake edible sandwiches from supermarket supplies, especially if one can count on animal hunger to dull per-
ception of the cheating, but there is nothing like good bread, to begin
with. It should be of firm texture, and at least a day out of the oven in the
presliced stuff we are growing used to. The filling should be of good quality, and should be spread or laid right to the sides of the foundation, and
even spill over a little if feasible, rather than lie lumpishly in the middle.
Sometimes sandwiches are good made with mayonnaise instead of butter,
with chicken for instance . . . and here I mean real mayonnaise, although
I have often settled for the boughten kind in jars, and some people insist
they prefer it. Common sense is called for, always: lettuce will wilt and be
slippery if it waits too long, and many people despise it with bread; jam
will make everything stained and soggy unless it is curbed by ample butter spread evenly on both slices . . .

The first day I went to a rural school, when I was almost eleven, my
bewildered mother packed a lunch for me. It was what the society editor
of the *News* would call "a dainty collation," and it cost me about two
weeks of trust and acceptance from my bucolic companions. The whole
thing was a humiliating disaster, decades beyond them in forgiveness and
generosity: a silver knife for spreading the neat packet of bread slices; two

small screw-top jars which had once held samples of some kind of face cream, now filled with mayonnaise and blackberry jam; salt and pepper in little folds of wax paper which spilled at once onto my skirt; a ripe sliced tomato which followed them into my lap and raised a good laugh from my fascinated mates as they downed their thick pieces of bread with a slab of last night's pot roast stuck between them. Marjie Thayer, who had been my ally for several years before we moved to the ranch next to hers, acted with therapeutic brutality and compassion and cracked me on the head with the hard-boiled egg in its shell which rolled out last. She knew just the strategic spot of tenderness, to make me run fast for the Girls' toilet, streaming with tears I must hide, and other juices. My poor mother was never told . . . but as far as I can remember, she never packed a school lunch again.

It is fun, though, in a certain amount of privacy, to make sandwiches as the appetite and the larder dictate, and often I set up a kind of buffet of two or three good breads and a few cheeses and sliced meats and so on, with bowls of mayonnaise and butter, generous knives, a few tempters like pickles and olives, and jams for the *bonne bouche*. And I know of one restaurant which in a few years has become famous on the highway between San Francisco and Sacramento, primarily because of the little loaves of good bread it serves, hot and fresh, one to a person on a generous cutting board, with another board loaded with foods to play with to make at least a dozen child-sized sandwiches, and above all with a knife worthy of the game. It is fun. It is relaxing. The stopping place has grown into an enclave of Disneyland-type entertainment, but still in dark corners there are Senators and schoolteachers and even parsons slicing seriously at their own small loaves, fabricating tangible dreams in the shape of four-bite morsels.

The formula for this amusing little bread has often been printed, and it is so basic and simple that I think it should go here too:

The first time I read this homely receipt, it was in an article written by one of the daughters-in-law of the legendary California family now so eminently busy and successful, and she said flatly, "Grandma's bread recipe has never before been given to anyone." Then she made a classic and tricky and even ambiguous remark: "The secret is yours." If it is true that five great artists will paint the same model in five different ways at the same time, so it is a somewhat more painful fact that five bakers, given this simple plan for making bread, will turn out five (or in this case twenty) different loaves. The secret . . . but which one? Grandma is chuckling.

It is plain by now, in this candid chronicle, that when I was a little girl in Whittier, we submitted to a series of cooks. My mother had been raised in Iowa, partly at least, in the days when "hired girls" were

Nut Tree Bread

1 cup lukewarm water
1½ tablespoons sugar
1 cake compressed yeast (or 1 envelope granular)
3 cups (about) sifted all-purpose flour
1½ teaspoons salt

Place water in warmed mixing bowl, add sugar and yeast, and stir until dissolved. Add half the flour, and the salt, and beat hard with a spoon or stick for about 2 minutes. Add rest of flour gradually, with the hands, to make a springy smooth ball of dough (about 5 minutes). Cover with towel and let stand in warm place until doubled in bulk (45 minutes). Flatten dough on oiled board, shape into four little loaves, and put into greased pans about 5 x 2½ x 1½ inches. Cover again, and let rise in warm place until tripled. Then bake at 400° for about 20 minutes, or until loaves are free from sides of pans. Turn out on rack, and cool.

dime-a-dozen, mostly from Sweden, eager to learn to speak American and deft with plain and familiar edibles. In California Mother faced new language hazards, and could not accustom herself to the hissing male college students who would later become Japanese admirals. In self-protection, perhaps, she hired some strange female characters, most of

them with motherly-looking Irish bosoms and hearts of solid pig iron. One of them I can remember only because she actually *made bread,* instead of our getting excellent supplies from one or sometimes two bakeries in the little town, depending upon which was the best advertiser in the *News*. And when I was between about five and ten, and when Grandmother was away helping God run her local, national, and celestial church, we would eat rare grilled steak and *Blotters*, made from good bread . . . and whether or not the current cook had just flounced away. Of course there were always a few other forbidden fruits on the table, like salad in a big bowl with "French" dressing, and red wine in stemmed glasses, but it was the *Blotters* that we lived for.

A recipe for them, like one for Railroad Sandwiches, is hard to make precise. First, though, the bread must be good, honest, slightly stale, cut fairly thickly, and not crumbly but not easily sogged and bogged. The steak must be juicy, so that its elixirs follow the knife down each quick cut, and then flow along the grooved platter to the well at one end. Our steak was always on an oak board fashioned correctly with the grooves and well of course, and it was as hot as the meat, so that the juices never turned chilly. At a certain moment, after the children had eaten nicely of their cut-up meat and vegetables, Father would lift his carving knife and fork in a certain way. Mother would nod yes. He would lay one slice of the bread from its battered silver plate into the well, and then judiciously turn it over to catch exactly the second half of the meat juice, and then put it back onto the plank and cut it neatly into two halves, one for my little sister and one for me, or in quarters if there were more of us. Perhaps he and Mother then made one for themselves? I do not remember anything past my own heady pungent enjoyment. It seems now to me that new life coursed through my small healthy body. And I know that such a moment is almost impossible to recapture physically, for there is seldom such good bread as we could still eat then, bakery-bought or kitchen-made by a passing doxy, and to my own taste meat itself is not as good. Mostly, I suppose, I miss some of that present company. *Où sont les buvards d'antan?* Where, in my local dialect, are the Blotters of yesteryear?

I am not sure that pancakes and waffles count as a form of bread, but since I believe, with the full support of my gastric processes, that one starch is enough for any meal, I think they are handy to know about, even if I seldom make them anymore. I really do not like the puffy thick kind so often served in American coffee shops and lunch wagons and airports, which are apparently savored by millions of us, if the sales of packaged mixes for them are a fair indication. I think they are dreadful. My paternal and Yankee grandmother, as opposed (as she often was) to my mother's Irish mother, used to make thin griddlecakes of home-grown buckwheat flour, and serve them with melted butter and wild sage comb honey from the hives Grandfather put up in the hills. It was a heady meal, but if I ate it now I might sink like a stone, for several hours at least.

I like the small slightly thick cakes the Swedes make in a *plett* pan, but I never had any luck with them, perhaps because I was not more than clinically eager to succeed, and used new pans. Once in a garden in Drottningholm I ate a stack of about five of them with crushed fresh strawberries between each layer and floating all around. Then I ate another stack, and then I divided one with my hostess, surely not from hunger but because I knew that I would never eat such a wonderful thing again.

I prefer very thin pancakes, like the French crêpes, and I think a little brandy is good in the batter. These cakes are easy to make, and will keep for a few hours, to be played with for any part of a meal, from *canelloni* to *suzette*. And the best recipe for waffles I have ever read or used, and I have

৶ Gigi's Waffles

2 eggs
1 cup rich cream
1 cup well-sifted flour
⅛ cup melted butter

Separate eggs, beat whites, and in larger bowl beat
yolks hard for at least 5 minutes. Add cream and
flour alternately, beating all the time. Then add
butter, beat more, and fold in the egg whites.

৶ Elsa's Banana Bread

1 cup dark brown sugar, pressed firmly
       to measure
½ cup soft butter
2 eggs
½ cup commercial sour cream
3 large ripe bananas, mashed
1 teaspoon soda
2 cups flour, all-purpose or whole wheat
1 cup chopped nuts (optional)

Cream sugar and butter, beat in eggs and sour
cream, and add mashed bananas. Sift soda twice
with flour, and stir slowly into bowl. Fold in nuts if
wished. Bake in slow oven (325°) for about 1½
hours, in greased bread pans, and let cool in them.
Turn out.

used it often with supreme confidence, is
called: ৶

Nothing could be simpler, surely! Gigi's
original directions said, ". . . beat until your
arm is numb." She is a highly dignified dowager by now, but I am sure she will not mind
my adding that she crossed out, on my treasured file card, "Keep beating hell out of everything . . ."

As for sweetened breads, I can and do
sometimes make them, usually with an egg
and baking powder riser rather than yeast,
which I am temporarily at odds with but know
I'll return to at a riper age. It is easy to tip some
extra shortening and more sugar and perhaps a
bit of leftover marmalade into a biscuit batter,
and turn out a commendable loaf to slice for
breakfast or tea. It smells good in the baking,
too. Perhaps the favorite one when my family
fattened on such nibbles was: ৶

This moist cake-bread keeps well, and even
to middle-aged and elderly people who have
lost their first happiness with the flavor of bananas, Elsa's invention is a good one. And
there are many others, made with orange and
lemon peels, juices, jams . . . even with
chopped apples, and of course dates and figs
and raisins, and the ubiquitous nuts. I would

not care if I were condemned to exile from them, for almost any reason, but I am glad that I can occasionally savor them mentally.

Muffins are good, not too sweet, not too crumbly, made from any of such trusted mixtures, and meant wisely to be eaten warm and at once, from the oven. Fresh fruits, rolled first in a little flour and sugar, are like delicious nuggets in them, and not only the familiar blueberries but canned peaches and pears cut into niblets are a pleasant change. I make such little breads for innocent palates. I think of the ancient English rhyme, so innately full of satisfaction:

> To market, to market,
> To buy a plum bun!
> Home again, home again!
> Market is done.

When I was little, it was a great treat to have popovers for lunch, and if we had been either good or downright exemplary, we were allowed to nip off the top of one of the tiny hollow soufflés, which is what they amount to, and fill the mysterious cavity with butter and strawberry jam, then re-cap it, and after a short wait eat the whole wild mess with a spoon. It was worth living for. So are popovers themselves, to many people, and now and then somebody will die for them. I know of a noted private baker, who promised to bring a big hot batch for breakfast one Sunday morning, and disappeared completely! He telephoned that he was on his way. He never came. His friends waited, and finally checked with everyone who might possibly have seen him carrying his big box of hot tiny balloons through the streets, but never again was he heard of. Was he robbed, and then carted off? He left no widow, no known children, and his apartment except for a neat pile of popover pans was empty. He and his gift were gone. *Misterio de las pampas! Mystère des mystères!* . . .

There is a kitchen reliable which is neither fish nor fowl, neither muffin nor sandwich, but a *loaf*. It is oddly quaint and old-fashioned, and fun to serve now and then. One of them, which like all proper sandwiches should be wrapped tightly to let sit (but not to be sat upon!), is: ℰ

One of the nobler ancestors of this concoction is a baked Oyster Loaf. It interests me, in retrospect, that I can evoke such succulent memories of the ones my mother reported eating voluptuously in boarding school, in "secret midnight feasts," since never did she cause one to be served forth to her children! I have had to go far afield to find a recipe that would satisfy my first burning dreams of such a dish, and I feel safe in saying that so far my evocation, at least, remains virgin. Not long ago, for instance, I ate a most delicious hot crisp redolent artful Oyster Loaf, and I enjoyed it clinically as well as gastronomically, especially since it was made by a true kitchen-friend. But it had eggplant in it. It was not quite right, quite pure enough, for my conditioned but hungry palate. I keep reading recipes . . .

There seem to be two schools of procedure, in making a true Oyster Loaf. Either you put the delicately cooked oysters with a lot of crumbs and butter and Béchamel sauce into the previously prepared belly of a crusty loaf, or you coat them with egg and crumbs and so on and deep-fry

ℰ A Toasted Cheese Loaf

2 cups grated nippy cheese
½ cup minced fresh herbs (parsley,
*   scallions, basil, etc.)*
    OR
¼ cup dried mixed herbs soaked in ½ cup
*   dry vermouth or white wine*
2 to 3 cloves garlic, finely minced or
*   mashed*
Juice of one lemon
Salt, fresh black pepper
Equal parts butter, olive oil, to make
*   spreadable paste*

Mix all well together. Cut long crisp French loaf down middle, end to end. Then slash into 1-inch slices, but not through. Spread the paste thickly on the halves, wrap well, and let stand at least two hours. Unwrap and heat slowly. When all is melted, broil for 3 minutes or until bubbling, and serve at once.

them and then put them quickly into the coffin, as such a hollowed shell
was called in Olde Englande. The lid is fastened down, perhaps after a

little thick cream is poured in. The whole is
baked, and then, no matter how it has been
filled, is whipped as hot as possible to the
table . . . or wrapped cannily to take on a
picnic or to a hungry friend. But I should
live so long, which I have already done, as
to see this properly produced! My mother's
ghost grows restless.

    Meanwhile, there are hot tarts. They are
not too far removed in character from such a
dream. I call them tarts because they are
made in pie tins but have no upper crust. If
they did, they would be pies, I think, and I
have eaten and even made many a good one
of meats or fruits, usually following English
recipes. But I like to make tarts too, with rich
bottom crusts and fillings of mushrooms,
olives, little shrimps, onions, cheese . . .
They are fine for an easygoing supper party,
with drinks and/or free-flowing simple

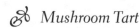 *Mushroom Tart*

1 thick half-baked pie shell
1 pound small mushrooms or sliced
      mushrooms (fresh if possible)
¼ pound butter
1 scant cup chopped parsley
4 scallions, finely sliced
1 cup sour cream
1 tablespoon Worcestershire sauce
2 or 3 eggs
Salt, pepper to taste

*Have pastry shell ready, and cooled. Brown
mushrooms in butter. Add herbs and scallions, stir
until limp, and let cool. Beat cream, sauce, and eggs
together, mix lightly with other ingredients, and pour
into shell. Pat smooth. Bake 25 minutes at 400°, or
until knife slid into center comes out clean. Serve
warm . . . or cold, second best but delicious.*

wines. They are fine for luncheons too . . . and even picnics. They are easy
to cut and serve. If the crusts are well-baked first (they can be half baked
and frozen . . .), they are convenient to fill quickly with any hot thick mixture one wishes, and then serve at table. For making ahead of time,
though, and to eat warm or cool or hot, they are best baked with their fillings in them, based on a mild unsweetened custard, and here is a good
recipe, stepchild of the classical Quiche Lorraine perhaps: &

A good variation is to use two cups of fresh cooked shrimps to one of sliced or tiny mushrooms. Another is of shrimps and chopped or sliced green olives. I feel sure chopped leftover chicken would be good . . . or fish . . . or why not anchovy fillets laid on the tart shell and then covered with an herby or even cheesy custard? A quick look into any good kitchen manual would lead on and on. . . . All that is needed is a pie shell and a custard!

This is true also of making a *pan bagna*, or pizza, or *pissaladière*, or *anchoyade*: once one has bowed with respect to the first classical requisite of some decent crust, invention can take command. All these heady things are nothing but pieces of dry dough! I myself seem to have grown past most reservations about such ancient formulas, always with proper humility of course, and I do not hesitate to cheat outrageously with something like the following brashly named: ॐ

This is so patently a shortcut that it does not deserve any kind of apology. It can be very good indeed. The secret, I think, is the two bakings: the pizza does not become soggy. It will stand quick reheating, and can be frozen for a reasonable time. Some people prefer it when I have peeled, chopped,

ॐ Pizza Presto

2 cups Bisquick
   AND
⅔ cup water
   OR
1 measure biscuit dough
½ cup olive oil
1 can anchovy fillets
Thinly sliced ripe tomatoes
Thin rings of green pepper
Finely chopped fresh herbs and parsley
Thinly sliced mild onions
Sliced green or black olives
Crumbled ricotta, mozzarella, any
    mild cheese
Etc., etc.

Mix Bisquick lightly with water, or make one measure of biscuit dough. Oil one large cookie pan or two cake or pie pans generously, and pat out dough with oily hands to cover the bottoms thinly and evenly. Bake 10 minutes at 450°.

Sprinkle liberally with more olive oil, the oil from the anchovies, and the rest of the ingredients. Bake 10 to 20 more minutes. Cut into wedges or squares, and serve.

and drained the tomatoes, but I think it tastes more "honest," in its own perverted and corrupt way, if the fresh whole slices are put first on the dough with the anchovies, and then covered with whatever is at hand. The cheese of course comes last, to hold down the whole wild mish-mash. I like a couple of cloves of finely minced garlic in with the scatter of herbs and olives and suchlike. In other words, nothing much can go wrong with this flouting of so timeless a staple as a slab of dough baked with olive oil and herbs.

I should probably be more hesitant than I am about pinning gastronomically traumatic experiences in my own life upon my grandmother, the one with the Nervous Stomach, but I do so with an increasing gratitude for the wonderful comparisons she unwittingly forced me to draw. I have fine memories of the Blotters we ate when she was away (they would have been considered too unmannerly, too rich, and above all too indulgent of our animal natures . . .), and when I look back to one of the best plain pieces of baked starch I ever ate, I immediately remember both it and the worst, and once more the worst was a favorite of my dam's. She called it Steamed Crackers, and considered it a panacea for an upset digestive system, whether from fever, disease, or the megrims. Perhaps it was not as bad when she made it or called for it as it would be today, for I feel sure we drank better water and bought better soda crackers fifty years ago than now. Even so, the memory of it turns my stomach one small queasy turn, and only clinical interest has made me search out a firm recipe to salve my unfilial conscience. I finally did find it, in Grandmother's own copy of Marion Harland's *Common Sense in the Household*. It is of course in the section called "The Sickroom," which was an important part of every decent culinary guide in the days when almost as many people were cured and killed by the cook as by twentieth-century miracle drugs.

The best thing about this recipe is its name, which was too "foreign" for Grandmother: ℬ

ℬ *"Panada*

"6 Boston crackers, split.
2 tablespoonfuls white sugar.
A good pinch of salt, and a little nutmeg.
Enough boiling water to cover them well.

"Split the crackers, and pile in a bowl in layers, salt and sugar scattered among them. Cover with boiling water and set on the hearth, with a close top covering the bowl, for at least one hour. The crackers should be almost clear and soft as jelly, but not broken.

　"Eat from the bowl, with more sugar sprinkled on it if you wish. If properly made, this panada is very nice."

Yes, I remember: it was that jellylike texture that made me gag . . .

And to relieve such a minutely odious condition, there is always the memory of a large generous woman who, every summer afternoon when I was about sixteen to nineteen, brought down to the Cove in Laguna, where we swam and sunned ourselves, a basket of hot wheels of Swedish rye-crisp.

"We" were a strange crew of cautiously daring adolescents and predacious admirers who might now be called pre-jet-set. We lived apart, or thought we did. Most of us were unaware of this state, and its ambiguity. We swam, talked, played card games in the sand. The beach was ours, we believed without question, and so were the ocean and the sun. There was surprising sexual disinterest. It was stylish to be supple and tanned, because Gertrude Lawrence was that way . . . We maintained a good direct supply of carnal wishes, being young and healthy, and probably our goddess was that large wonderful woman who every afternoon stood at the top of the Cove cliff and hollered for one of her numerous sons to come and get it, get the warm full basket.

Her method, I learned later, was to paint rounds of the flat hard bread with a mixture of half olive oil and half butter, let them heat well in a mild oven, salt them, and then wrap them in a clean bath towel for the trip to the Cove. And what pure pleasure it was for us, to swim and frolic like minor dolphins and cope with the tricky tides, and then pant onto the sand and eat a fragment of this unquestioned offering to our youth! Salt water ran down our faces, and tasted good on the crisp pungent hard-tack. It made for a fine moment, every day at four . . . for a while . . .

ℰℓ | A Plethora of Puddings

WHO WAS GEORGIE-PORGIE? According to Mother Goose as well as the Oxford Press, he was perhaps Charles II of England, a regally licentious character of the seventeenth century who kissed the girls and made them cry and then ran away when other boys arrived for the same purpose. Charles was a pleasure-loving and generally immoral fellow, somewhat affectionately referred to as Old Rowley, and Georgie-Porgie may first have been called Rowley-Powley in a typically roundabout British way of royal mockery, and that in turn may have given a roly-poly pudding its name, or vice versa, and all in all it is easy to think of the nursery familiar as a porkish (Georgie-Porkie?) delinquent, thick and pallid and slack-lipped, not attractive in spite of his amorous activities. According to most illustrations, he escaped with a sweet pudding under one arm and a large meat pie on the other. I cannot believe that his chosen diet did much to augment his sexual prowess: even reading the recipes of his probable times brings on a sympathetic lethargy.

And I have news for Georgie, aside from my bilious scoffing at his general antics: there are cakes and cookies and fritters and jellies and a thousand other sweet things worth stealing, perhaps not as easy to run with, but potentially dainty and delicious, and even refreshing. If he had preferred a bland and very British Trifle, for instance, to an equally ethnic Hunter's Pudding ("Tie firmly in a cloth, and boil for six hours at the least, or seven or eight would be still better," says one Victorian manual, not too long after his time), he might have had a little more trouble outrunning the other boys, but he himself would have been a less soggy swain.

A trifle can be a pretty thing, and it needs a pretty dish, one with a stem. I have one which is properly a Swedish vase, standing about eighteen inches tall, with fluted edges, veins of color in the glass, and other flighty and endearing qualities. It is predestined, once or twice a year but most often around Christmas, to hold a monumental chilled pudding made from sponge cake, macaroons, jam, brandy or whatever liquor seems indicated, custards, whipped cream. All this is light and fanciful, not what one friend boasts of turning out infallibly, a bulletproof dessert.

How I prefer to cope with this occasional sweet debauchery would horrify a purist, but perhaps that is good too, occasionally? Since I usually feel a trifle coming on around the winter holidays, I splurge on cans of the best possible peaches, apricots, plums, cherries, mandarin sections. If the pudding is to remain innocent I simply drain them. Otherwise I drain and then marinate them separately in a good liquor, usually kirschwasser or brandy. Somebody in the family with a steady hand and a peaceable disposition then lines the almost transparent Swedish bowl with the beautiful fruits, whose colors take on stained-glass patterns, heady or pure. I eschew the crumbled macaroons and slices of sponge cake demanded classically, and instead serve fragile unassertive little *biscuits* alongside, things like *langues de chat* or small unsugared sugar cookies.

Into the fruit-lined bowl I pile a thick English or French pastry cream (*crème anglaise*), which has been allowed to set and then has had folded into it generous amounts of either sour cream or whipped sweet cream, flavored to taste. More of the cream can be built smoothly over the dome, and then that dome itself is a field day for local artists, as long as they work fast and delicately. Our trifles have been ornamented with every-

thing from slices of hazelnut sticking out like spines between rows of brandied raisins, to animals carved from peach halves, to slivered ginger with a Japanese midget's parasol at the top. Mrs. Beeton wrote in 1861 that a trifle may be "garnished with strips of bright currant jelly, crystallized sweetmeats, or flowers; small coloured comfits are sometimes used for the purpose . . . but they are now considered rather old-fashioned." This is probably fortunate for modern teeth: coming upon a hard little comfit, no matter what its color, could be as potentially disastrous in a suave pudding as biting down on a large pearl in an oyster stew.

In England the correctly named *dessert* at the end of a meal consists of fruits and nuts. It does in France too, with cheeses and sometimes a sweet concoction which formerly would have preceded the last course. In America a dessert means a pie or pudding, or a plain or fancy cake with something like ice cream, or cookies or fritters. Occasionally fruits are served, but in general they are cut up or cooked or otherwise disguised, and are seldom presented in their natural state. I have yet to meet a handful of homegrown compatriots of any age or sex who could or would contend with an unpeeled orange or banana at table, or even a ripe peach or pear, and come off the winner. We are raised on variations of the fruit cup, which to many Western diners is often served at the beginning rather than the end of important meetings of the luncheon clubs and other conclaves. I can and sometimes do join foreign critics of this national peculiarity, but it is enough to state here that it is too bad, both colloquially and literally.

We are lucky in the United States, though, that the mid-Victorian slant to our native cooking has come into focus with the passing of our grandmothers' kitchen habits, at least in regard to what is still considered in England to be a true pudding. If we ended every main meal with one, we would be as liverish as we would if we drank French-style or Italian coffee from morning until night instead of our own comparatively watery brew. We have been beneficently influenced by the Continent in our general insistence upon ending dinner with a sweet something, and the typical English pudding, wrapped like a solid cabbage in cloth and then boiled or steamed for a long time, finally to be served with one kind of sauce or another, is almost unknown in America, at least since the turn of the last century.

Until then, all commercial cooking guides were full of hideous recipes for them. By now, one of our few reminders of this heartier age is the traditional Christmas treat, which very few people bother to make in its old way, thank God. Mrs. Beeton publishes perhaps the most merciful version of it, called Baroness, a recipe "kindly given [to the family of the editress] by a lady who bore the title here prefixed to it," and even in 1861 this was a guarantee of quality. A mixture of suet, raisins, flour, milk, and salt is duly chopped, bruised, and blended, and tied in a cloth which has been wrung out in boiling water and then floured. It must then be submerged and boiled "without ceasing, four and one-half hours." Mrs. Beeton, after stating that the results cannot be too highly recommended, adds, "Nothing is of greater consequence . . . than attention to the time of boiling, which should never be for *less* than that mentioned."

This is a typical rich pudding of the last two or three centuries in England, and perforce in America before much later, and according to those dubious customs and especially the dictates of Francatelli, the Queen's Chief Cook, ". . . when done, dish it up with a German custard-sauce spread over it."

In the Yankee amalgam of any such gastric hazard, well proved in Marion Harland's *Common Sense*, puddings were an important part of dining, but there was a new feeling of caution about their potential sogginess, especially as the climax of noon dinner; at the end of a recipe for Huckleberry Pudding made with yeast, Mrs. Harland says, "This will be found lighter and more wholesome than baked pastry." She then gives many formulas for the latter, all made with thick lardy crusts well stuffed with everything from blackberries to orange marmalade . . . American versions of the old British roly-poly!

There was a pudding mold at home, dutifully transported from the Whittier house to the Ranch after uncharted family wanderings, but as far as I can remember it was never used . . . one happy result of Grandmother's adamant stand against most sauces and seasonings as unseemly fripperies. It was a mysterious and rather handsome metal thing, with a bottom that seemed to buckle onto the fat ridged and dimpled top. It would have made a fine toy in the sandbox, but was sacrosanct because every house should have one somewhere in the kitchen. As far as I know, it receded farther and farther into the cupboard, and finally went down with the house, in front of the bulldozers after my father died and we turned that part of the Ranch into a children's park.

Two or three times in my youngest life I remember eating, with some pomp, a Treacle Shape at Aunt Gwen's. (She lived next door to us in Whittier, but several thousand miles away culturally.) I took a polite but restrainedly dim view of it, and can recall it only as a dank brown lump. My aunt's compatriot Mrs. Beeton wrote of one, "We have inserted this pudding, being economical, and a favorite one with children: it is, of course, only suitable for a nursery, or very plain family dinner." Such a compromise with patriotism and genteel poverty was correct in every way for Aunt Gwen, who had been swung through the New Zealand brush before she was a week old, with her missionary-doctor mother in a ham-

mock behind her in the packtrain of aborigines. After some fifteen years
of this peculiar introduction to British mores, my aunt (who was not in
any way related to us except by love) was shipped to a miserable school
run for dependents of the Anglican Church in Liverpool or thereabouts,
where she developed a protective shell of chauvinistic loyalty to exactly
the culture best expressed by Isabella Beeton. By the time the magnifi-
cent Gwendolyn, fortunately built like the Nike of Samothrace, came
into my life when I was barely four, her delayed sense of Empire had left
her with a sort of Puddlian-Tribal accent, thick enough to slice with a
spade (in which she read to us lengthily from *Uncle Remus*, my strange
introduction to the "Southern drawl" . . .), and a dutiful dependence
upon things like mint sauce, pickled beets, and a mercifully rare gesture
named Treacle Shape. She also knew, thanks to her earlier training or
lack of it, how to grill kelp leaves as well as marshmallows and wienies on
the beach; how to bake eggs in hot ashes, and potatoes in hot coals; how
to skin an eel and stare down a rattlesnake; how to gather mussels and
steam them in a five-gallon oil can with one little vent cut at the right
place with a pocketknife. She *also* knew how to make fried egg sandwiches that would keep a Foreign Legionnaire going for a week. She was
a wonder, except for those puddings.

It is a quick and basically logical jump from the steamer to the oven,
and we make dozens and perhaps thousands of so-called puddings in
America: *rice*, for instance. Most people like it best with a lot of raisins in
it, if they can face it to begin with. It is perhaps meant for the nursery, as
Mrs. Beeton stated about her own monstrosity, but that is where we
should all return now and then, to simplify ourselves.

The first such combination of soaked or cooked grain and seasonings
was, at least in Anglo-Saxon culture, called frumenty, and it is older than

England. It is mildly hysterical to read about its regional preparations, but the fact remains that it can be a good dish, even when made with some such packaged modern thing as "kosher groats." To do it right (and to do right by it!), one carries wheat to the village mill and has it cracked a little. Then, in Somersetshire for example, one stops by the smithy and lays the grain upon the hot anvil to add to its flavor. It is then creed. (That means stewed.) When it is soft, it is drained and mixed with milk or cream, raisins and currants, honey, cinnamon, a little nutmeg. It is cooked some more, but "not too much."

If this recipe sounds vague, others can be consulted, like this one from a manuscript written about 1399: "Take clene qwete and bray hit wele in a mortar that the holles gone all of . . ." And so forth and of course! And what one gets is a sweet nourishing dish, warm or cold, perhaps flavored with rare saffron and thickened, at the end, with beaten egg yolks. It would be called a *potage de frumenty*, thanks to the refining influences of William the Conqueror, whose sissified Normans changed several of the names of Britain, in and out of the kitchen.

If one leans more toward the stark Scottish than the bastardized cuisine, here is what sowans is or are: a fermented mixture of sids (and sids are the inner husks of the oat grain) and warm water which before it has rotted and bubbled along for a few days is of course called a serf. Finally it is strained. The sids are thrown away, after having been squeezed and pressed with native thrift to extract all the sediment in them. This sediment after a day or two will sink to the bottom, and then it is of course known as woans, and the liquid is logically called swats. As wished for, which according to English historians used to be very often in Scotland, the sediment is thinned with water, salted, and boiled until it thickens. It is served in bowls, with milk in a pitcher to thin it further. Its effect, which

seems to have been more direct than its directions, is described for seekers
of gastronomical clarity by Robert Burns:

> *Till buttered son's wi' fragrant lunt*
> *Set a' their gabs a'steerin',*
> *Syne wi' a social glass o' strunt*
> *They parted aff careerin'*
> *Fu'blythe that night.*

Of *course.*

Rice pudding is more fun, more intelligible, semantically. I make it
fairly often when the house holds young and/or old people. It is a good
little "snack" after school. It is excellent for breakfast, and why not? It is
pleasant to eat in bed with Music-till-Dawn turned on low-low. It will
bring sweet dreams. It should always have nutmeg on the top, like an
eggnog, and it can be made from uncooked or even leftover rice. Often
I use a pasta (noodles, vermicelli, especially capellini) instead, to surprise people and apparently to please them. This is definitely a slap-to-
gether, from long experience, but I suppose the proportions are two cups
of rice or pasta, lightly cooked and drained, and four eggs and two cups
of creamy milk, with brown sugar and raisins to one's taste, some dabs of
butter on top, and the all-essential nutmeg. This is baked in a well-
buttered dish or pan until set, in a 350° oven. My family prefers it made
of capellini and made in a large flat pan, to be cut like a tart. It qualifies
as one more Innocent.

The first time I knew that a pasta could be served without tomato
sauce on it was, I think, when I met a young Turkish student in Dijon.
Once he asked my husband and me to tea (mint, of course), and we
chewed for a long time on the sweetest, oiliest dessert I have ever faced in
my life. It was made of cooked vermicelli, floating in honey and vegetable

oil and baked slowly for several hours. Our friend cut it in small pieces, which helped somewhat, and so did the tea, but my teeth still cringe as I remember the lengthy little party.

Sometimes I use Japanese noodles instead of the Italian pastas. They are very thin, even more so than capellini, but although I follow both the directions and my own curious nose they stay tougher. I like them, I admit, partly because of the label, which describes them as "Soup eating, Dry eating, Cold eating, Sweet eating." For the last, one is directed succinctly, "Mix with milk and sugar, or jam." I have never been to Japan, nor to Hong Kong where this pasta is made for the islands, but I like to think that it would be easier there to find honey and oil for Sweet eating than either jam or milk . . .

Francatelli gives a tedious but basically good recipe for a vermicelli pudding, and I don't know why this surprises me, unless I am conditioned to feel that my early table habits were largely based on what his employer Queen Victoria unwittingly taught my grandmother, and certainly we never thought of such a heathenish thing! In fact, at home we never ate any pasta except a rare casserole of spaghetti, baked with ample cheese to hide its leftovers from Father. It was not until I went to college, and plunged into *la vie bohème* and postfootball orgies of Tony Fazzoli's 75¢-Full-Course-Dinner-with-(bootleg) Wine, that I met and enjoyed the many dubious platters of spaghetti loaded with watery tomato sauce that hopefully kept me in touch with worldliness.

Now and then I like to make a hearty pudding which I think is German-Jewish. I take liberties with it, depending upon the weather and the eaters: I use very thin noodles instead of broad ones; sometimes I mix the raisins and nuts into the whole, instead of making a layer of them; occasionally I use a general mount of black currants and thinly sliced tart apples in their place. Chopped cracklings (*groben*) can substitute for the nuts, and of course chicken or goose fat for other shortening. To make a richer dish, melted fat can be poured lightly over the crumbs. Honey or brown sugar are good instead of white sugar. And so on. And here is the basic recipe for a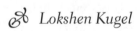

 Lokshen Kugel

½ *pound broad noodles*

1 *teaspoon salt*

2 *quarts boiling water*

2 *to 3 eggs*

¾ *cup sugar*

½ *teaspoon cinnamon*

　　OR

1 *tablespoon lemon juice*

4 *to 6 tablespoons shortening*

¾ *cup chopped seedless raisins*

½ *cup chopped almonds or walnuts*

½ *cup bread crumbs*

Cook noodles in boiling salted water until tender but not soft. Drain well and rinse under hot water tap. Beat eggs with sugar and spice or lemon juice. Mix well with noodles. Melt fat in baking dish, coat it well, and then pour fat into mixture. Turn half into dish, cover with raisins and nuts, add rest of mixture, and top with crumbs. Bake 45 minutes at 400°, or longer at 350°.

If this were made in a round flat pan, and cut in wedges as my family likes to do with a "capellini tart," it could be called a pie instead of a kugel, but Georgie-Porgie would never admit it as such. A pie to him was perforce enveloped in crusts of dough, under and over and usually around a filling made of everything from four-and-twenty blackbirds to eels, but seldom anything sweet, at least in the century when he and Charles II were kissing and running. A pie was a pie then, and a tart was a tart, and they still are, in England. Once I stayed for most of a winter in London, and nourished my soul as often as possible upon the hot plum tarts with Devonshire cream at Simpson's. (At home they would have been called deep dish *pies*.) There, correctly for there, a pie held meat or fish or fowl, and was no lightsome thing with only a top lid to it . . .

Our American fruit pies are, as far as I can tell, unique to our culture. Most often they have two crusts. They are round and are rather flat and

solid. They pack well, and frontier wives discovered that they also froze
well, which they still do. And hinterlanders still eat them at breakfast, and
what is wrong with that, if the crust be light and the apples and cinnamon
and sugar and butter a commendable mixture? Why complicate life by
combining much the same things all over the table: buttered toast and
jam, a bowl of applesauce? On the other hand, and this direful doomy
phrase is especially true when applied to pies, they can be dreadful. The
thought of facing a slab of some of the neo-Gothic monstrosities called
Ma's Best Apple, before a day of work or any time at all, makes me feel
that Lizzie Borden's prelethal breakfast of bananas and cold mutton
broth, for her doomed parents, would be less risky.

Certainly some of the pies we make with only a bottom crust, piled
with fluff, are ours alone! They are ingenious, in that one pie can serve
at least six or eight people, and the cook does not have to make that
many little pastry shells. And statistics, which I seldom believe, assert
that the American male prefers, after a good rare steak with baked potato
and tossed green salad, a slice of lemon meringue pie . . . the kind
Mom used to make (and not apple as I might have surmised). At the risk
of possible libel, I can say that I have known several American males, in
the best senses of the words, and not one of them liked lemon meringue
pie. And it was family legend with us that after many years of listening to
my father speak nostalgically of the rhubarb and gooseberry and even
apple pies he ate when a child on the Peachblow Farm in Iowa, Mother
had a temporary cook who could present him with a shining example of
each . . . but he could not eat them because they were too light, too delicate, too digestible . . .

I think that in our kitchen vocabulary a real pie has two crusts, and
anything with only the bottom one is a tart. I state, therefore, and often,

that I prefer to make tarts. I like them. Other people do too. Mine can of course be filled with fish, vegetables, meat, cheese, and best of all these, fruit, in the fully plural sense. The crust, really a kind of shallow case or box, can be unbaked, half-baked, or thoroughly golden and crisp and ready for a delicate or sturdy cooked filling. The occasional perusal of a good classical cookbook is indicated, if a part-time or even professional provider feels a deadly blank when confronted with the request for "a nice tart" for the evening dessert. One pattern easy to follow is to bake a pastry shell, prepare a *crème anglaise* and drained fruits and a glaze of jelly or jam, and construct the lovely thing just in time to let the glaze settle over the beautiful strawberries or cherries or whatnot, which in turn lie in neat patterns upon a bed of thick "pudding" upon the flaky crust. (Some good cooks varnish a tart shell with white of egg or milk before baking it . . .) Every kitchen buff has a few tricks: I for instance like to rinse and hull strawberries, or stone cherries, and roll them in kirshwasser before I lay them in circles on the custard. If I am going to make an orange tart, I do the same with rum on the skinned sections of the fruit. They must not be too moist when they go onto the custard.

And with this last I often cheat arrogantly, and so far nobody has chided me except perhaps my own conditioned conscience. In loose or lazy moments I use the best procurable packaged "mix" for vanilla pudding, grate some lemon or orange rind into it, and add one half cup less liquid than the idiotically simple directions say. Once cooked, I leave the pap in its pan, covered directly onto its surface with waxed paper or cellophane. When it is cool, I stir into it a cup of commercial sour cream. This shoddy and unreasonable facsimile of a pastry cream I spread, almost unblushingly, upon a baked shell either round or oblong. The fruit goes on, according to the cook's whims as well as the season's. It is fun to make a

tart of several kinds of fresh or canned things like plums, apricots, cherries, pineapple, peaches, in their own rings or squares, and cut and shaped and stoned according to their natures. The tart will be a mosaic, especially when it has been glazed evenly with a mixture of jam or jelly and lemon juice or liqueur (one cup to one tablespoon, melted together). A lovely thing! And if one is as dishonest as I sometimes am, according to both the classics and one's innate instincts, there are decent sticks of half-frozen pastry in the markets. To be vaguely jesuitical, is it much shadier to use a preconfected dough or pudding mixture than a jam or jelly already in its jar? Perhaps the whole trick is to enjoy making it and then serving it forth . . .

Pastry crusts are good to know about, and to use from one end of a plain or fancy meal to the other. Never more than one appearance per meal, though! I knew a retired *chef-pâtissier* in Provence, very fat and married to a wife his size. They had a fox terrier to match. The three ran a small restaurant near Aix, and from the hors d'oeuvre through the dessert every course was based on or accompanied by a variation of his conditioned accomplishment: plain hard and plain flaky pastry, brioche pastry, cream puff and puff pastry, in shells-squares-timbales-pies-tarts-molds, fleurons, sticks, hot and cold pâtés. He made pastries of butter, suet, lard, oil. He was a maniac, not able to sleep much, potentially dangerous unless he was kneading and rolling and baking. He would stand at the door of the small dining room and watch as we ate, at first with delectation and then more slowly, until he could produce his predictable surprise, a dessert never on the menu, which a man with a gun at his temple could not but savor. We stopped going there.

Some people have a natural "hand" for making pastry dough, and although I have been told that it depends upon everything from the body's metabolic speed to the kind of water added to the paste, I suspect that most dough, like everything else, is produced by people who know what they are doing. They have practiced and studied, and observed and judged. They are skilled. I am not, by comparison with almost any of them, partly because my own meals lean toward cheeses and fruits at the end, but I do know a few rules about pastry making, and I follow them dutifully. Everything is cool or cold; hands should stay off as much as possible, helped by cloth or cellophane; the rolling should be light. If a single (bottom) crust is to be half or wholly baked before the filling, it should be pricked. It should be baked in a hot oven (400°–450°) for about five minutes, and then at about 350° until it is lightly browned, if one wishes a finished crust. For vegetable and fruit tarts which will need more baking after they are filled, I take the shells from the oven in 5 to 8 minutes. I have good luck, because I am not shy about consulting better cooks and perhaps because I am equally brash about cheating, with things like prefab dough! (It is called the green luck of the Irish, but often I am honest and true-blue . . .)

There are other than dough crusts in our days, made with crumbs of various kinds, and butter or one of its bedfellows. Probably the best one I ever make, but rarely because it is somewhat overpowering, I got from a package of moist grated coconut. (This convenient product also comes in cans.) I fill the crust at the last minute with good ice cream, but it will hold up well with a *crème anglaise*. I feel sure everyone knows it and likes it as much as my occasional guests seem to, but in case its delicious monstrousness is not widely known, except by the forty million people who look at the sides of packages, here is the recipe: &

 Coconut Pie Shell

2 to 3 tablespoons soft butter
1 package or can (1½ cups) moist coconut

Spread butter evenly in 9-inch pie pan. Pat coconut smoothly into butter on bottom and sides. Bake at 350° for 12 to 15 minutes, or until lightly brown and crisp. Cool before using.

Now and then, to startle our favorite *bourgeois* at table, I make what for some reason is called a pudding in England but which I cannot think of as anything but a tart. It has an intense taste to it, and I notice that it is always eaten to the last rich crumb, and slowly . . . and best savored with a glass of good port: ℰ

ℰ A *Duke of Cambridge Tarding*

Rich pastry dough

¾ cup candied fruit peel or preserved fruits

Kirsch or rum to cover fruits

¾ cup butter

¾ cup sugar

4 egg yolks

Line 9-inch pie pan with pastry, making rim around edge, and chill. Cover fruits with liquor for ½ hour. Drain them, and scatter evenly over bottom of pastry. Put marinade, butter, sugar, and egg yolks into top of double boiler and cook gently until thickened enough to coat spoon. Pour over fruits. Bake in 400° oven until top is rich brown and crinkled. Serve warm or cold.

And of course there are cakes, both baked in their pans and fried in rounds on a griddle, and there are fritters. One reason I loved to go to dinner at Mrs. Thayer's, when I was young, was that there might be little hot crisp fritters, pineapple or banana within, and a lavish dusting of sugar without. Sometimes, I think, they might have been apple. A long time later I lived in France with some people who made *beignets* of everything from old turnips to gooseberries, and they were uniformly delicious, because of this excellent conditioning to the appreciation of Forbidden Fruits (Grandmother did not believe in hot fat), but I myself have never made a fritter in my life, because I do not own a frah-kell. I am almost tempted to make place for such a foreign gadget, however, when I read old recipes and remember my apparently harmless sensuality at the Thayer ranch. Perhaps half a century might make the calories more of a menace than they were then. But what could be more fun, at the season when the grape leaves are small and succulent in my wine valley, than to follow a receipt like the one for Vineleaf Fritters in my copy of *Everybody's Pudding Book*, which was published in London in

1866? Since they do not even need a frah-kell, I would call them. &

These of course were not fritters in the correct American or French
sense, but were a kind of pancake. They
make me think of a good trick my friend
Elsa used to pull with plain sweetened pancake batter: she had a plate of sliced bananas beside the griddle, and on the uncooked topside of each cake she would
quickly scatter several pieces of the fruit,
before it was time to flip them. It made a
most delicious dessert, sprinkled with sugar
and lemon juice, and I always thought it
would be even better if she used a thin
crêpe batter instead of the somewhat puffy
American version. I suppose good cooks

 ## *St. Helena Flimflams*

*Gather some of the smallest vine-leaves you
can get; cut off the stalks, and lay them to
soak in a little French brandy, rasped
lemon peel, and sugar. Then make a batter
with flour, water, and the white of (an) egg;
drop a small portion here and there over
the pan, lay a vine-leaf upon each, fry them
very quick, and when done, strew sugar over
them. Glaze them with a salamander, and
serve with lemon-juice and sugar.*

have been making banana pancakes for decades, and even blueberry
pancakes and peach pancakes. I am ignorant about the situation, but
feel tempted to investigate . . . for I *like* pancakes, except for breakfast,
when they make me sink like a stone. They are very good piled up with
crushed fresh fruit or jam between them, and cut in wedges. They are
good rolled into *canelloni,* and even folded for *crêpes* more-or-less
suzette. These last attention-getters can be flabby and completely confused in flavor, depending upon the showmanship rather than the aesthetic honesty of the cook behind the flame, and in general they are to
be avoided in "grand" restaurants. (If there are impressionable adolescents of any age in the party, a Baked Alaska is more fun . . .) The best
liquor-logged crêpe I ever ate was on a cold dusty street in Provence at a
fair of some kind, when they were being sold for about ten cents apiece

to advertise a new after-dinner drink. They were hot, fresh, and generous, and very messy to eat, dripping with melted butter, sugar, and booze, and the professionally fat and jolly vendor poured barrels of his heady product into apparently thin air, for I never heard its name again. Sometimes I wonder if he was a retired broker or dentist who had been advised by his psychiatrist to steal a carload of something like Grand Marnier and make all the pancakes he had ever dreamed about . . . (I also knew a nice old lady who when she died was found to have hidden several hundred plain flapjacks in a big trunk in the attic, neatly packed with layers of moth repellent. Of course she may have been raised to think of them colloquially as flannel cakes, which would make the camphor a natural precaution, but I am conditioned to believe that a mysterious liqueur might have done as well, if perhaps more stickily.)

And then there are cookies, which for children should be as large as crêpes, but stiffer, and for people at parties should be no bigger than a nibble. Some of us like soft cookies, but mostly the good ones are crisp and thin. Now and then, though, they are like gentle lumps, and can have icing on them, which perhaps moves them one notch over in the dessert hierarchy, to become small cakes. My Uncle George married a girl named Georgetta, which was always good for a quiet family titter, and she made a preteen dream of delight for us at Christmas and scattered festivals. They were rich but firm, sometimes with walnuts in them, about two inches tall but uneven in shape. The dough was darkly thick, to stand up that way, and very darkly chocolate. On top was a fine fat swirl of even darker fudge frosting. Bliss! And at the other end of the stick, and giving as much pleasure in a more Spartan way, were Oatmeal Rocks, which were as thick and heavy but perhaps a tenth as rich. They had no chocolate anywhere, but they were loaded with raisins, and what child could ask for better? Given a couple of them as we raced out the back door after supper, which we usually ate early so that Father could get to a meeting, we were set for hours of Run, Sheep, Run through the orchards of young orange trees and old walnuts, where now a hundred thousand people live on a thick crust of asphalt. The Rocks are still good, and any honorable recipe for oatmeal cookies will suffice, to be dropped generously upon a baking sheet and then into the pockets of omnivorous children.

Such small baked cakes must have evolved from the cooking of the early Scots, and then further back, but they seem very American in their gastronomical importance. Cookies are made commercially, and sold in uncountable shapes, flavors and sizes, usually packed in cellophane envelopes, in California supermarkets and Missouri crossroads stores, and whereas a French schoolchild would snatch a slice of bread with some jam on it, our children prefer the convenient and more varied (and perhaps richer and sweeter) little pastries. Truck drivers munch them for hoped-for nourishment on long hauls. Schoolteachers and stenographers nibble low-calorie Vanilla Gems and high-calorie fig bars during Free Period. Dutiful daughters-in-law placate Gramps with a honeyed soft confection tactfully free of seeds, nuts, roughage, and other geriatric hazards. And I am told that chocolate brownies are "a universal favorite," although I would hesitate to serve one to a Jordanian or even a Marseillais.

The nearest I ever came in another country to what I suspect is our own national invention was when my landlady in Aix gave tea parties for two Swedish aristocrats who added luster to her circle and loved pastries of all kinds as long as they were rich and sweet. The cook always made, among other dainties, a *biscuit au chocolat*, which I never would have tasted otherwise, just as I never would have been invited with the other more socially acceptable guests if the Swedes had not liked me and the cake too. It was a large flat round dusted with confectioner's sugar, and of an almost chewy texture which reminded me of our cruder brownies. I think it would have been much better at the end of a light meal, perhaps served with *crème Chantilly*: it called for coffee and not tea, or better yet a cool merciful glass of wine. But we all tucked into it, no matter how awkwardly on our tiny balanced plates, as we sat in a large circle in the drawing room, and when it had vanished there was a great bowing and hand kissing and the Swedes and I ran up to the Cours Mirabeau for a quick beer . . .

A noted home economist once wrote asking me the origin of our brownies, and I had to plead real ignorance, except for their possibly elegant beginnings in a chocolate biscuit. She said, "I have made them all my life and since friends old and young like them so much I have become curious." I looked in many books, with no luck except for the dependable Mrs. Rombauer, who gives several recipes for them, starting out #1 flatly by stating, in a rare burst of prose, "Than which there are no others." She reneges a little with #2, saying of it, "A lighter Bar than Brownies #1, and even better." I always believe this lady without cavil, if not always with full obedience, and I am sure her recipes are the best for what I described to the home economist as having to be "rich, chewy, sticky, full of walnut or pecan meats, indigestible, and generally delicious."

I should perhaps have added, "to them as likes them," for by now in my progress toward the pap and pabulum of senility I would rather do several other unpleasant things than eat one. We seldom had them at home: Mother was liverish, and rightfully ascribed dangers to chocolate which she managed to ignore in the huge amounts of butter we downed at the Ranch. (I know, because for several years I did the Saturday churning. It was a strangely satisfying but irksome job, and when I showed signs of rebellion I was easily conned back to the chore by crass flattery for my knack of turning out much better butter than could, or would, any other available slavey.)

On cookie baking days now, usually when young people will be around, I pour the dough into pans to make squares, or drop it bit by bit on cookie sheets. I admire the thinly rolled kinds, but am lazy about them, perhaps because of my innate lack of interest in the national nibble. I have found that rather moist dark spicy cookies are generally pleasing, to eat with a glass of milk if one is growing fast or is in other ways needful of soothing. I used to make a good kind with fresh or frozen persimmons, and cooked pumpkin or apple sauce will serve as well. Other people, which means older than perhaps eighteen, like this baked in small loaves and sliced thin for tea. Most cookie buffs believe that raisins or currants are, to purloin a phrase, the *raisins d'être* of any and every excuse to eat them, but I myself like occasionally to use moist dates cut into bits, and I think that morsels of candied fruit first marinated in a little brandy make a slightly festive addition. And nothing is better, now and then, than some leftover orange marmalade!

My younger daughter, who has always had a light wrist at the oven, went through a delicious period of turning out Brandy Snaps. It was plainly to avoid studying chemistry and thinking about the fact that she was in love with a dashing Italian who loved another girl, a tiny blond German instead of a large dark Irish-Russian. It is possible that a few tears salted the Snaps, but we continued to devour them delicately, which is the only possible way to respect their fragile pungency. Their name sounds rakish, perhaps Georgian or even Edwardian, but they are teetotal, although they could fittingly be *served* with a strong punch or eggnog. ✄

✄ *Brandy Snaps*

1 ¼ cups flour

½ cup molasses (light for delicate flavor, dark for stronger)

½ cup butter

⅔ cup sugar

½ teaspoon grated lemon rind

1 teaspoon lemon juice

Sift flour once, and measure. Combine molasses, butter, and sugar, and heat until sugar dissolves. Add lemon rind and juice. Add the flour, and mix well. Drop by small teaspoonfuls on a greased baking sheet, leaving plenty of room to spread. Bake in hot oven (425°) about 5 minutes. While still warm, loosen cookies with spatula and roll over a knife blade or wooden spoon handle. If cookies do not loosen easily, return to oven to reheat slightly. Store when well cooled.

My poor girl, lovelorn but not lazy, found that the recipe would make about four dozen elegant rolls, but that if the dough was dropped by the half teaspoonful it would make about twice as many flat crisp Snaps with half the bother. Once she was hoist on her own petard and spent hours making what must have been several hundred tiny brown coins which, since she knew she had already flunked chemistry and the telephone had not rung for days, she piled right side up and precisely on plates, to serve to some cousins and other human beings her age. She was forever disillusioned with such fiddle-faddling when she watched the boys open their mouths and literally toss handfuls down their gullets, as if they were eating popcorn. She never made Brandy Snaps again, but now and then I do, to keep green the memory of her oven days . . . and my own wrist supple.

Another tedious but rewarding cookie, and this time surely of German origin and never as good as when it is made according to whatever is Hoyle in High German, is a peppernut. They were made long before Thanksgiving at home, thanks to my mother's years in Dresden trying not to develop either her lovely contralto voice or her ladylike skill at the pianoforte, and also to the inexplicable fact that Elizabeth Klein elected to spend several years in our kitchen. They were stored in tight canisters which had once brought tea from Peiping via Dublin. They were lightly glazed, and never given a lazy coating of thick powdered sugar to drift down one's front as are the modern boughten kinds. They demand not only a good wrist but three or four of them, and strong arms and fingers. They also take a fanatical and occasionally desperate patience, as I once found when I launched on a program of sending them to my Chosen Few for Christmas.

The kitchen was usurped by their kettles and trays, the house by their pervasive and insistent odor, and my full attention by their rigorous demands. It threatened to become a debacle rather than a jolly preholiday rite. I soon called on my sister to come help, and she did, with two very small children to add to mine underfoot. After about twenty-four hours of this domestic madness, my husband, who was writing a novel, left, simply left. I waved a stained floury arm as he drove down the hill. I wanted to go with him, and later come back with him to a tranquil sweet-smelling house, and I did not blame him, then or now, for using the turmoil and general *kuchen und kindern* ambience as an excuse for what he wanted very much to do anyway. I was stern with myself for a moment, and then returned to the fantastic process going on in an almost mesmeric fashion in the big kitchen, all the rolling, baking, glazing. Once more the need to nourish stayed a cracking heart, perhaps.

Here is the recipe I like. There are many others, and some are easier. My first mistake, maritally disastrous but ultimately delicious in itself, was to double the formula. This formed an almost solid rock of dough which made it seem impossible to reduce to a thousand pebbles. I could not stir it alone, for more than a few strokes, but my sister and I used a dogged combination of long spoons, hands, and stubbornness, and I had a feeling, probably correct, that we must not cheat by adding a little extra moisture. The whole caper need not be this arduous, with a single or half measure and perhaps a more charitable climate than our high dry perch in the mountains north of Mexico. ℬ

Anyone mad enough to start peppernuts will finish them and never be sorry, but they need at least four arms, as far as I am concerned, and perhaps should not be planned for the dark of the moon.

As is plain in any kitchen book, including this one, it is hard to draw lines between the conventional categories of food, especially when one approaches the real dainties of our human fodder, things like jams as compared with preserves, baked custards with pastry creams, cookies with cakes. A cake is, actually, a big airy cookie. And a sponge cake is nothing more than a soufflé . . . and so on.

For practical purposes, picnics and such, I lean toward cakes made in loaves or flat ob-

ℬ Pfeffernüse (Peppernuts)

1 pint corn syrup
1 pint dark molasses (New Orleans sorghum)
½ pound butter
½ cup lemon juice
1 teaspoon soda
2 teaspoons cinnamon
1 scant teaspoon cloves
2½ pounds flour
½ pound citron
½ pound unblanched almonds
Rind of 1 large or 2 small lemons

Warm syrups together, and add butter and lemon juice. Sift soda and spices with flour, and add gradually. Put citron, almonds, and lemon peel through medium food grinder, and add. Make a very stiff dough, adding more flour if necessary. Let stand overnight. Roll with hands into balls the size of marbles. Place on well-greased pans and bake at 350° for about 20 minutes. When cool, roll around in the following glaze, a handful at a time in the double boiler, and then place separately on waxed paper. Let dry well, and put in tightly closed boxes for at least two weeks. (Half an apple in each box will keep them from getting too hard.)

GLAZE:

1 cup confectioner's sugar
2 tablespoons boiling water (more if needed)
1 teaspoon vanilla, if wished

Melt together in double boiler, and keep hot while glazing peppernuts. Add another measure or half measure when the supply grows low.

long pans, and left uniced. I am assured that most people, especially men, want frosting on their cakes, but I have yet to find anyone so frustrated by a light dusting of powdered sugar that he would not eat his share and more. I prefer the type of cake called biscuit in French cooking to our American layer cakes piled high with fillings and frostings. It seems to me that as the availability of packaged mixes for both cakes and their garnishings increases, our average cakes, the kinds that sell well at Girl Scout Bake Sales and are devoured at the

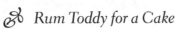 *Rum Toddy for a Cake*

½ cup brown sugar
1 cup fresh orange juice
⅓ cup dark rum

Dissolve sugar in orange juice over low heat. Remove, add rum, and pour slowly over hot cake. Let stand in tube pan or spring mold until cool.

monthly meetings of the Potluck and Bingo Marching Society, grow taller and frothier and less significant on the palate. There are special knives for cutting and serving them from plastic cake stands with transparent domes, through which the eager eaters can gaze with anticipation on their prospective treats, airy nothings made of Aunt Susan's Lemon Chiffon Delight and piled with one of her immediate relative's secret formulas for the foamiest lightest yummiest almost-genuine Peach-Fondant Butter Whip anyone ever ate. My stand against such gagging structures is firm if not actively militant, and when I make a cake I tend to keep it very flat in appearance and very simple in ingredients: a small protest, but mine own.

I like to split a cake baked in an oblong pan or in two round layers, and fill it with a thick pastry cream flavored with lemon or orange, and dust it at the last minute before serving. A little jam is good on the inner slices before the cream goes on. And a plain yellow cake in a spring mold, pricked when fresh from the oven and bathed with the following booster, is pleasing to all but the teetotalers: *&*

It is therapeutic for a cook to depart from reality now and then and go

right through the looking glass, and any classical manual will encourage
such an occasional trip. It may only go as far as a trifle, and then only once
or twice a year, like mine, but it will clear the kitchen air of any lurking ennui and cynicism. Of course there are the Unattainables, too, the high-
culinary almost-legendary near-mythical dishes one reads about and
knows firmly one will never taste, much less reproduce. There is for instance a recipe in Francatelli's *Modern Cook* (London, 1846) for a *"Mille-
feuilles cake à la Chantilly,"* which has long obsessed me, mostly because I
know that never would I try to follow its fairly simple steps. It starts out,
"Give ten turns to one pound of puff-paste, then divide it into two pieces,
and roll them out to the thickness of the tenth part of an inch . . ." There is
a stark little engraving of this complete improbability in my life. And further along in the section Queen Vic's cook called Ornamental Entremets
there is an almost equally discouraging recipe, unfortunately without an il-
lustration, for making a "Savoy cake in the form of a glazed ham." This
must have roused many a merry moment at court, compared with some
others of those interminable dinners. I know ways to make people laugh
that are easier . . .

I also know that I shall never eat a Sacher torte that fits my mind's image. For a long time I thought perhaps . . . maybe this time? I looked at
them on pastry trays in gilt-edged restaurants and in fashionable cake
shops and in relatively low-class delicatessens. But no. I shall continue to
read about this peculiar product of the Hapsburgs, which is easier on both
the imagination and the liver. And the same is probably true of a recipe
somewhat ambiguously called a *cassata alla siciliana*. To me, nurtured
during three short fattening years in the tea shops as well as the cafés of Dijon, a *cassata* means a rich frozen dessert, to be eaten in small voluptuous
bites. This dessert sounded like a chilled cake. I looked more attentively at

the formula for one more obviously qualified Unattainable, and decided
that it was a version of the *pouding anglaise* served superbly in good Italian
hotels and infamously in bad ones. It is nothing but pound cake sliced
horizontally, spread then with a creamy and alcoholic mixture of whatever
the cook feels at that moment is creamy (and potable), and then coaxed
into shape for a chilling of several hours. The delicately stodgy edifice is
then masked with a good bitter mixture of chocolate and butter and perhaps strong coffee, and is chilled again, at least overnight. It can be decorated, and it is served in thin slices after very rich meals, just as a reputable
Sacher torte should be.

Once in the Galeria in Milan I ate unashamedly of a cake so ephem-
eral that I knew I too was floating with it for the rest of a fine long day. That
happened another time, in a Corsican restaurant on the Left Bank in
Paris. We plainly had both time and money to spend, and still it was clear
that we liked good food and wine to match our quiet squanderings, and
halfway through the afternoon, when the place was empty, a young chef
came out with a huge pan covered with a glazed meringue. He would like
us to taste what he had created. It was for the night's menu. As I remember, it was painful for us to break into the thing at all, for we felt delicately
surfeited, knowingly and lightly sated. But he was suddenly speaking in
tongues, gastronomically. He served us too amply in his pride, and we
steeled ourselves, and cut into one of the two most delicious and unattainable cakes I have ever met, in print or at table. As I now remember, it
was at least three layers of a "biscuit" filled with a pastry cream amply but
still discreetly flavored with either kirschwasser or Cointreau. The top of
the big oblong was covered with a meringue, "set" in the oven and then
glazed daringly with a red-hot salamander. Perhaps there were flavors of almond, vanilla, hazelnut. It was an extraordinary thing, born to die and per-

haps never live again in quite the same form. We asked the young chef what he called it, and he said, "It is mine, the Cook's Cake." Then he sat down and we all ate another piece and drank some strong coffee and some brandy. Everything was fine, for that day.

This quality of being for once only, of being unreachable, can touch all directions in the kitchen. For desserts, sometimes the peaches are exactly right, or the melons. But not often. Sometimes in a cherry tart a stone has been left in, and the one person who should not find it bites down upon it. Ah, well . . . fruits are fruits, like cooks. In general I would rather depend upon a plate of seasonal fruits from the supermarket than a careless pastry cook. Winter or summer, I think the best dessert in the world, after no matter how plain or elaborate a meal, is what is at its peak of ripening from the fields and orchards. There are grapes, and apples, and pears-cherries-apricots-peaches-plums-oranges-nuts-dates-figs-raisins according to their natural and enforced seasons, and almost anywhere one or another of them can be found, the year around. I do not like them chilled, for they lose much of their intangible fragrance and savor. If they must be washed, it should be as fast as possible, with a quick gentle drying.

I learned in northern Italy to sprinkle strawberries with fresh orange juice. I learned from a Finnish girl to coat blueberries (and currants and ripe gooseberries) with egg white beaten with some water, and then with sugar, and to spread them on waxed paper to dry and make their own sweet shells. I was probably born knowing that an acid will keep some fruits from turning dark, so that without being told I coat bananas and pears and a few other things with fresh lemon juice. But I cannot remember who first showed me how to open a can, which I often do! A compote made of firm halves of pears, peaches, apricots, pineapple, either fresh or all shameless from the grocer's shelves, can be a fine thing, the latter if they are drained well and then covered again with a syrup made of one cup of their mixed juices and one of sugar, reduced to one scant cup. (I like to use brown sugar, and the juice that tastes best . . .) On the side, a can of stoned black cherries can be drained, and covered amply with kirsch, or a can of drained tangerine sections with rum. I pour the hot sauce over the first fruits in a big bowl, and let them chill. At the last, I add the marinated fruit and its heady juice. Sometimes when I am trying to please or cajole I serve this fine mixture with another bowl of a stiffish *crème anglaise*, but I really prefer it by itself . . . with, of course, a plate of thin plain cookies alongside.

Apples are important in any kitchen scheme, and are a perfect end to a simple meal, cool but not chilled, and especially with some cheese, depending upon the season, the food, and the people gathered for it. And they are good cooked, in a hundred ways, and one of the treats of my childhood was to have apple dumplings appear, each ready to burst with steamy richness from its solid wrapping of crust. While Grandmother was there we doused the dumplings in our big soup plates with her approved mixture, really not bad, of hot milk mixed with cinnamon and sugar and a smidgin of butter, but at the Ranch, where we no longer had my dam but did have a generous cow correctly named Bessie, we reveled in cold thick cream over the hot delights.

Plain baked apples are good, hot or cold. Apples filled with mincemeat or chopped dried fruits and plenty of butter are good. Any honest American cookbook will prove their goodness. Sliced apples baked into things like Brown Betties are good. We had one cook who made big pans of something she called Apple Crisp, with a kind of topping of sugar and butter and flour on it, and cold or hot it was good. I always tried to get a leftover piece of it for breakfast.

Applesauce can be one of the best dishes on earth, especially with hot gingerbread, and my mother persuaded all her cooks, including me and no matter what our ages or IQs, to turn out commendable facsimiles of her own occasional masterpiece. The quartered and peeled apples, usually small and tart, were boiled fast with a modicum of water. They spat viciously as they were stirred. When they started to fall to pieces, plenty of dark brown sugar was beaten in, and they were taken from the fire. A generous amount of butter was added, perhaps a teaspoonful for each cup. The hot lumpy mess (we *liked* it lumpy!) was poured into a big bowl, and immediately dusted with cinnamon, and before long it was gone and the cook started over again. The actual cooking went fast and was odorous and fun. It was peeling the fruit that was a bore, but we put up with it philosophically, knowing no alternative.

Now I often cheat with unsweetened canned applesauce, which can be made with better fruit than I might find, and I am always conscious of how shocked my mother would be. I heat it, adding brown sugar and the ritual dollop of butter at the end if that is indicated, and it is good enough. Depending upon its purpose, I can season it with grated lemon peel, spices, rum, cayenne . . . and here is one recipe I learned from a Russian woman when I lived in Vevey. It is easy, and refreshing in winter ℰ

 ### *Pommes Russes*

Butter

6 to 8 dry ladyfingers, split

¾ cup fruit juice (orange, pineapple, apple . . .)

2 tablespoons honey

¼ cup kirsch

3 egg yolks

2 cups sweetened spiced applesauce

3 egg whites

Line well-buttered flat baking dish with ladyfingers. Mix the fruit juice, honey, and liqueur, and pour the syrup over the cakes. Let them soak thoroughly, and then pour off any extra liquid. Beat the yolks and mix into the applesauce. Beat the whites and fold in. Pour over the ladyfingers. Bake about 20 minutes at 375°. Serve hot with thick cream to which a little kirsch has been added.

And here is a strange recipe given to me by an American Lady who lived far too many years in a château near Perpignan. I have made it often, and it is delicate almost to the point of what my grandmother and Marion Harland would call Invalid Cookery, but after a possibly heavy meal it is what my father would more correctly term Salubrious. ℰ

This sounds stark, but it is merely airy, with a subtle tang. It is easy to think of many other ways fruits are cooked which have not these tenuous qualifications, ending probably with one of the boiled puddings Georgie-Porgie, as a true Englishman of his times, felt worth running away with. I have more than a nodding acquaintance with tricks richer than my expatriate friend's, but lighter than a Baroness, and here are a few of them to amuse and perhaps please jaded and even plain hungry diners:

 *Apple Snow*

1 large or 2 smaller sour apples
½ cup powdered sugar
2 egg whites
2 cups "fine smooth" crème anglaise

Peel and grate apple(s) into large bowl. Sprinkle with the sugar, add the egg whites, and beat the whole fiercely until very firm and light. Heap in a flat dish and pour the custard around it.

Soak 10 to 12 large ripe figs, which have been peeled, quartered, and slightly mashed (canned ones will do in a pinch), in kirsch for two hours. Fold the whole into a generous quart of soft vanilla ice cream, and refreeze for at least a half hour.

Spear sweet ripe oranges on a fork, and peel them deeply enough to take off all the white. Cut out the sections into a bowl. Add approximately one part of light or dark rum (or kirsch) to every part of the generous juice, sprinkle the whole with powdered sugar, and let sit in a cool place for at least two hours. This is pretty to serve in stemmed goblets, so that one can drink the elixir at the end . . . but never with any wine alongside that I can conjure to my mind's palate!

To make Ambrosia, a classical American dessert, especially in the South and especially for Christmas in days not so olden, slice nicely peeled oranges crosswise very thinly. Lay them in a pretty cut-glass dish if you were brought up on the right side of the fence, and over each layer sprinkle freshly grated (or moist tinned) coconut and sugar. Let them stand. Serve them forth. They will make a naïve and pleasing dish, worth new favor.

Wash some peaches or pears or apricots or plums, split them to remove the seeds, and lay them in a flat buttered baking dish. Put about a teaspoonful of brown sugar or jam in each, a dollop more of butter, spices to taste, a good sprinkle of cake crumbs if wished. Add a thin bottom of white wine, vermouth, port, or plain water. Cover them closely with foil or a tight lid, and bake in a 350° oven for about a half hour. Take off the lid and broil for a minute at the end, if wished. They are delicious cold or hot with a pitcher of cream alongside, or a bowl of sour cream, or servings of vanilla ice cream . . . or even *flambé* with a little brandy or rum.

Make a generous core in unpeeled apples, cut a thin line vertically around them so that they will not burst, and fill them with a fruit jelly. Top them with butter. Bake them as one would the fruits above.

And so on.

Every plain cook, which means a day-to-day cook enjoying and learning from experience, will have dozens of such easy and generally unwritten maneuvers ready to use. It is good to read classical manuals for both help and pleasure, and to look also at whatever drifts into view from the fastly rolling culinary presses of America and the rest of the world. There are astonishing variations on the old themes . . .

I feel like a patriot named Pareto, who in 1900 or so exclaimed about a totally opposite subject, "Give me a fruitful error, and time, full of seeds, bursting with its own corrections!" Georgie-Porgie, you may keep your sterile truth for yourself, and let boys, and girls too, burst with their own corrections of the stodgy things you stole along with the kisses! There is plenty left. *Fall to, therefore!*

Some Ways to Laugh

For anyone who "drinks his wine with laughter and with glee," as it says we do in the song about the tavern in the town, it will perhaps seem odd for me to include coffee-tea-milk in a list of potables, and certainly they do not qualify as *apéritifs* or cocktails. But I am putting them here because they are liquid and a part of our life and I want to get them out of the way. Other people have written about them, with greater skill and knowledge, from Brillat-Savarin to Soyer and beyond, and their words are available in most libraries, for those of us whose opinions can accept some embellishing.

In the same way, it is wasteful of me to say much about either spirits or wines, in the face of bad to wonderful books about them which continue to be written after several thousand years of steady praise and some blame. As for beers and their like, I agree with A. E. Housman, who wrote as one who should know,

Malt does more than Milton can,
To justify God's ways to man.

I love good beers and ales, and served in the English way, not numb with cold. But I have an instinctive feeling which may well be mistaken that it is foolish to mix the grape and the grain, and since I like wine better than beer, I usually choose to drink it.

I indulge in some drinkin-likkas which I do not approve of on aesthetic grounds, but because they interest or enliven me and occasionally because I am by nature courteous. I like a good dry martini, and I do mean good (made of the best procurable ingredients, and with care) and I do mean dry (not sweetish or weak or drowning over ice cubes). I also like a potion which never fails to baffle and even repel the bartender: dry or occasionally sweet vermouth, half-and-half with gin, and at room heat. This qualifies as the old-fashioned gin-and-It of English pubs, but in German Switzerland, where I first met the shocker, it was bluntly referred to as *ein Gift* (Poison!). It suits me, in my present chronological status, especially at off-times of the day when either duty or dallying tells me that a mild yet forthright nip is indicated. I like French and Italian *apéritifs*, especially the bitter ones, either straight or with soda water. I like brandy-and-water, about half-and-half again, and only now and then; it is a good restorative for weariness. After good meals I sometimes like cognac or *marc* or a rare taste of fruit alcohols like kirsch, but I have not drunk any sweet liqueurs since I was first feeling my way, alcoholically at least, in my very early twenties.

As for wines, they are for me. I like honest wines as such, all of them and always. Of course some are better than others, and I like the best ones the most. But I could and would forgo any other liquid forever, as long as I might drink one humble wine with my daily bread. I like wine before, during, after, and in between meals, if things point that way. I like to know, and to use, local wines, which is probably why I have managed to live near the grapevines since I was four. If I were told today that even one more sip of wine would kill me, I might *believe* it, but I know that I would also investigate the prognosis, weigh its validity, and then decide for myself. If I agreed to abstain for survival's dubious benefits, I could at least taste vicariously by continuing to serve wine to my friends and, like old George Saintsbury in his *Cellar Book*, grow mellow on memory.

Water should be man's first and finest tipple, but seldom is, these days. It is easy to say that a good spring or well is the remedy, but even that becomes doubtful as chemicals and wastes infiltrate the earth we blandly and ceaselessly defile. I have strong personal reactions to this subject, and am inclined to splutter about it, and I know that my own final blow will come on the day a reputable vintner tells me that even fermentation is not ridding his wines of fallout. After that, what? Where?

Perhaps fortunately, I have never prescribed a rule for how to boil water, a topic open to plagiarism from all sides. My own opinions were formed early in life, from hearing my mother sum up an ignorant housewife as one who could not do it, and a reclaimed soul as one who could not when she married but had overcome this handicap. In a casual way I have kept my eye out for actual formulas for such a delicate barometer of one's kitchen and marital eptitude, and not long ago I found a good mention of it in the 1886 edition of Mrs. Rorer's *Philadelphia Cook Book*:

> Wash out the tea-kettle thoroughly, fill it with fresh cold water, stand it over a quick fire and bring it to boiling point. Use at its first bubbles, or it parts with its gases and becomes flat.

I really knew all this anyway: use fresh water; never let it boil too long; throw it away and start over again for anything but rinsing the cups. At home we had a special kettle for water for the tea, and it never occurred to us to deviate from the unwritten rules. The inside of this battered old utensil was encrusted with perhaps an inch of tumorous deposits of a chalky and distasteful gray-brown, never disturbed. My grandmother believed them to be a salubrious sign that the water, in heating, had left them there in a sort of purification ceremony as it came each day to the proper bubble. In other words, she preferred to assume that this horrid encrustation stayed in the kettle instead of lodging in our hearts, brains, or gizzards.

The water, once correctly boiling, was poured immediately upon the tea leaves, which had been flicked into a heated pot, Crown Derby for company and plain bone-ware for everyday. As I remember, we always drank tea for lunch, very black (except "cambric" for us children of course) and "strong enough to trot a mouse on." As my mother grew older and assumed her position as Lady of the House after her dam's death, there was simple tea in the English style at about four o'clock, and in spite of the bother (and I feel rather strongly about this because I was usually the one who assembled the whole seemingly easy ritual and then cleared it away), it was a pleasant thing to be there in front of the fireplace and to hold a cup of the hot delicate brew against one's lips, for after high noon we drank pale green tea, not the throat-rasping potent black.

Naturally our supplies, even through a couple of wars, came in occasional shipments in tin boxes from Dublin. We held firm to Grandmother's edict that the first-grade was perforce kept in China, the next best was sent to Ireland, and the rest was shoved off on England. I shun thinking of what the old lady would have said about the stuff in tea bags, but fortunately she never knew of them. . . . (Who invented them? Was a new star sighted by anyone?)

Myself, since about my twenty-fifth year I get drunk on tea, so that like any controlled alcoholic I steer clear of my poison except in emergencies, when I know that I must be overbright for a time, and not have to drive a car. One cup of even the lowly Orange Pekoe will make me talkative, and after two I am tittery and flushed. Three will lift me that many feet off the ground, not safe to be behind a wheel. It is with regret that I choose to stay sober, for I have a vain dream of being able to sniff imperceptibly at the liquid in a shell of Belleek and know at once if it is Gunpowder or Young Hyson. This snobbish but detached satisfaction must remain beyond my personal horizon, the way the decadent beauty of a pink fresh *foie gras* stays unattainable to a person prone to gout.

The water that goes into an honest teapot, and for that matter any pot at all, including the human, is of increasing concern, even without my own splutterings. Detergents, insecticides, and what I think of as plain wastes but are now referred to more elegantly as effluents: they all flow-seep-percolate-drift into our diminishing supplies of potable waters, on this enormous and generous continent. We absorb them at home and in public, even on the washed vessels for our food and drink. (The filthiest bar I ever went into was in Cristóbal Colón, and I held a shot glass of rum in my gloved hand and hoped as I tipped it down my throat without touching it to my lips that the raw alcohol would probably protect me, but no spirits can eliminate the chemicals in "detergent film," as far as I know . . . even if we rinsed all our plates and glasses in straight C_2H_5OH). We accept, physiologically at least, surprising amounts of all this, as yet unmeasured but guessed at by horrified ecologists and such. We drink fallouts in our coffee cream. And vegetables and animals and other supplies of human provender are fed on the effluents piped into our ever-greener valleys from prosperous sewage plants which convert waste into "harmless" water . . . which somehow and strangely seems to be discouraging the fish in streams, lakes, bays, oceans . . .

The history of the human body indicates that with time, given that time, it will erect its own fortress, the way the common fly has done in areas systematically bombarded with DDT: bigger and better flies. People may be walking around, in a few decades, so full of chemical poisons that they will be impervious to threats not yet invented. It is an interesting sur-

mise, in the face of my own smug assurance that I shall escape it, and in
the meantime I refuse to drink most tap water (or to use it for any food
but soups, which is inconsistent). I prefer to die from something gutty and
nostalgic like undulant fever, or botulism. I want to encrust my arteries
with the natural calcium of bottled water rather than the stinking liquid
from my kitchen faucet, which has been chlorinated, irradiated, iodized,
fluorinated, and otherwise raped for my safety.

As for making good tea or coffee in these protected days, the best thing
to use is the water bottled for drinking. Unlike most liquor, it can be
bought in five- and ten-gallon jars, nicely provided with legs by its merchants, and worth whatever it may cost, which is much less than alcoholic
spirits of course. Even a tea bag or a mug of instant coffee tastes better if it
has been made with water drawn from the *olla* on the back porch.

I do not have an encrusted kettle anymore. All that the stuff from my
taps does is make strange rings on things, in the house, and attract perverted or desperate snails and earwigs in the garden. It also kills many cut
flowers in their vases, before their time to die, which is ominous.

But here is a trick I have often used if there is no pure spring nearby
and not even a *bottle* of good water to buy: fill a quart or half-gallon jar or
a pitcher from the tap, swish through it a handful of clean grass, and chill
it. Wheat grass is apparently most potent, and it can be grown in a box of
earth wherever there is moderate air and sun. A few sprigs of alfalfa will
do well too, and they are easy to grow in any kitchen plot or border. (They
are also pretty, and are fine in posies when the deep purple-blue flowers
bloom.) But green weeds from meadows or ditches, or good plain *grass*,
will do. For an hour or so the water will taste faintly green, of chlorophyll.
Then it will be fresh and sparkling, and miraculously will not leave a ring
on the jar.

When I am alone, and needful of an outer goad, I bring to the boil a measure of good water in a Teflon pan, put a teaspoonful of instant decaffeinized coffee and a half teaspoonful of "espresso" grind into about an ounce more of water in a mug, and then pour the hot water into it and cover it tightly. In four or five minutes it is steeped. Now and then I add one small-size saccharin tablet and a little rich milk which is probably from radioactive cows. This is a private show of quasi-independence, certainly, from my intrinsic recognition that caffein and I are enemies. In public I permit myself two sips of it, no more, when the after-dinner coffee is, as Brillat-Savarin wrote, ". . . so steaming hot and so crystal clear that its perfume fills the room." Even two sips can be a voluptuous delight, when they are taken knowingly.

At home, when friends come, I make "real" coffee, and with care. I use a drip pot lately, but think I prefer a Chemex, with its filter. I use freshly roasted and ground beans when possible, or buy the smallest available cans, since I do not serve the brew often enough to justify keeping supplies on hand. I make it "strong enough," and add up to one-third over-roast or espresso grind according to my guests. I serve it only after an evening meal, unless there is a beloved barbarian or a dietary eccentric at table whose demands are worth being satisfied without cavil. This is seldom the case, fortunately, although I do number one or two former alcoholics among my oldest-and-dearests, who need and get countless cups of coffee while we sit drinking our own poison from stemmed glasses.

On afternoons when two or three of the few tea lovers I still know will feel limber enough to come to my fireside, we drink that brew in correct style, and I make it the way I learned to as a child, but in an enamel or Teflon pan. And meanwhile tea bags and "instant" drinks are with us. It is repellent to me to be served a cup with one of the umbilical strings hanging over the edge, but it happens in otherwise dignified homes and public places. I agree with several people that in an emergency the dreadful bags can be used, but always removed in the kitchen before the tea is served, and I know that this brew can be controlled and even good. In the same way, I believe that instant coffee can be a very decent beverage, if made with a little care and respect. The operation is perforce a makeshift one . . . and it is probable that it would taste somewhat like hot coffee if the water from the tap came from the powder room on the fifty-second floor of an insurance building, and not my *olla*. Since this book is a collection of my own gastronomical prides and prejudices, I can admit that I am not proud of such a compromise. I am intrinsically *agin* instant coffee, even if it claims to be 100 percent pure and blended to suit my nationwide personal taste (what impudence!). I am even more agin instant tea, which sometimes contains the additional affront of sugar or mint or jasmine flavoring built into it, plus other chemical properties which make it soluble in cold water, to pour over ice cubes!

It would be an amusing job to compile another anthology of literary titbits about tea and coffee, which through their cheerful noninebriation have inspired some surprisingly lusty prose and verse. The beverages are fairly strong in natural drugs which are listed as stimulants and even excitants in our pharmacopeia, but which we absorb as a routine part of our culture. Fortunately in America, where the coffee break is an essential in office management and coffee often accompanies all three of our daily meals, it is usually a weak brew compared to the European half cup served after eating, or mixture of hot milk and coffee which is breakfast or part of a simple supper. Otherwise we would be twice as jittery as we already are. In the British Isles, and perhaps in some of their former colonies, strong black tea is served at eleven and again at five in offices and factories, and with "suckie-sweets" tucked into the cheek is what has kept many an otherwise miserable employee on his feet . . . toothless but vertical.

❧ A Tea

1 or 2 tablespoons tea (My grandfather
    would be incredulous!)
1 quart cool water
1 sprig mint, if desired

Let stand in hot sun 3 or 4 hours. Chill.

My father's father, a prairie giant in looks and behavior, gave up stimulants forever when he was forty—or at least he believed so. He "saw the Light," and became a militant Christian. This included forswearing liquor as a tool of the devil in those days, but he drank a brew of his own, hot and cold and all day long, steeped each morning from a half pound of freshly ground beans or a large cup of tea leaves, and one quart of water and a cup of sugar, which he sipped like cough medicine if his huge frame felt like sipping, between the floods of strong black coffee and tea which went with every meal. He was the man who now and then, on market days, would buy a little bottle of rootbeer extract, the size meant to make several gallons, empty it into a tumbler of water, and toss it off, firm in his faith in his own abstemiousness. Where a lesser human being would shake to death or at least fall down, he simply prayed a little more . . .

Here is a recipe which reminds me somewhat of the caffeine punch the old man devised. I first heard of it from a woman born and raised in Vermont instead of Iowa, who assured me of its potency: ❧

And this reminds me of another New England drink, called Switchel, for haymakers and other people working in the fields in summer: 2 tablespoons molasses, 1 tablespoon vinegar, a pinch of powdered ginger, for each cup of cold water. (Grandfather would shrug pityingly . . .)

Cokes, equally puny shadows, but still slaphappy with cola and sweetening, are often said to be our national drink. Tea-coffee-milk, though, are standard in restaurants and many homes, to be drunk with meals.

Milk is mistakenly used as a beverage instead of a food, and has proba- bly killed more adults with its double socko of proteins than it has nursed through their infancy and old age, where it naturally belongs as a substi- tute for the human mammary fluid. It is useful in cooking, and when it is fresh and raw ("certified" when it can be bought, and thus unquestion- ably of surer quality than the pasteurized, homogenized, and vitamin- enriched products commonly consumed by publicity-conditioned Ameri- cans), it can be a very pleasant and nourishing addition to a light meal or nibble, or as a restorative.

Tea I have implied that I appreciate, and even know how to make correctly, but seldom do. Coffee, I state firmly, at the possible risk of an- other plagiarism suit (this time from the Old Spanish Proverb Protective League), must be hot, black, fresh, and strong. Tea can fairly commend- ably be served with or after luncheon, and toasts or dainty cakes and cookies are good with it in the late afternoon. Coffee, I believe without doubt, should never be served *with* any meal but breakfast. In fact, it is actively revolting to me to try to taste with my mind's tongue its flavor and beautiful aroma with meats or green salads or pasta or fish, al- though when I was much younger I loved to eat rich chocolate desserts with a cup of it.

If considered as a cultural compulsion, a near-steady flow of hot weak liquid perhaps acts like the pill patterns of many modern people; one cup or capsule to relax, then one to stimulate, and so on. We are in much the same conditioned behavior with common salt, which most recipes list as an essential ingredient of everything from soup to gingerbread, reducing a

strong and distinctive flavor to nothingness. (In our language, the word "darling" is in the same sad state, without flavor because of its thoughtless abuse and overuse . . .) Perhaps we should take another *taste* of coffee and tea, and even milk, and consider them for a few minutes as new and peculiarly delicious, something to be savored and used sparingly, judiciously. We have too much of them. When they are in short supply, they become a luxury. We can live without them (even milk!), unless we are infirm or very young or old . . . and even then, we can remind ourselves that the South Sea Islanders never saw a cow before the white invasion, but still had beautiful teeth!

In the case of these three liquids, which my grandfather sternly preferred to consider nonstimulating but which send me quickly into the dizzy jitters or nudge my liver to give out a firm warning, I do not think of any of them as the beginning of a meal. Unless a true friend *asked* for a glass of milk, for instance, I would not serve it as an *apéritif*. But there are many discreet and even appetizing things to be drunk "safely" while other people are roaring it up over their dry sherry and their martinis and scotches, and I have spent years unobtrusively concocting them: margaritas without tequila, Gibsons of pure water, bourbon-and-branch made of apple juice. What we drink, before a meal which we will share with friends, is unimportant. The basic reason for this remains as true as it is primitive: a man or an animal cannot swallow well if he hates or is fearful. And that is why I like always to sip slowly at almost any liquid, and with chosen people aged from a few months to near a hundred years, before we sit down together.

Of course there is nothing better than a cup of strong hot coffee made from freshly roasted and ground beans, but this ideal is seldom attainable, especially on trips. Two traveling-friends of mine once devised a kind of elixir, which countless of us have since made and carried in flasks on our long and short safaris, and which most of us keep on hand in the home-based refrigerators. Two table-spoonfuls of this powerful brew in the bottom of a cup, and enough boiling water to fill it, will make a breakfast drink which is probably better than anything procurable for miles around . . . or two *demitasses*, a pure godsend after a motel-diner meal and highly recommended even at home (perhaps with a little rum floated judiciously onto them . . .):

 *The Welton Brew*

1 pound regular grind coffee
8 cups cold water
Filter paper

Soak the coffee in the water for 12 hours, covered. Strain through a fine sieve, and then filter the liquid through a paper or cloth. Keep the elixir in icebox. (And a hundred years ago this recipe would end, "Dry the grounds to stuff pincushions . . ." Today, out with them!)

This trick is one of the Tried-and-Trues, and especially handy for people who live alone and cannot keep ground coffee fresh enough with the small amounts they use. It is also recommended to lazy people, which includes me. How pleasant to have a pungent cup ready in as long as it takes to boil six or eight ounces of water, with no boring pot to clean!

I, being both slothful and the possessor of a Curious Nose, have evolved an interesting combination of this elixir and my grandfather's heady brew, plus a touch of the tropics which I must have read or dreamed about. True to form, I store it in the icebox, ready for unexpected guests or even, now and then and very cautiously, a small taste for myself. (For this last, the weather both within and without must be Fair . . .) A generous tablespoonful of it in a cup of hot milk makes a pungent kind of *café au lait*, and since powdered decaffeinated stuff can be used instead of the comparatively honest "regular," it is safe to serve as a nightcap to soothe the sleepless. It makes a good *demitasse* at the end of a meal (with or without rum!): 1 tablespoon in the little cup, then filled with boiling water. &

& *A Tropical Brew*

> *1 cup water*
> *½ to ¾ cup instant coffee (add 1 table-*
>   *spoon espresso grind for added flavor)*
> *½ cup brown sugar*
> *1 tablespoon Angostura bitters*
>
> *Stir ¼ cup water into coffee. Add sugar to ¾ cup*
> *water, and boil five minutes. Add to dissolved coffee.*
> *Add bitters, stir rapidly, and pour into jar or bottle.*
> *Cover at once. 1 to 2 tablespoons will make 1 large*
> *cup of coffee.*

There is no question in my mind about punches: I really do not like them. Perhaps this is because I usually do not like the parties at which they appear. It is also because I do not like several flavors mixed together, especially in what I drink. I would rather be served a glass of champagne brut than no matter how sutble or historical a blend of rum, cognac, Grand Marnier, Moselle, and spices. There are times, though, especially if one knows children and old people as well as wedding guests, when a punch or "cup" of nonalcoholic dignity is needed: easy to serve and not clogged with floating remnants of fruits, harmless to Cub Scouts and ancient insomniacs, and yet with its own wallop to it. By good luck, I came upon just such a jewel, in 1961.

I knew at once that it would fill my stern requirements, for I am stuffed with prejudices about giving harmless people of any age the powdered and packaged "drink mixes" which bewildered PTA mothers and Begonia Club refreshment chairwomen fob off in their hurried attempts to avoid contributing to the delinquency or broken hips of their thirsty guests. "My" punch, which has brightened many an eye in this part of Northern California since I first spotted it in Craig Claiborne's *New York Times Cookbook*, has gradually been changed almost beyond recognition, but it can never be called anything but the right and perfect name for it, and one I hope he would not begrudge us: &

The magic although obviously non–Secret Ingredient in this recipe is, I suspect, its generous amount of good strong tea. It brightens the eye, loosens the tongue, and I have watched many experienced tipplers return happily to the big bowl for more unbelieving that it does not have a "stick" in it.

People have asked me about robbing it of its virginity, and although I am purposely ignorant about punch-making in general, I am not too timid to surmise from reading about it that a fifth of good brandy could be added to the mixture, once cooked, and champagne used instead of ginger ale. This would make a light and not too heady drink, correctly pink and pretty (and free from unidentifiable floating objects), but one that should probably be renamed Loss of Innocence. My own integrity or stubbornness forces me to mention again that I would rather be handed a glass of cold dry wine than any such pretty mish-mosh . . . or at the next Mothers' Meeting at the schoolhouse a paper cup of plain fruit juice. Ah, well . . .

 Age of Innocence Cup

*1 quart freshly brewed tea (12 tea bags
        to 1 quart water)*
1 quart fresh unsweetened orange juice
1 pint fresh unsweetened lemon juice
3 pints cranberry juice
*2 cups sugar syrup (2 cups sugar, 1 cup
        water, boiled briefly)*
4 quarts chilled ginger ale

Make tea by removing rapidly boiling water from heat, pouring over tea, and steeping for 5 minutes before removing bags. Mix tea, juices, and syrup, and store in icebox in quart jars. To serve, pour 1 jar of mixture and 1 quart of ginger ale over large chunk of ice in punch bowl.

Advantages of this recipe: nonalcoholic but with good "kick," no messy floating fruit, nice color, easy to make in big batches and store in icebox, easy to measure quart for quart.

❧ | The Secret Ingredient

IT IS COMMON IN SMALL COMMUNITIES, especially if they are far from towns, for one person or another to become known for a special power. A man may have some control over sick frightened animals which gradually extends to his own friends and is interpreted as miraculous or divine healing. A woman may be of a hypersensitive nature which with time develops into an intuitive "clairvoyance" about other people's dreams and hopes. In the same way, there are men and women who have a special nose for mushrooms, or an inimitable hand with pastry and jellies. At present, I, living less than a hundred miles from a big city and with about two thousand other townspeople, do not know of any local witches or warlocks, but there are several people here who seem to have an uncanny power over food. They manage to keep to themselves whatever it is that makes their creations subtly and definitely better than any attempts to approximate them. They are even willing to make knaves and clowns of themselves, to protect their recipes . . .

I have known one of these passionate cooks, and for many years. By now she is retired from her kitchen. (Actually she married an even more ancient man who fell in love with her food and now holds her and it for himself alone, to our hungry chagrin.) While she was practicing, I did my best in both overt and underhanded ways to learn her secret ingredients, but I remain foiled.

She had been very lonely after her first husband died, and to keep herself from the river, perhaps, she began to cook about three dishes for local

families smart enough to recognize her superiority. The routine of ordering and then fetching one of her preparations was rigid, and involved ap-
pointments, reservations, and occasional frustrations if Bertie Bastalizzo's
schedule was full. She was very fussy about the kind of dishes her creations were to be served in, and several of us invested in large handsome
pottery baking dishes which are unused since that old robber stole Bertie
from us. We knew her instructions about how long to let the food "rest"
before serving it, what temperature to let it rest in, and even what to do
with it once it was at its peak of restedness. In fact, she dictated everything
but our actual digestion, serene in her power over our palates, for she and
we knew, with conditioned fatalism, that never again would we taste the
likes of her delicate little dumplings of herbs and chicken, her flat tarts of
thin noodles and mushrooms, her feathery mixtures of *capellini d'angelo*
and a kind of *pesto* which was, naturally, "secret."

One summer I spent several weeks flattering her into letting my
younger daughter, who had all the makings of a good cook as well as a
private investigator, act as her kitchen helper. I kept notes unashamedly
on the reports of this sorceress' apprentice, my underage spy, but any results I produced were nondescript. Something was simply *not there*, and
neither my accomplice nor I could guess what.

Much later Bertie offered blandly, as if to punish me for my obvious
breach of trust, to write her recipe for the dumplings. I felt humbled and
grateful, as if a small halo had suddenly been awarded me in spite of my
sins. I have kept her large piece of pink butcher paper to remind me of
these mixed emotions, for its scrawl is unintelligible to me, completely
meaningless, cryptic anyway. It lists ingredients which are never mentioned again. It notes measurements ranging from "some" to a monstrous
"10½ pounds" (of salt!). Perhaps Bertie believed that she was giving me

her true recipe. Perhaps I cannot translate it because her own English was too limited to write it. Perhaps she was trying to make a culinary monkey out of me.

I still like her, and regret that since she succumbed to a second love we no longer taste her beautiful dishes. But part of me rebels at her seeming trickery. Her scribbled directive is one more exhibit in my private Hall of Gastronomical Ill Fame, for I really cannot believe that a good cook will distort a prideful recipe. I continue this stubborn and obviously naïve faith in the face of many more such pitiable little tricks, and prefer to console myself by thinking back on the wonderful odorous kitchen I would go to when it was time to pick up one of Bertie's mammoth casseroles.

This was a ritual, as well as a pleasurable ordeal, for I had to be there exactly when I had been told to, or a little before, and on each of countless times I was instructed in how long to let the dish rest and was quizzed sternly about what else would be served. If Bertie approved, occasionally she gave me a jar of her fresh pickled zucchini as a tacit benediction. And always, as if she could not bring herself to let one more creation leave her own familiar kitchen for a stranger's, I had to sit down and consume a beaker of one of the worst drinks I can remember in a long life of polite subjection to them.

It was kept in a half-gallon jug in the icebox, and drunk straight, from cottage cheese glasses with daisies on them. The recipe, always reverently accredited to the deceased Mr. Bastalizzo: Pour one pint from a full half-gallon jug of dark sweet vermouth made by a local vintner, add one pint of bourbon whiskey, shake a little now and then, and enjoy. Simple, near-lethal, and challenging!

One time there was some delay in getting the dish from Bertie's hands into mine: she ran out of aluminum foil to cover it and had to find a new roll, perhaps. It was much like the way a mother will nearly miss the train that is to take her tender child to camp . . . I drank two tumblers of her husband's brew, and with the flash courage of unexpected inebriation I asked my friend point-blank if she had really meant ten and a half pounds of salt. She simply cackled, like a tipsy old Mona Lisa. I reeled carefully to my car, my arms filled with another proof of her culinary mystique.

We are so conditioned to this threat of the Secret Ingredient, and this acceptance of trickery, that even honesty has become suspect when we are brash enough to ask for recipes. My own mother always disclosed calmly her "secret" in making the best mustard pickles in the world, but almost nobody believed her, simply because she *told* it. She made the pickles according to a fairly standard recipe, almost measure for measure like many I have read, BUT she added one eight-ounce jar of Crosse & Blackwell's Chowchow to it. There was no substitute, she said, and it was the honest truth, as anyone could prove by trying. Here, because it seems the right place, is her method:

Edith's Mustard Pickles

1 quart very small whole cucumbers
1 quart sliced large cucumbers
1 quart sliced green tomatoes
1 quart peeled small white onions
1 large cauliflower in small floweriets
1 pint 2-inch (cut) green string beans
4 green peppers in 1-inch cubes
4 quarts water
2 cups salt
1 cup flour
6 tablespoons Coleman's mustard (dry)
1 tablespoon turmeric
1 cup sugar
Vinegar
1 8-ounce bottle Crosse & Blackwell's Chowchow

Let vegetables stand overnight in brine of water and salt. Heat to scalding point and drain. Make smooth paste of flour, mustard, turmeric, sugar, and enough vinegar to make 2 quarts. Cook in double boiler until thick. Add chowchow. Mix with vegetables. Heat through, and bottle.

And here, almost in refutation of my mother's candor, is the best version I have yet evolved from Bertie's directions, for her

 Pickled Zucchini

Leave 6 to 10 small crisp zucchini whole, or slice thickly, lengthwise.

Brown gently in olive oil. Pack vertically in wide-mouthed jars.

1 cup vinegar
1 cup brown sugar
4 cloves garlic
1 cup chopped parsley
1 tablespoon oregano
1 tablespoon salt
1 teaspoon pepper

In same oily skillet, boil vinegar and sugar. Add rest of ingredients, boil gently 5 minutes, and pour over zucchini to cover. Add more oil on top if needed to make ¼-inch cover. Keep in icebox. Serve drained and cold for antipasto or with cold meats.

Needless to say, this translation is *not* exactly right, but its result is a fresh delicious hors d'oeuvre in the summer, kept for even two weeks or so in the icebox, and made if possible from vegetables fresh from the vine and not more than four inches long. (It is also very good with any kind of supper entrée, hot or cold.) I honestly have no idea what the Secret Ingredient might be, but charity will excuse my obtuseness, perhaps, if I give one short example of Bertie's prose, found under my door apropos of a later rendezvous for ten dozen of her mystery dumplings: "Please If you fene time, cools me up abaut 5 pm clook up." Add measurements to this, and you have an undecipherable code!

People like Bertie, and even my honest mother, are increasingly rare, and I have a dismal feeling that they may soon disappear completely. It is not as much a question of their supplies as it is of their own unquestioning demand for quality. The things they used in their recipes were not hard to grow, or buy, and while they bowed to seasonal riches, and made pickles when the vegetables were at their best, because that is the way they had to, we can buy zucchini and beans and even green tomatoes all year in the supermarkets. We can assemble everything directions call for, from vinegar to turmeric and, with a little effort, Crosse & Blackwell's Chowchow (and none other!). But do we? Why bother? Why clutter the icebox with a couple of jars of chilled zucchini? Who wants a dozen bottles of mustard pickles sitting around? Who has the time, when you come right down to it, to fuss with such maneuvers? Such-and-such is almost as good, and a lot less trouble . . .

An interesting and grim proof of this conjecture that the Berties are doomed happened lately in our town, when the second of two birthday parties was given for an honorable old lady of ninety-eight. Ten years before, when we celebrated her comparatively youthful anniversary, we did special honor to her by blackmailing another friend of almost the same age to make hundreds of her famous sand tarts to eat with the punch. They were delicate thin little wafers, light and crisp and not the classical sand tart at all, and for decades her recipe for them was her sternly guarded secret. Perhaps it was age that softened her pride, for when I discreetly and admiringly asked if perhaps a hint of old-fashioned lemon extract might be the Secret Ingredient, she gave me a pleased nod . . . and later the receipt! On it she wrote at the end, ". . . and ½ teaspoon of ? ? ?" —our private joke.

So the ten years passed, and when the time came to deputize a few of us to supply soppets for the ninety-eighth birthday punch, I proudly produced the famous sand tart recipe, feeling sure that the old lady who had not been able to reach that age would never begrudge it in honor of the one who had. But nobody had time enough to follow it . . . or rather, it was mutually and immediately vetoed in favor of a wonderful new trick (. . . just as good!) which involved packaged mixes of both cake and custard, frozen lemon juice, and sweet sherry, ". . . really fun to make . . . so quick and easy . . . and all you do is *slice* it . . ."

That is the end of the story. Or is it? Where are the witches of yester-year, the strange old women with their dogged involvement, their loyalty to true flavor and changeless quality? If at times they protected their "secrets" to the point of knavery, at least they had the courage to stay passionate about it. Perhaps that was the Secret Ingredient: the blind strength of timeless passion?

And here, without secrecy anywhere or of any kind, are some recipes which seem to have outlived the nineteenth century, our Golden Age of Pickling. Like most family jewels, they are called Sarah's This and Aunt Maggie's That, and in one way or another all of these people were witches, so that I have carefully tested their brews, and often, to prove them honest. I can vouch for the following ones, which in slightly different forms are surely in any standard American cookbook, if not in the tattered blotchy notes still pushed to the back of a few old kitchen cupboards. There are shades of exotic and ethnic backgrounds in them, but basically they are still-living proofs of the passionate romance between Midwestern housewives and the Mason jar, which filled shelves with gleaming beautiful vessels of cooked fruits and vegetables, all dirt cheap in season and rare as toad gems in the long winters fed on potatoes, cabbages, and parsnips, with fresh celery such an honored treat at Christmas that cut-glass vases were especially designed and named for it.

"Canned" fruit was very different from the jams and preserves that women also "put up," and so were canned vegetables and even meats: lightly cooked in thin sugar or brine liquids according to their natures, and packed into sterilized jars, to supplement the tedious meals of winter and help hold at bay the rickets, diarrheas, and suchlike that haunted prairie mothers. "Preserves" were in turn different from "conserves," and both were different from jams. And pickles were not relishes!

Here are some proofs of this mysterious and ritualistic protocol: ⅋

In other words, preserves are kept whole, and cooked gently in heavy syrup. A conserve, however, is made from cut-up fruit, sometimes of two or three kinds, with raisins and nuts in it: a more exotic mish-mash, often served with meats, as would be a chutney made hotter with spices, garlic, chilies, and so on.

"Jams" are like preserves, except thicker, with one or occasionally more than one fruit in bits and pieces, and "honeys" are even thicker, and very smooth. (The prime one at home was Grandmother's Quince Honey, which took days to make, involving tedious grating of the fruit and long, slow stirrings. It was finally one of the most beautiful colors I have ever seen, of a deep subtle orange, like stained glass, in constant danger of "sugaring" in its little jars, and so sweet that even thinking of it makes my teeth shudder.) "Jellies" are, of course, the clear juices strained from fruit, and they depend upon natural or added pectin, or a judicious dosing of fresh lemon juice if they are too bland in taste, to attain and keep a delicate stiffness.

⅋ Anne Lodge's Strawberry Preserves (Delaware)

1 cup firm strawberries, slightly crushed
     or left whole
1¾ cups sugar

Cook together on slow fire until sugar dissolves. After boiling point is reached, boil slowly 8 minutes for 1 quart, 10 minutes for 2 quarts, taking care never to cook more than 2 quarts at a time. Pour into large bowl, and stir or push down now and then until cold. Let stand overnight. Put in jars and seal well with wax or paraffin. Extra syrup may be kept for desserts.

⅋ Edith's Plum Conserve (Iowa via Pennsylvania)

5 pounds plums or fresh prunes, stoned
     and sliced
5 pounds sugar
3 oranges, sliced very thin
1 pound black seeded raisins or currants
1 cup slivered almonds or broken walnuts

Boil plums and sugar slowly until thick, stirring. Add oranges and raisins, and cook until tender. Add nuts at last. The conserve should be thick.

"Marmalades," most often made with citrus fruits, are a skillful compromise between jellies and jams, and when at their best are six of one and a half a dozen of the other. A thick, stodgy orange marmalade bound with added pectin is barely palatable if one is used to a product made with time and patience, as was my mother's. We accepted it without question as the best on earth, even though it appeared as regularly as hot toast on our breakfast table every morning of the year except Christmas. It was, that is to say, and it still is, as normal a part of our family life, now largely nostalgic, as Edith's mustard pickle.

It took three days to make. The first day the fruit was quartered and cut into very thin strips, a juicy odorous task that puckered the fingertips. If the cook was one of our happier ones, in a long string of them ranging from euphoric to deeply misanthropic, the seeds were pushed to one side and tied into a little cloth bag to soak and simmer in the brew and lend their gentle, bitter flavor until just before the final boiling. The whole sloppy mess was soaked overnight in exactly three times its bulk of water, and then cooked fast for twenty minutes and allowed to cool again for twenty-four hours. The third day, it was carefully measured, one cup of juice and fruit to three-quarters cup of sugar, and was cooked about a quart at a time, quickly, until it passed the classical test for jellying, as given in any kitchen manual. This was a tedious but pleasant-smelling chore, as indeed was the whole process, and we all knew how to lend a hand . . .

The marmalade was put into pint jars for family use, with prettier, smaller ones for giving to its admirers. (People seldom left the Ranch without something in their hands, and seemed to shun us only during the green bean season, when they got tired of the large baskets of excess produce they had to smile at and accept. There were temptingly long rows between the orange trees in those days, and my father and the Hired Man of the Moment thought nothing of planting beans a hundred yards at a time . . .)

The whole marmalade ritual took place several times a year, thanks to our having rotated crops of Valencias and navels at the Ranch, and in off-seasons, when the fruit was sweet and soft, a final addition to the pot would be some fresh lemon juice, to pick up the flavor and help the jellying . . . or perhaps a few lemons or grapefruits sliced into the stuff at the start. This last trick we accepted with adequate grace, but we felt that it was not quite kosher.

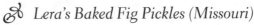

Lera's Baked Fig Pickles (Missouri)

10 pounds firm fresh figs, white or black
Whole cloves
5 pounds sugar
2 cups cider or wine vinegar

Wash figs, and stick 1 clove in each. Make thick syrup of sugar and vinegar. Pour while hot over figs in uncovered roasting pan, and leave in very slow oven (225°) for 2 hours. Let stand overnight, without touching. Repeat baking. Put into jars, and pour syrup to top of each jar.

The basic way that conserves and preserves differ from relishes and pickles is that the first must be made only with sugar and the second with varying amounts of sugar or salt, vinegar, and perhaps spices. (Relishes are usually chopped or ground vegetables, and pickles are either whole or sliced.)

The "Relishes" section of almost any decent cookbook of the last century will make one think that our grandmothers could and did bottle anything that stood still, and many of the receipts are best left to armchair speculation, or at least a detached scientific reorganizing. Perhaps that is why a file like mine is relatively safe to work from, for it holds nothing but my own Tried-and-Trues, like this somewhat odd variation on a familiar theme: ᪲

These succulent and heady figs are delicious with cold meats, or baked ham, and they taste almost Near Eastern in what I assume is an

American custom of putting one or two side dishes of sweet and sour relishes upon the dining table, at least for Sunday and "company" meals.

 Lera's Sweet Pickles

> *4 large dill pickles (not kosher style)*
> *2 cups sugar*
> *½ cup vinegar*
>
> *Slice pickles thin, put half of them in large jar or crock, and add 1 cup sugar. Add rest of pickles and sugar, and let stand overnight. Add vinegar and stir up. Good any time. Eat fast or put in jars.*

Green beans, ripe and green tomatoes, eggplant, cucumbers . . . cherries, and green and ripe peaches and grapes and melons: they can all be treated much as Bertie did her zucchini, or according to the more Anglo-Saxon way of soaking them in brine and then covering them, lightly cooked, with plain or seasoned vinegars in jars and crocks. They are fun to play with, even if they are of largely clinical interest to people like me, who find that their acidity quarrels with the enjoyment of a glass of wine alongside the dishes they usually accompany. Pickles can be crisp and refreshing, admittedly, and they war less pugnaciously with a good pint of ale or beer than with wine, great or small. They are, I think, pure pizen with milk, tea, coffee . . .

Here is an easy compromise between the unadorned sour cucumber flavored with dill, which I acknowledge can be delicious on a hot day and preferably on a picnic, and the fancier mixtures called names like Bread and Butter, Luncheon, and so on. Once more, it comes from a favorite witch:

It is rash of me to state, or even imply, that every recipe in my card file has been tried and found true. A few are there because they are forever mysterious and tantalizing, like Bertie's. They act as a catalyst, to test my wits, and they undoubtedly hide a Secret Ingredient to be decoded by a more skillful or more patient cook than I. Here is one I cannot recommend, therefore, for anything but its evocative rhythm. It is from a long-gone friend reared near an Arkansas crossroads. I have often eaten this tart crisp relish and admired it, and it is the way the recipe was written for my future pondering:

Lera's easygoing recipe is a far cry from the classical soakings and simmerings of a backwoods cook, but comparatively plain when one reads some of the ways American housewives managed to circumvent decay and death during the rich summer canning seasons, not many decades ago. There were standard formulas, of course, but each family had its own tricks, even with such an Eastern and Midwestern favorite as Corn Relish (mostly vegetables of several kinds, with fresh kernels of corn predominating, and a sweeter taste as it went into the hotter regions, where it would spoil more quickly), and Governor's Mixture, traditionally made of green tomatoes and onions and spices instead of the onions and cucumbers of a banal Bread and Butter. Chow-chow was a crude shadow of my mother's own Mustard Pickle, and piccalilli, which is somewhat like India Relish, was country cousin to Mother's elegant

Addies Sisters Pickels

"Soak pickels 6 or 7 days in Salt Brine Strong enough to hold up an Egg or 1 lb Salt in a Galon pump Water take out of Brine & Wash in Cold Water (drain) than soak pickels in Alium water 3 days 2 Tabelspoon full to a Galon water and drain. Start with 3 cups of Suggar covering Pickels with Vinegar Simmer 3 mornings (Not boil) Keep adding Suggar each morning."

Baltimore Relish (Michigan?)

2 quarts ground tomatoes, ripe but firm
2 quarts ground green tomatoes
1 large cabbage
12 large onions
2 to 3 cloves garlic (optional)
4 green peppers
½ cup salt
2 quarts good white vinegar
1½ pounds sugar
½ cup white mustard seed
½ cup grated horseradish
1 tablespoon celery seed

Grind vegetables coarsely, add salt, and let stand overnight. Drain. Add rest of ingredients and boil until thick, stirring now and then.

Like most such concoctions, this seems better after a few weeks, and in my own home the current cook kept a sharp eye on the jam cupboard on the back porch, and saw to it that there was enough of last year's supply of full jars of our favorites to last until new ones had ripened. We did not have a cool dark cellar at the Ranch in California; it was a wooden house built during the Gold Rush, flat on the ground, to last a dozen years or so until a proper adobe structure could be made, which it never was. So we never could use the common big stoneware crocks, which, if kept cool and dark enough, would hold a winter's supply of some of the Midwestern standbys that my grandmother and mother were accustomed to. We kept everything from "canned" peaches to chili sauce in Mason jars on the back porch, cool enough in winter, and we trusted to luck and artful dodges in the summer, when a lot of reinforcements were on the way from the garden, anyway . . .

A direct opposite of this somewhat haphazard ritual of using acid and heat and spices to preserve food (actually a form of embalming) is the agreeable and perhaps alien method of serving fresh fruits and vegetables in a raw chilled hash, which if cooked would be like a chutney or a relish. It is often found, even now, in homes which have been swayed by British colonials reliving their pukka-sahib days, even unto the third and fourth generations. I have inherited several recipes from them. Here are a couple, historically pungent and socially proven of worth: ❧

 Harvy-Scarvy (Norfolk, England)

2 cups crisp finely chopped celery

2 cups finely chopped apples, cored but not peeled

2 cups finely chopped onions

Salt, freshly ground pepper to taste

½ cup vinegar

½ cup salad oil

Add vinegar and oil to celery, apples, and onion, and stir well. Chill for 1 or 2 hours, and stir again just before serving. Good with any cold meats, but preferably pork chops.

Some outlanders may not relish the idea of a cold pork chop, but I can say that one that has been properly cooked and drained and chilled, and then married with a generous serving of this fresh bright relish, makes a fine meal indeed. In the same way, Puchidee, served as amply as a vegetable, is a tantalizing companion to almost any cold meat or fish or poultry. It is somewhat more complex than a Harvy-Scarvy, but can be made in the same way, using a modified vinaigrette instead of sour cream: ❧

An ancient friend of mine who had spent perhaps sixty years in Injah used to serve a wild-eyed relish at her Sunday night suppers. I cannot find the recipe, which is perhaps as well, although I have followed it many times with awed success. It is never served with anything but cold rare roast beef, as far as I know, or, oddly enough, fuming Boston baked beans in winter. It is hot as the hinges of hell's front door, with real chili pepper chopped into it, and is made of coarsely ground apples and onions bound with *finely* chopped orange, peel and all! It is further confounded by a generous dousing of Scotch whiskey instead of a more conservative and economical vinaigrette. It sounds like gastronomical mayhem, but I can recommend it as something to be considered and even toyed with in the kitchen. Perhaps it is a fair antic for the occasional warlock who must

 *Indian Puchidee*

6 *large sour apples, cored and peeled*
1 *large red sweet pepper (or 1 cup canned pimientos)*
1 *large green pepper*
1 *large onion*
2 *cloves garlic (optional—not with poultry or fish)*
Salt, pepper, curry powder to taste
Sour cream (or unflavored yogurt)

Put apples and vegetables through coarse food grinder, season to taste (remembering that a good curry powder will increase violently in flavor), and chill well. Mix lightly with sour cream before serving. (A few chopped mint leaves can be added with the cream . . . good with poultry and especially with cold lamb.)

survive any covey of witches! There is no Secret Ingredient in it, but it is plainly a recipe dependent upon personal courage . . . and in what amounts?

ℰ | Conclusion

Oh, turn not from the hum-ble Pig,
My child, or think him in-fra dig.
We oft hear lit-er-a-ry men
Boast of the in-flu-ence of the Pen;
Yet when we read in His-to-ry's Page
Of Hu-man Pigs in ev-e-ry age,
From Croe-sus to the pre-sent day,
Is it, my child, so hard to say
(De-spite the Scribe's vain-glo-ri-ous boast)
What Pen has in-flu-enced Man the most?

Oliver Herford (1863–1935)
A Child's Primer of Natural History

Index